Intellectual Property Prot€
for AI-generated Creation

This book explores the intersection between artificial intelligence and two intellectual property rights: copyright and patents. The increasing use of artificial intelligence for generating creative and innovative output has an impact on copyright and patent laws around the world. The book aims to map and analyse that impact.

The author considers how artificial intelligence systems may aid, or in some cases substitute for, human creators and inventors in the creative process. It is from this angle that the copyright and patent regimes in four jurisdictions (Europe, the United States, Australia and Japan) are investigated in depth. The author describes how these jurisdictions look at works and inventions generated through a process where artificial intelligence is present or prevalent, and examines how copyright and patent regimes should adapt to the reality of artificially intelligent creators and inventors.

As the use of artificial intelligence to generate creative and innovative products becomes more common, this book will be a valuable resource to researchers, academics and policy makers alike.

Ana Ramalho is Copyright Counsel at Google, and a Guest Lecturer at Leiden University, The Netherlands.

Intellectual Property Protection for AI-generated Creations

Europe, the United States,
Australia and Japan

Ana Ramalho

Routledge
Taylor & Francis Group

LONDON AND NEW YORK

First published 2022
by Routledge
2 Park Square, Milton Park, Abingdon, Oxon OX14 4RN

and by Routledge
605 Third Avenue, New York, NY 10158

Routledge is an imprint of the Taylor & Francis Group, an informa business

British Library Cataloguing-in-Publication Data
A catalogue record for this book is available from the British Library

Library of Congress Cataloging-in-Publication Data
Names: Ramalho, Ana, 1976- author.
Title: Intellectual property protection for AI-generated creations Europe,
    United States, Australia and Japan / Ana Barbara Quintela Ribeiro Neves
    Harmer Ramalho.
Other titles: Intellectual property protection for Artificial Intelligence-
    generated creations Europe, United States, Australia and Japan
Description: Abingdon, Oxon [UK] ; New York, NY : Routledge, [2022] |
    Includes bibliographical references and index.
Identifiers: LCCN 2021046399 (print) | LCCN 2021046400 (ebook) |
    ISBN 9780367415617 (hardback) | ISBN 9781032163031 (paperback) |
    ISBN 9780367823290 (ebook)
Subjects: LCSH: Copyright—Computer programs. | Computer
    programs—Patents. | Artificial intelligence—Law and legislation. |
    Intellectual property.
Classification: LCC K1443.C6 R36 2022 (print) | LCC K1443.C6
    (ebook) | DDC 346.04/8—dc23/eng/20211028
LC record available at https://lccn.loc.gov/2021046399
LC ebook record available at https://lccn.loc.gov/2021046400

ISBN: 978-0-367-41561-7 (hbk)
ISBN: 978-1-032-16303-1 (pbk)
ISBN: 978-0-367-82329-0 (ebk)

DOI: 10.4324/9780367823290

Typeset in Bembo
by Apex CoVantage, LLC

To the memory of my grandmother

Content

Acknowledgements

This book would not have been possible without the help, understanding and encouragement of many people. I'd like to thank Siobhán Poole at Routledge, for her infinite patience and support throughout this process, and Vanessa Biermannova, for her generous and skilful research assistance.

A few friends have also given their contribution, in one way or another, to this book. Special thanks go to Kim de Beer, whose cheering-on capacities are second to none; to José Paredes, who doubles up as the friendliest of havens and as patent consultant extraordinaire; and to João Almeida, who is and always has been a remarkable example to aspire to. I am unbelievably grateful for their presence in this process (and in my life in general).

Finally, no acknowledgement note would be complete without mentioning my family and their incredible support. My deepest thanks go to my mother and to my sister, Sara, for always being there no matter the storm I end up getting myself into, and to my husband James for being able to magically lift me up and keep me grounded at the same time.

1 Introduction

AI has a profound impact on society, including the way people work, create and socialize. Indeed, businesses can significantly improve their services by using it. Yet, behind the hype, there are serious limitations. AI tends to require too many repetitive tasks to be feasible, and it requires too much human labour to become mainstream. In the long run, as business process workers transition to human employees, their number may be reduced due to automation.

I didn't write that first paragraph, save for the first sentence in bold. Since this is a book about artificial intelligence (AI) systems and their creations, I thought it only polite to give them the first word. The paragraph was written – following the prompt of the sentence in bold – by Talk to Transformer, a neural network that completes text.[1] Coincidentally, one of the main goals of this book is to investigate whether AI systems' creations and inventions require a human being – and if so to what extent they do, and how that impacts copyright and patent laws (or, in Talk to Transformer's version, whether AI "requires too much human labour to become mainstream").

The term "artificial intelligence" can be used to describe either a scientific field or a technology. This book deals mainly with the latter, although a couple of approaches and techniques from the field of AI as a scientific discipline – such as machine learning techniques – will be mentioned where relevant to explain the workings of the underlying technology. The topic of the book stands at the intersection of AI in the sense just mentioned, and two intellectual property fields: copyright and patents. The starting premise is that the intervention of AI in the process of creation of works or inventions has an impact on, respectively, copyright and patent laws (although that impact might not be the same in the two legal disciplines because copyright and patents function differently in terms of, e.g., requirements for protection). Creation of works by, or with the help of, AI systems raises questions of autonomy (i.e., how autonomous an AI is in creating works and inventions, and the relation that autonomy has to human input), and of how copyright and patent laws treat and should AI-generated content.

---

1 *Talk to Transformer* <https://app.inferkit.com/demo> accessed 3 June 2021.

DOI: 10.4324/9780367823290-1

To be sure, the general idea of making machines that can mimic human thought and behaviour has been around since antiquity.[2] It is the increase in computer power, together with developments in AI technology and access to more training datasets, that has kick-started a new AI era.[3] The pervasiveness of AI systems and applications has in turn prompted many policymakers to address the impact of AI on several areas, including copyright and patents. For example, as recently as October 2020, the European Parliament has even classified it a priority in the area of intellectual property law to assess intellectual property rights in light of the "growing autonomisation of certain decision-making processes [that] can give rise to technical or artistic creations," with the objective of fostering "an environment conducive to creativity and innovation by rewarding creators."[4]

Chapters 2 and 3 will analyse in-depth, respectively, AI and copyright protection, and AI and patent protection. Each chapter starts by exploring the way in which AI can generate products that, if created by humans, would likely qualify as, correspondingly, copyright protected works and patentable inventions. New AI applications emerge every day, so the chapters will offer some illustrative examples that can help paint a picture of AI capabilities in the realm of works and inventions, but they do not purport to be exhaustive.

Next, each chapter examines the justifications for granting copyright or patent protection, as such rationales can provide a sound basis for discussing whether protection should be available. In other words, only by considering the

---

2 Mizuki Hashiguchi, 'The Global Artificial Intelligence Revolution Challenges Patent Eligibility' (2017) 13 *J Bus & Tech* 1, 7: "In Greek mythology, the masterful Hephaestus built a gigantic robot that patrolled the island of Crete, monitoring whether laws were properly implemented. Hephaestus even created intelligent tables that automatically supplied food and drinks. During the Italian Renaissance, Leonardo da Vinci drew mechanical lions that moved autonomously. One of them was designed to present a cluster of beautiful lilies" (footnotes omitted). See also, on how AI has been around for a long time, Ryan Calo, 'Artificial Intelligence Policy: A Primer and a Roadmap' (2017) 1–2 <https://papers.ssrn.com/sol3/papers.cfm?abstract_id=3015350> accessed 3 June 2021; Peter Stone and others, 'Artificial Intelligence and Life in 2030. One Hundred Year Study on Artificial Intelligence: Report of the 2015–2016 Study Panel' (2016) 50–52 <http://ai100.stanford.edu/2016-report> accessed 3 June 2021. Michael McLaughlin, 'Computer Generated Inventions' (2018) 8–9, <https://papers.ssrn.com/sol3/papers.cfm?abstract_id=3097822> accessed 3 June 2021.

3 See e.g., Explanatory Statement to the European Parliament (Committee on Legal Affairs), 'Report on Intellectual Property Rights for the Development of Artificial Intelligence Technologies' (2020/2015(INI)) 12 <www.europarl.europa.eu/doceo/document/A-9-2020-0176_EN.pdf> accessed 29 May 2021.

4 Ibid. Note that already in 2017 the European Parliament had adopted a Resolution with recommendations to the Commission on Civil Law Rules on Robotics, where it called on the Commission to "support a horizontal and technologically neutral approach to intellectual property applicable to the various sectors in which robotics could be employed." The explanatory statement accompanying the Resolution clarified in that context that "the elaboration of criteria for "own intellectual creation" for copyrightable works produced by computers or robots is demanded." See European Parliament Resolution of 16 February 2017 with Recommendations to the Commission on Civil Law Rules on Robotics (2015/2103(INL)). <www.europarl.europa.eu/sides/getDoc.do?type=TA&language=EN&reference=P8-TA-2017-0051> accessed 3 June 2021.

underlying justifications for copyright and patent protection can a grounded conclusion be reached regarding whether AI-generated content should be protected by copyright and patent laws.

The following section of each chapter analyses relevant elements related to copyright and patent protection in four jurisdictions: Europe,[5] United States (US), Australia and Japan. The criteria for the choice of these specific jurisdictions were wide geographic area coverage, balance of common law and civil law countries, and advancement of AI developments, both from a technological and legal perspectives. The relevant elements explored were chosen according to their relevance to the question of protection (or lack thereof) of AI-generated content, and vary from one chapter to the other, due to differences between copyright and patent law. For copyright, the elements selected for analysis, which will be examined in relation to which jurisdiction, were protected subject matter (including conditions for protection, such as originality), authorship and other forms of protection, like neighbouring rights regimes, where applicable. For patent, the analysis will focus on patentable subject matter; the patentability requirement of inventive step or non-obviousness; the requirement of enablement or sufficient disclosure of the invention; inventorship; and other forms of protection such as utility model or similar regimes, where applicable.

Other elements of copyright and patent law regimes, while relevant for the broader topic of AI and intellectual property, are outside the scope of this book. One example is the issue of ownership, which differs from rules of authorship and inventorship. This is because this book seeks to investigate the legal status of AI creations, which include who the creator might be; ownership questions, while relevant, bring little to this discussion. This book will also not examine the protection available for the AI system itself, since the goal is to zoom in on output created by the AI system, but not the AI system itself.

Chapter 4 wraps up with some conclusions and recommendations. Building upon the previous Chapters, it will be highlighted that both copyright and patent laws require a human creator, and that the key question then becomes which type of human contribution to an AI-generated work or invention can give rise to authorship or inventorship claims. Specific recommendations in relation to future policy- and law-making in copyright and patents will also be recalled, and patterns that emerge from those recommendations – namely, the possibility of creating new rights to protect AI-generated content – will be further analysed. These recommendations are, to the extent possible, jurisdiction-agnostic, as the idea is to aim for an alignment of the different jurisdictions. Patent and copyright laws exist against the background of some level of international harmonisation

---

5 For copyright, the analysis will focus on European Union (EU) law in the field of copyright. The EU has played a fundamental role in the harmonisation of copyright laws of the member states. For patents, because there is no horizontal harmonisation of patent law at the EU level, the jurisdiction analysed will be Europe, and the basis for analysis will be the European Patent Convention of 5 October 1973 (EPC), which is a multilateral treaty rather than an EU instrument.

(which is in place due to several treaties and conventions[6]); building on the work of that harmonisation and continuously monitoring the development of national or regional laws is key, since harmonisation increases legal certainty and trust of users in the patent- and copyright legal systems.[7] Chapter 4 will finish by highlighting some points of attention for policymakers, which may also amount to possible topics for other research. These will consist of exceptions that can accommodate machine learning (since AI creation of works and inventions is dependent on a previous stage of machine learning), ownership issues and moral rights.

References

Primary sources

Agreement on Trade-Related Aspects of Intellectual Property (1994)

Berne Convention for the Protection of Literary and Artistic Works (1886)

European Parliament (Committee on Legal Affairs), 'Report on Intellectual Property Rights for the Development of Artificial Intelligence Technologies' (2020/2015(INI)) <www.europarl.europa.eu/doceo/document/A-9-2020-0176_EN.pdf> accessed 29 May 2021

European Parliament Resolution of 16 February 2017 with Recommendations to the Commission on Civil Law Rules on Robotics (2015/2103(INL))<www.europarl.europa.eu/sides/getDoc.do?type=TA&language=EN&reference=P8-TA-2017-0051> accessed 3 June 2021

European Patent Convention (1973)

Paris Convention for the Protection of Industrial Property (1883)

Patent Cooperation Treaty (1970)

WIPO Copyright Treaty (1996)

Secondary sources

Calo R, 'Artificial Intelligence Policy: A Primer and a Roadmap' (2017) <https://papers.ssrn.com/sol3/papers.cfm?abstract_id=3015350> accessed 3 June 2021

Hashiguchi M, 'The Global Artificial Intelligence Revolution Challenges Patent Eligibility' (2017) 13 *J Bus & Tech* 1

McLaughlin M, 'Computer Generated Inventions' (2018) <https://papers.ssrn.com/sol3/papers.cfm?abstract_id=3097822> accessed 3 June 2021

---

6 See e.g., on patents the Paris Convention for the Protection of Industrial Property (1883) and the Patent Cooperation Treaty (1970); on copyright, the Berne Convention for the Protection of Literary and Artistic Works (1886) and WIPO Copyright Treaty (1996); and on both patents and copyright, the Agreement on Trade-Related Aspects of Intellectual Property, or TRIPS Agreement (1994).

7 This has been highlighted recently, in relation to patents, by the President of the European Patent Office, 'Update of Legal Aspects of Artificial Intelligence and Patents' (October 23, 2020) 2<www.epo.org/modules/epoweb/acdocument/epoweb2/468/en/CA-PL_5-20_en.pdf> accessed 3 June 2021): "Continuous monitoring of the technical developments and exchange of policies and practices between the patent offices and beyond contributes to aligning practices and increases legal certainty for the users of the patent system.").

President of the European Patent Office, 'Update of Legal Aspects of Artificial Intelligence and Patents' (October 23, 2020) <www.epo.org/modules/epoweb/acdocument/epoweb2/468/en/CA-PL_5-20_en.pdf> accessed 3 June 2021

Stone P and others, 'Artificial Intelligence and Life in 2030. One Hundred Year Study on Artificial Intelligence: Report of the 2015–2016 Study Panel' (2016) <http://ai100.stanford.edu/2016-report> accessed 3 June 2021

Talk to Transformer <https://app.inferkit.com/demo> accessed 3 June 2021

2 AI and copyright protection

2.1 Introduction

The act of creation is traditionally equated with a human being. However, developments in the field of artificial intelligence (AI) are challenging this notion. We currently have machines that can create books, music, paintings and other subject matter that would come under copyright protection when created by a human being. Non-human creations that amount to literary or artistic products thus raise questions regarding the legal status of AI creations.

The intervention of AI systems in the creative process implies a re-evaluation of key concepts in copyright, (such as authorship and conditions for protection), against a revision of the rationales underlying copyright protection (since they justify the granting of exclusive rights in the first place).

This chapter will start by exploring the notion of AI systems as creators (2.2). For that purpose, it sketches a definition of AI systems and of the way they work, while pinpointing the stages at which human involvement might still be needed (2.2.1). The next section describes examples of early AI creators (2.2.2) and of more recent AI applications (2.2.3), which will provide an idea of the evolution in the area of AI systems capable of generating creative products. Section 2.2.4 will build on the previous ones and investigate what creativity means in the context of AI creations.

The next section (2.3) will revisit copyright rationales and describe the main theories that justify the grant of copyright protection. This will provide a basis for the conclusions later in the chapter – the question as to whether copyright can or should provide protection for AI-generated works must start with unveiling what justifies that protection in the first place.

Section 2.4 follows to analyse a few elements of the copyright laws in the jurisdictions selected. The elements to be analysed are those deemed the most relevant for the topic of this book. The first one will be copyright's protected subject matter (which comprises the conditions for protection). It will be assessed what the eligibility criteria are, and to what extent that criteria can accept creations where an AI system is part of the creative process. The second element to be assessed will be authorship. The analysis of authorship for each of the jurisdictions will focus on whether the concept of authorship can

DOI: 10.4324/9780367823290-2

accommodate non-human creations. Finally, in an ancillary fashion, alternative forms of protection, such as neighbouring rights regimes, will be briefly considered where the jurisdiction concerned comprises such regimes.

The last section of this chapter will provide some conclusions and recommendations, based on the previous sections. The conclusions will highlight that a human being is always present at some point in the creative process. Since the current common rules and practices of the four jurisdictions require human intervention for a work to be protected by copyright, a test will be suggested to assess when the intervention of a human being during the creative process is enough for an authorship claim to succeed. Moreover, beyond the finding that authorless works cannot be copyrightable, this Section will look into whether they should be. Hence, this part will investigate the adequacy of the regime of computer-generated works – which can be found in jurisdictions other than the ones examined in this book – to protect authorless, AI-generated output. At this point, it will also be examined whether protecting such output would be compatible with the copyright rationales earlier explained in section 2.3, and then the chapter will briefly consider the advantages and drawbacks of creating a sui generis, neighbouring right or a similar regime specifically designed to protect AI-generated works and encourage their dissemination.

2.2 Artificial intelligence systems as creators

2.2.1 Setting the stage

Even though there is no universally accepted definition of AI, AI systems have been defined as machines that imply a human-type of behaviour, in the sense that it is meant to signify actions done by computers that require intelligence when done by humans.[1] This indicates that the concept of intelligence is key

---

1 Jack B. Copeland, 'What is Artificial Intelligence?' (*Alan Turing*, May 2000) <www.alanturing.net/turing_archive/pages/Reference%20Articles/What%20is%20AI.html> accessed 5 May 2021; Ryan Abbott, *The Reasonable Robot – Artificial Intelligence and the Law* (Cambridge University Press 2020) 22, defines AI as "an algorithm or machine capable of completing tasks that would otherwise require cognition." The author goes on to explain that "[c]ognition refers to mental capabilities and the process of acquiring knowledge and understanding through thought." See also Stuart Russell and Peter Norvig, *Artificial Intelligence – A Modern Approach* (3rd ed., Pearson 2014) 1–2, according to whom four different approaches can be followed to define the term "artificial intelligence": thinking humanly (which measures closeness to human thought processes); thinking rationally (measuring the thought process against an ideal performance as embodied in rationality); acting humanly (measuring fidelity to human behaviour); and acting rationally (where it is considered that a system is rational if it does the "right thing"). Note however that, for some schools of thought, "intelligence" requires understanding, which would mean that acting humanly or rationally should not be considered a measure of intelligence, as the AI system would not be aware of what it is doing. Expanding on this point (albeit concluding that "AI does not need to mimic human thought processes or perceive the meaning of its actions") see *Abbott* (ibid.) 25–27. It should also be acknowledged that the term "artificial intelligence" is equally used to define a broad area that comprises inter alia reasoning and knowledge representation, robotics, natural language processing, and machine learning – see Michael

when trying to identify the meaning of AI. One difficulty in defining the term "artificial intelligence" though is that "intelligence" in itself is not a monolithic concept; in fact, there is no single or absolute measure of intelligence.[2] This assumption is reflected in the fact that human actions can take a myriad of forms. Humans can use logic and reasoning to find a solution to a problem; but they can also use their creativity to produce artistic works, for instance. And indeed, even though there is no unitary view of what "intelligence" means, it is arguable that human intelligence is an ensemble of several components, and that creativity is one of them.[3] It can also be maintained that a "higher human intelligence," which involves intention and content states like belief and desire,[4] is part of a broader concept of intelligence (one that would be out of reach for AI systems, which cannot – or not yet – achieve such content states).

But besides intelligence, AI also presupposes autonomy.[5] Autonomy implies that the work produced by the AI system results from it acting independently from the constant input of a human operator.[6] Beyond that, autonomy can be defined as a matter of scale, according to the level of human involvement, and not necessarily in the binary state autonomous–non autonomous.[7] There are

---

McLaughlin, 'Computer Generated Inventions' (2018) American University Washington College of Law <https://papers.ssrn.com/sol3/papers.cfm?abstract_id=3097822> accessed 22 May 2021.

2 Francisco Câmara Pereira, *Creativity and Artificial Intelligence – A Conceptual Blending Approach* (Mouton de Gruyter 2007) 10: "[I]ntelligence is not monolithic: there is a multitude of factors to take into account and one cannot find a unique and absolute measure."

3 Ibid., 10. See also David Levy, *Robots Unlimited – Life in a Virtual Age* (Taylor & Francis 2005) 149 and *Copeland* (n 1) (the latter pointing out other examples, such as learning, reasoning, problem-solving, perception, and language-understanding).

4 Richard McDonough, 'Machine Predictability versus Human Creativity,' in Terry Dartnall (ed.), *Artificial Intelligence and Creativity – An Interdisciplinary Approach* (Springer 1994) 117. The author holds that "higher human intelligence is inseparable from the sort of cultural activity which distinguishes persons from animals or machines."

5 In the 'European Parliament Resolution of 16 February 2017 with Recommendations to the Commission on Civil Law Rules on Robotics' (2015/2103(INL), European Parliament 2017) <www.europarl.europa.eu/sides/getDoc.do?type=TA&language=EN&reference=P8-TA-2017-0051> accessed 7 May 2021, it is considered that a smart robot will imply "the acquisition of autonomy through sensors and/or by exchanging data with its environment (inter-connectivity) and the trading and analysing of those data." See also Madeleine de Cock Buning, 'Autonomous Intelligence Systems as Creative Agents Under the EU Framework for Intellectual Property' (2016) 7 *European Journal of Risk Regulation* 310, 312, explaining that autonomy is a necessary element of artificial intelligence and is "related to the level of control or involvement a human operator has in a system."

6 Margaret A. Boden, *The Creative Mind – Myths and Mechanisms* (2nd ed., Taylor & Francis Group 2004) 163: "[W]hat must a program be like, to appear creative? . . . The results must often be individually unpredictable, although they may all possess a recognizable conceptual style. They must be generated by the program acting alone, relying on its own computational resources rather than constant input from a human operator."

7 For an alternative classification of autonomy, see The Royal Academy of Engineering, *Autonomous Systems: Social, Legal and Ethical Issues* (The Royal Academy of Engineering August 2009) <www.raeng.org.uk/publications/reports/autonomous-systems-report> accessed 5 May 2021, explaining that systems can range from controlled, implying a high level of human intervention (such as a car);

several levels of autonomy, with some AI systems being more autonomous than others.[8]

At the low end of the spectrum of autonomy, machines are mere tools, whereas at the high end they will amount to an AI system capable of autonomously creating works, with little to no human input. The middle of the scale blends human and AI participation, and it is arguably where the grey area and most problems for now lie.[9] The level of involvement, or autonomy, of AI in the act of creation is related to the distinction that is sometimes made between AI-assisted and AI-generated content, where the former represents situations where the AI is a tool in the hands of a (human) creator, and the latter amounts to content autonomously generated by an AI.[10] Assessing the level of involvement of an AI system in the creative process is relevant for a discussion on copyright and on whether copyright is or should be granted to AI-generated works, insofar as, if a human or humans is/are traced in the process of creation, that intervention might amount to (human) authorship. However, while it is helpful to conceptualise AI-generated works in different categories according

---

to automatic, which carries out fixed functions (such as an elevator); or to autonomous, at the low end of human intervention, which are systems that can learn and make their own decisions.

8 See Ana Ramalho, 'Will Robots Rule the (Artistic) World? A Proposed Model for the Legal Status of Creations by Artificial Intelligence Systems' (2017) 21 *Journal of Internet Law* 13 and references cited therein. See however European Group on Ethics in Science and New Technologies, *Statement on Artificial Intelligence, Robotics and 'Autonomous Systems'* (Publication Office of the EU March 2018) 9–10 <https://op.europa.eu/en/publication-detail/-/publication/dfebe62e-4ce9-11e8-be1d-01aa75ed71a1> accessed 5 May 2021, stating that the term "autonomy" has an ethical dimension, as it is connected to human dignity and human agency. In this construction, "autonomy" can only be attributed to human beings, and therefore "automation" is a term better suited for machines. Throughout this book, I will use the term "autonomy," as it has gained wide recognition in AI research (without prejudice to recognising that "autonomy" in a narrow sense can only be applied to human beings).

9 Jani McCutcheon, 'The Vanishing Author in Computer-Generated Works: A Critical Analysis of Recent Australian Case Law' (2013) 36 *Melbourne University Law Review* 915, 931–935.

10 See advocating for this distinction e.g., Josef Drexl and others, 'Comments of the Max Planck Institute for Innovation and Competition of 11 February 2020 on the Draft Issues Paper of the World Intellectual Property Organization on Intellectual Property Policy and Artificial Intelligence' (Max Planck Institute for Innovation and Competition 2020) 2 <https://pure.mpg.de/rest/items/item_3193085_1/component/file_3193086/content> accessed 22 May 2021. Jane C. Ginsburg and Luke A. Budiardjo, 'Authors and Machines' (2019) 34 *Berkeley Technology Law Journal* 439, add a third category, which somehow reflects more accurately the spectrum of involvement of AI in the act of creation. They conceptualise outputs originated in an AI as three different types: "Machines designed to create outputs which reflect only the creative contributions of the users are 'ordinary' tools, and we should treat them in the same way we treat cameras, word processing programs, and other mechanical or digital adjuncts to the creative process. Machines which, instead, are capable of producing outputs with minimal user input are 'fully-generative' in that their outputs necessarily flow from the creative contributions of the machines' designers – who, accordingly, are the authors of the resulting works, even if someone other than the machine's designer operates the machine. And machines which produce outputs reflecting the creative contributions of both the designer and the user are 'partially-generative' in that the machines do not wholly generate the expressive content of the resulting works, but instead rely on the contributions of users."

to the level of autonomy of the AI system, it is less advantageous to do so in a binary (or even tripartite) fashion. As shall be apparent from the discussions in this book, AI systems can blend human and machine contributions to many different degrees. A more granular approach is therefore preferred, and accordingly the spectrum of autonomy referred to above is deemed more useful for analysing AI-generated content and its treatment under copyright law.

A number of authors hold that there isn't at the moment an AI at the highest end of the spectrum of autonomy, i.e., a true form of "strong AI," "a self-conscious and self-expanding system . . . which is capable of establishing its own rules and thus of expanding its code, function and purpose by itself."[11] Indeed, many commentators agree that currently AI exists only in the shape of "weak AI" or "narrow AI," which are AI systems that can perform specific tasks in well-defined fields (as opposed to a general intelligence like the one displayed by humans).[12] For instance, while evolutionary programmes can change their own rules in ways not foreseen by the programmer, so that they can generate outcomes that they would not have been able to generate in the past,[13] an initial programming of the AI system (by a human being) is still necessary. In fact, in order to think and act humanly and/or rationally, AI systems need to "learn." The system does not "learn" in the traditional (human) sense of the word, but it does so in a functional sense by changing its behaviour based on experience in order to enhance its performance.[14] This concerns a subfield of AI as a scientific area, called "machine learning": an automated process designed to find patterns in data, to then apply those patterns to new data.[15]

11 See e.g., Tobias Rothkegel and Mark Taylor, 'What Characterises Artificial Intelligence and How Does It Work?' (2016) 22 *Computer and Telecommunications Law Review* 98. See for an in-depth development of the concept of strong versus weak AI, *Russel and Norvig* (n 1) 1020ff. See also European Parliament (Committee on Legal Affairs), 'Report on Intellectual Property Rights for the Development of Artificial Intelligence Technologies' (2020/2015(INI)), European Parliament 2020) 13 <www.europarl.europa.eu/doceo/document/A-9-2020-0176_EN.pdf> accessed 22 May 202: "The prospect of a 'strong' AI, that is to say one that is conscious of itself, seems after all still to be very futuristic."

12 See 'Public Views on Artificial Intelligence and Intellectual Property Policy' (United States Patent and Trademark Office October 2020) section ii. <www.uspto.gov/sites/default/files/documents/USPTO_AI-Report_2020-10-07.pdf> accessed 20 May 2021. See also Juan Pavón and María J. González-Espejo, 'Fundamentals of Artificial Intelligence,' in María J. González-Espejo and Juan Pavón (eds.), *An Introductory Guide to Artificial Intelligence for Legal Professionals* (Kluwer Law International 2020) 7.

13 Margaret Boden, 'Creativity: How Does It Work?', in Michael Krausz, Denis Dutton and Karen Bardsley (eds.), *The Idea of Creativity* (Brill 2009) 245: "Whether a computer could ever come up with a new style is a hotly disputed question. It is not obvious that it could not, because some programs are able to alter their own rules in unpredictable ways, so that they can generate structures on Tuesday, which they could not have generated on Monday. These are the so-called evolutionary programs, which contain mechanisms – 'genetic algorithms' – that can make random changes in the program's rules and select the most promising for further 'breeding.' Sometimes, the selection is done at each generation by a human being. But sometimes, the programmer chooses a list of criteria – the 'fitness function' – by means of which the program itself selects the winners automatically."

14 Harry Surden, 'Machine Learning and Law' (2014) 89 *Washington Law Review* 87, 88–90.

15 Josef Drexl and others, 'Technical Aspects of Artificial Intelligence: An Understanding from an Intellectual Property Law Perspective' (October 2019) Max Planck Institute for Innovation and

Machine learning can be done in a supervised or unsupervised way, or also as reinforced learning. In supervised learning, the machine "learns" from data that is already labelled, i.e., the AI is given concrete examples labelled with the right answers (such as pictures of dogs and wolves with those names on the images).[16] Once the AI is well trained on the labelled data, it can give quick and accurate answers to new inputs, but it is difficult to adjust it to changing environments.[17] By contrast, in unsupervised learning the data used as learning input is unlabelled. This means that the right answers are not provided to the AI system (for instance, the system could even just be told to find out how a dog looks like, and for that it would go on the web with the help of a search engine and retrieve images of dogs, to then learn what was common among those images).[18] Because the AI system learns through its own observation, it can more easily adapt to changing environments (although the solutions it finds are not always the ones intended, as they depend on the experience gathered throughout the learning process).[19] Finally, in reinforced learning, the AI makes its decisions freely, and a human being provides a reward signal in relation to each decision which tells the AIs whether the decision is good or bad.[20]

In both supervised and unsupervised learning, human intervention is present at some point (although admittedly at different degrees). Thus, when an AI system generates a creative output, human intervention can still be traced at a few stages in the process. The collection of reliable data and its preparation is heavily human-dependent, for example (especially if quality of data is an issue, which will require e.g., filtering bias).[21] In supervised learning, a human being will have to label the data, but even the indication of a concept in unsupervised learning is triggered by a human action (and in any case, in unsupervised learning, human intervention to interpret the AI output will be more extensively

---

Competition Research Paper No. 19–13, version 1.0, 3 <https://ssrn.com/abstract=3465577> accessed 21 May 2020.

16 Yorick Wilks, *Artificial Intelligence – Modern Magic or Dangerous Future?* (Icon Books 2019) 126–127.

17 *Pavón and González-Espejo* (n 12) 14.

18 *Wilks* (n 16).

19 *Pavón and González-Espejo* (n 12) 14.

20 European Commission Independent High-Level Expert Group on Artificial Intelligence, 'A Definition of AI: Main Capabilities and Disciplines' (European Commission 8 April 2019) 4 <https://ec.europa.eu/digital-single-market/en/news/definition-artificial-intelligence-main-capabilities-and-scientific-disciplines> accessed 22 May 2021.

21 1 *Pavón and González-Espejo* (n 12) 13: "One of the most time-consuming tasks in this process [of machine learning] is the acquisition and preparation of data sets. . . . They usually come from different sources, so they have to be integrated, cleaned, filtered and converted into a convenient format (normalized) to be processed by the available ML tools." See also Amanda Levendowski, 'How Copyright Law Can Fix Artificial Intelligence's Implicit Bias Problem' (2018) 93 *Washington Law Review* 579, 591: "Good training data is crucial for creating accurate AI systems. The AI system tasked with identifying cats must be able abstract out the right features, or heuristics, of a cat from training data. To do so, the training data must be well-selected by humans – biased training data can result in both false positives and false negatives" (footnotes omitted).

required[22]). In reinforced learning, a human being provides feedback to the AI regarding its decisions. In the stage where the AI creates the work it is also possible to have human intervention – for instance, a human might want to give instructions for an AI to modify the work – even though this is not necessarily the case. Moreover, in some cases, post-production of a creative product (choosing between different AI outputs, perfecting the chosen one, etc) will also be necessary (and performed by a human being).

There are a number of methods of machine learning. One that has gained prominence is neural networks – networks of small processing units inspired in the human brain, with several weighted connections among them.[23] The connections' weights are trainable parameters, i.e., numeric values which evolve during the training process.[24] One of the most successful neural network modalities – because it is more accurate and less dependent on human guidance – is deep learning.[25] In deep learning, the processing of data takes place through several layers, from raw data to greater levels of abstraction (each layer being thus a more granular representation of reality).[26] Each layer takes care of a specific task: for instance, if the input data is a photo of a cat, the first layer can take its pixels, the following layer can e.g., try to identify edges in the picture, the next one tries to connect those edges to certain shapes, the following puts together different forms to obtain parts (such as a tail, a nose or a leg), and all the layers together will lead to the conclusion that the photo depicts a cat.[27] During the training process, a weight is assigned to each input received from an input in the previous layer, so that it is possible to identify specific patterns.[28] Neural networks require a large number of parameters and neurons, thus being dependent on high computing power and specialised knowledge (as it is a difficult task to design the network and the interconnections between the different layers).[29] According to Pavón and Gonzalez-Espejo García, however, the main issue with neural networks, specifically deep learning, is traceability: i.e., because it is based on trial-and-error, the final result or output can be hard to explain if there is no access to all the iterations that led to the result.[30]

A special type of neural networks are generative adversarial networks (GANs). GANs consist of two models (a generator and a discriminator) that

---

22 *Drexl and others* (n 15) 8.

23 *European Commission Independent High-Level Expert Group on Artificial Intelligence* (n 20) 4.

24 *Drexl and others* (n 15) 6.

25 *European Commission Independent High-Level Expert Group on Artificial Intelligence* (n 20) 4.

26 Compare with Copyright Clearance Center, 'Written Comments to the Content of WIPO Conversation on Intellectual Property and Artificial Intelligence (Second Session)' (Draft Issues Paper on Intellectual Property and Artificial Intelligence, World Intellectual Property Office 2020) <www. wipo.int/export/sites/www/about-ip/en/artificial_intelligence/call_for_comments/pdf/org_ccc. pdf> accessed 28 May 2021.

27 *Pavón and González-Espejo* (n 12) 15.

28 Ibid.

29 Ibid., 16.

30 Ibid.

interact with one another.[31] GANs feed on random input (noise), and as their training progresses – through the interplay between the generator and the discriminator – they are able to produce output based on a real dataset that they are also provided. The discriminator's role is to detect whether a piece of data is part of the real data set or whether it was generated by an algorithm, while the generator's function is to create output that resembles as much as possible the real data set.[32] The data that GANs are provided with is usually unlabelled – thus, any underlying structure or pattern is not evident to humans and/or cannot be easily discovered by other techniques. GANs have been used in a variety of applications, including novel paintings[33] or music,[34] and even in more specific applications like the generation of fake content[35] (e.g., videos, "deepfakes").

2.2.2 Early AI creators

Early AI systems that produced creative output achieved levels of relative independence. A few examples are worth mentioning: AARON (for artistic works), BRUTUS (for literary works) and the Computoser (for musical works).

AARON is the name of a program created in the 70s by Harold Cohen – an art professor and an artist himself. Its works have been exhibited in many galleries and museums around the world, and private collectors have paid considerable sums for AARON's art.[36]

The program generates drawings and paintings (with real paint and canvas, as Cohen built a painting machine that works together with the AI system). The first versions of the AI system were simple: Cohen defined a small set of rules and shapes, and AARON used those to compose drawings.[37] Since the 70s and until 2016 (when he passed away), Cohen worked on refining AARON's code,

---

31 Ian Goodfellow and others, 'Generative Adversarial Nets,' in Zoubin Ghahramani and others (eds.), *Advances in Neural Information Processing Systems* (NIPS 2014) 2672–2680.

32 *Drexl and others* (n 15) 8. See also *Pavón and González-Espejo* (n 12) 16–17.: "For instance, there could be a generating network that creates images of fake cats that look real. The other is the discriminator network, which examines the pictures and tries to determine whether they are real or fake. This competition between the two networks makes them perform better."

33 Ahmed Elgammal and others, 'CAN: Creative Adversarial Networks Generating – "Art" by Learning About Styles and Deviating from Style Norms' (arXiv 2017) <https://arxiv.org/abs/1706.07068> accessed 28 May 2021.

34 Li Chia Yang and others, 'MidiNet: A Convolutional Generative Adversarial Network for Symbolic-Domain Music Generation' (arXiv 2017) <https://arxiv.org/abs/1703.10847> accessed 28 May 2021.

35 Ming Yu-Liu and others, 'Unsupervised Image-to-Image Translation Networks', in Isabelle Guyon and others (eds.), *Advances in Neural Information Processing Systems* (NIPS 2017) 700–708.

36 Richard Moss, 'Creative AI: The Robots that Would be Painters' (*New Atlas*, February 16, 2015) <http://newatlas.com/creative-ai-algorithmic-art-painting-fool-aaron/36106/> accessed 18 May 2021.

37 Chris Garcia, 'Harold Cohen and AARON – A 40-year Collaboration' (*Computer History*, August 23, 2016) <https://computerhistory.org/blog/harold-cohen-and-aaron-a-40-year-collaboration/> accessed 18 May 2021.

and enhancing its knowledge of artistic elements such as colour or form.[38] Cohen used his own knowledge to do so; reportedly, he would first reflect on how one would approach the production of art, to then turn the answer into executable commands.[39] The body of knowledge that AARON relies on to produce paintings and drawings is comprised of both external-world objects and representation-building processes.[40]

Once the program is running, AARON makes its own decisions and it is not possible for a human to modify the drawings as they emerge.[41] Each drawing is unique because it is the result of millions of possible decisions that AARON makes as it draws.[42] In other words, AARON creates the works autonomously, though based on the "teachings" of Cohen. For example, in 1985 Cohen described the Statue of Liberty with sufficient detail to allow AARON to produce a drawing depicting it.[43] However, AARON's artistic decisions are also constrained to a certain degree by some technical issues. Namely, it is unable to correct or erase what it creates as it goes along, and it always starts in the foreground moving towards the background of the drawing.[44] For that reason, AARON is unlikely to draw big objects in the foreground, because that would block things drawn in the background; therefore, it either places small objects in the foreground, or it draws there the main subject of the drawing (often, people).[45] Some of the decisions that AARON makes seem random, just like human decisions would be – e.g., whenever the program has to make a decision and there is no particular reason to choose one course of action over another, it will make a seemingly random choice.[46]

BRUTUS is a story-generating program that was developed by Selmer Bringsjord and his collaborators. Its authors recognize that BRUTUS lacks consciousness; in fact, it is precisely its lack of consciousness that gave rise to the hardest of the authors' initial questions: how could they build the program so that the stories it generated were rich in consciousness?[47] BRUTUS uses two distinct levels: the knowledge level and the process level. The knowledge level contains representations of the types of knowledge necessary to write a story, namely domain knowledge (such as places and behaviours), linguistic

38 Annemarie Bridy, 'The Evolution of Authorship: Works Made by Code' (2016) 39 *Columbia Journal of Law and the Arts* 395, 397., Boden, *The Creative Mind – Myths and Mechanisms* (n 6) 159ff.

39 Pamela McCorduck, *Machines Who Think. A Personal Inquiry into the History and Prospects of Artificial Intelligence* (A K Peters 2004) 518.

40 Pamela McCorduck, *Aaron's Code: Meta-Art, Artificial Intelligence, and the Work of Harold Cohen* (W.H. Freeman & Company 1991) 202.

41 Ibid., 201.

42 Ibid.

43 Harold Cohen, 'The Further Exploits of AARON, Painter' (1995) 4(2) *SEHR*.

44 McCorduck, *Aaron's Code* (n 40) 202.

45 Ibid.

46 Ibid.

47 Selmer Bringsjord and David A. Ferrucci, *Artificial Intelligence and Literary Creativity: Inside the Mind of BRUTUS, A Storytelling Machine* (Lawrence Erlbaum Associates 2000) 67.

knowledge (words, sentences, etc) and literary knowledge (e.g., literary structures or story grammars, which includes principles of storytelling and readers' engagement).[48] The process level comprises the processes that use the knowledge level to produce a story.[49] The specific stories created by the program are mysterious and have betrayal as their main theme.[50] Apart from grammar rules and general vocabulary, BRUTUS was given a database of information about the world and the language of academia (the setting against which the story develops), as well as specific representations (for example, a mathematical representation of betrayal, defined e.g., in terms of actions and goals of the characters).[51]

Besides AARON and BRUTUS, it is worth mentioning the Computoser[52] – a somewhat more recent AI, but whose system still denotes a simple architecture. The Computoser is a rule-based, probability-driven algorithm which generates music by following a pre-established (albeit loosely defined) set of rules.[53] The preparation stage of the algorithm involved retrieving 500 popular songs details, analysing 50 MIDI files of classical and modern composers, and extracting rules from different sources about music theory and composition.[54] Users can listen to the music generated by the Computoser by merely pressing the "play" button, or can instead choose certain parameters that the autonomously generated track should follow (mood, tempo, accompaniment, instrument, scale, drums, dissonance or whether they want a more classical or electronic-like track).

2.2.3 Evolution: GPT-3, DeepDream, Next Rembrandt

More recent AI systems are based on artificial neural networks. For example, the GPT-3, arguably the largest language model created to date, has 175 billion parameters (weights of the connections between the nodes of the neural network).[55] It can generate any kind of text, such as songs, essays, press releases, guitar tabs or even computer code; however, it is still prone to mistakes like

---

48 Ibid., 165ff.

49 Ibid.

50 *Levy* (n 3) 160ff.

51 Ibid.

52 See 'Computoser' <http://computoser.com> accessed 22 May 2021.

53 Bozhidar Bozhanov, 'Computoser – Rule-Based, Probability-Driven Algorithmic Music Composition' (December 2014) 1 <https://arxiv.org/abs/1412.3079> accessed 22 May 2021: "While progressing with the composition, decisions between multiple allowed alternatives are taken based on predefined probabilities, drawn from both existing musical practice and the analysis of sample data."

54 Ibid.

55 Tom B. Brown and others, 'Language Models are Few – Shot Learners' (May 2020) <https://arxiv.org/abs/2005.14165> accessed 28 May 2021; Will D. Heaven, 'Open AI's New Language Generator GPT-3 is Shockingly Good – and Completely Mindless' (*MIT Technology Review*, July 20, 2020) <www.technologyreview.com/2020/07/20/1005454/openai-machine-learning-language-generator-gpt-3-nlp/> accessed 28 May 2021.; James Vincent, 'Open AI's Latest Breakthrough is Astonishingly Powerful, but Still Fighting its Flaws' (*The Verge*, July 30, 2020) <www.theverge.com/21346343/gpt-3-explainer-openai-examples-errors-agi-potential> accessed 28 May 2021.

producing biased text, or generating incorrect facts or information.[56] Mistakes made by the GPT-3 are supposedly due to the large amounts of data it ingested without any human supervision or rules (as human intervention would make the model too resource-intensive).[57]

Another example is DeepDream, an artificial neural network developed by Google. DeepDream finds patterns in the images that it is fed and enhances them. This is done by making different layers of the neural network emphasize specific features of the image.[58] The result is a psychedelic, sort of augmented version of the original image. In the field of artistic works, another known example is the Next Rembrandt project, where an AI system can generate works in the style of Rembrandt. The researchers involved in the project examined the entire collection of Rembrandt's works using 3D scans and digital files upscaled by deep learning algorithms. This allowed the AI to grasp the painter's use of geometry, composition and painting materials to then replicate the style of Rembrandt in a new painting.[59]

2.2.4 Creativity in the context of AI

The functioning of recent AI systems and the examples mentioned above beg the question as to whether machines can really be creative. Since creativity is considered part of the notion of "intelligence" – which is itself an essential element when defining AI – shedding some light onto the concept of creativity becomes key. It should also be recalled that this book concerns AI systems which generate (creative) output that may potentially be considered for copyright (and also patent) protection, and therefore it is relevant to investigate what creativity means in the context of AI-generated creations. Scholarship on creativity is available in numerous fields, such as psychology, neurobiology, philosophy or computational creativity (the latter looking specifically at machine creativity). They all study and attempt to define creativity in different ways and employing different methods.

In psychology, consensual definitions of creativity focus on the creative outcome, rather than the creative process or the person who created the product, as ultimately the identification of a process or a person as creative depends heavily on the tangible outcome being creative.[60] It is therefore such creative product that will be subject to a creativity assessment.

---

56 *Heaven* (n 55).

57 *Vincent* (n 55).

58 For a detailed explanation, see Alexander Mordvintsev and others, 'Inceptionism: Going Deeper into Neural Networks' (Google AI Blog, June 17, 2015) <https://ai.googleblog.com/2015/06/inceptionism-going-deeper-into-neural.html> accessed 28 May 2021, and 'Tensor Flow Tutorial on DeepDream' <www.tensorflow.org/tutorials/generative/deepdream> accessed 28 September 2020.

59 For more detail on each of the stages of creation, see 'Next Rembrandt' <www.nextrembrandt.com> accessed 28 May 2021.

60 Teresa M. Amabile, *Creativity in Context* (Westview Press 1996) 33.

Psychologists consider that creativity encompasses at least two elements: novelty and appropriateness. In other words, the creative product must be new and valuable.[61] However, these terms are used in a vague way and it is not clear for whom and to which degree a product must be new and valuable to be considered creative.[62] Beyond these two elements, there is little consensus in psychology as to what creativity is or what it entails.[63]

Some psychologists expressly hold that, in order for a product to be creative, the underlying process must be heuristic (where the path to the outcome is not straightforward) rather than algorithmic (where there is a clear and straightforward path to the outcome).[64] The example that Amabile gives of the latter is telling: "[A]n artist who followed the algorithm 'paint pictures of different sorts of children with large sad eyes, using dark-toned backgrounds' would not be producing creative paintings, even if each painting were unique and technically perfect."[65]

The author goes on to explain that a task or process might be heuristic or algorithmic depending on the creator in question, stating that "if the task is heuristic for the individual in question, then novel and appropriate solutions generated by that individual can be considered creative." This suggests that, according to this theory, an assessment of creativity needs to focus on the outcome, but also on the process of creation – with the consequence that an outcome that is the result of a heuristic process can be considered creative, while a similar outcome resulting from an algorithmic process will not be.

From the perspective of cognitive theories, there are different ways of being creative, and some of them do not involve a conscious effort to create.[66] Some authors even hold that irrationality, intuition or unconsciousness are necessary parts of any creative process – even in fields traditionally embedded with rationality, such as exact sciences.[67] Neurobiologists have a holistic view of creativity, in the sense that all the different facets of creative activity occur within the brain – which is why, according to this field of science, both intuitive and analytical thinking are necessary to generate creative outcomes,[68] even though creativity processes differ from one human brain to another.[69]

61 Panagiotis G. Kampylis and Juri Valtanen, 'Redefining Creativity – Analysing Definitions, Collocations, and Consequences' (2010) 44(3) *Journal of Creative Behaviour* 191, 203; Margaret A. Boden, 'Computer Models of Creativity' (2009) 30 (3) *AI Magazine* 23, 24.

62 Boden (ibid.)

63 Beth A. Hennessey and Teresa M. Amabile, 'Creativity' (2010) 61 *Annual Review of Psychology* 569, 572.

64 *Amabile* (n 60) 35.

65 Ibid., 36.

66 Mark A. Runco, *Creativity: Theories and Themes: Research, Development, and Practice* (2nd ed., Elsevier 2007) 37.

67 Arhurt Koestler, 'The Three Domains of Creativity' in Michael Krausz, Denis Dutton and Karen Bardsley (eds.), *The Idea of Creativity* (Brill 2009) 263.

68 Gregory N. Mandel, 'Left-Brain versus Right-Brain: Competing Conceptions of Creativity in Intellectual Property Law' (2010) 44 *UC Davis Law Review* 283, 333–334.

69 *Runco* (n 66) 108.

The field of philosophy is similar to that of psychology: in order for a product to be creative, it must be new and valuable.[70] Newness or novelty is used in the sense that a work must be different from other creations in order to be considered creative,[71] even though that in itself is a matter of degree.[72] As pointed out by Gaut, however, this (traditional) definition is product-oriented: the creative process is irrelevant for an assessment of creativity.[73] For Gaut, then, one more creativity requirement should be added to the list: that the creative process involves "flair" (as opposed to a mechanical or accidental process).[74] Hausman also adds another criterion for assessing creativity, which is that the work is the result of both spontaneity and direct control (the latter because, inter alia, the creator also exercises "critical judgement in deciding what to accept and reject when possibilities occur to him.")[75]

The definition of creativity in the field of computational creativity[76] is also similar to the one in psychology: for an AI system to be considered creative, it needs to aim to produce solutions that are not replications of previous solutions that the AI system knows (corresponding to the requirement of novelty in psychology); and it also needs to aim to produce solutions that are acceptable for the task it proposes (corresponding to the requirement of appropriateness).[77] In computational creativity, creativity is also a matter of scale – for example, the ability to reason at different levels of abstraction or the ability to work in more than one domain without reprogramming would be considered to be at the high end of the creativity spectrum.[78] It has been pointed out that, in order to be creative, the AI computation must involve judgement and minimum randomness; self-criticism should be a trait at all times.[79]

From the approaches taken by the different disciplines, it is possible to reach an understanding of the concept of creativity that can shed some light into creativity in the context of AI. It is clear that most disciplines call for a multifaceted, non-linear definition of creativity. It is thus necessary to consider not only the creative product (the work), but also the process of creation by which

---

70 See e.g., Carl R. Hausman, 'Criteria of Creativity,' in Michael Krausz, Denis Dutton and Karen Bardsley (eds.), *The Idea of Creativity* (Brill 2009) 12; Berys Gaut, 'Creativity and Skill,' in Michael Krausz, Denis Dutton and Karen Bardsley (eds.), *The Idea of Creativity* (Brill 2009) 83–85.

71 Hausman (ibid.).

72 Gaut (ibid.).

73 Ibid., 85.

74 Ibid., 84–85.

75 *Hausman* (n 71).

76 Computational creativity refers to the use of computers to generate creative results, such as art, scientific theories, or engineering designs – see Margaret A. Boden, 'Foreword', in Tarek R. Besold and others (eds.), *Computational Creativity Research: Towards Creative Machines* (Atlantis Press 2015).

77 *Câmara Pereira* (n 2) 36–37.

78 Ibid.

79 Boden, *The Creative Mind – Myths and Mechanisms* (n 6) 163. See however *Levy* (n 3) 150ff., arguing that "every computer operating in a creative field utilizes some form of randomness in its decision making. . . . The use of randomness breeds creativity because the very process of creativity requires that some decisions be taken for no particular reason"

the work comes into being. This process should be taken holistically, so that not only intuition and spontaneity are relevant, but also conscious control and rationality must be accounted for. Purely mechanical or accidental creations fall short of being creative, as suggested by Gaut. Creativity is also equated to newness or novelty, not in the sense used in patent law (absolute novelty),[80] but rather as something surprising, because different from what existed before (even if only slightly different, because creativity is a matter of scale).

An interdisciplinary definition of creativity, one which borrows elements from different scientific fields, would label many AI-generated outputs as non-creative. Indeed, in addition to clearly mechanic or accidental creations, other types of output could also be considered non-creative. For example, in the case of AARON, if judgement and self-criticism are taken as benchmarks, it is doubtful whether any of its paintings could be considered creative. AARON will create different paintings, but it will not be able to change its style unless it is programmed to do so. It needs to be fed knowledge and experience to be able to produce works. AARON needs to know the things it depicts in its art, which is done through a generative system – a set of abstract rules which specify the anatomy of the human body (two legs, two arms), but also how body parts look like from different points of view (for example, in a painting depicting several people, someone's arm behind someone else's body will be invisible).[81] The program can thus paint people with only one arm visible, but cannot paint one-armed persons, since its model of the human body does not comprise that possibility.[82]

The inability to change through self-criticism and judgement also means that the program has constraints to its creativity. To be able to transform its style, the program would need to be programmed in a way that would allow it to drop constraints (i.e., programmed to consider two limbs as the general default rule, but allowing for one or zero limbs, for instance).[83] Unlike a human painter, AARON cannot imagine things it has never seen. It is this lack of imagination that can be a key difference between human and many machine creators.

Conversely, GANs may be considered to change through self-criticism and judgement due to the interaction between the discriminator and the generator, although they still lack intuition and spontaneity, as well as imagination, at least in the traditional (human) sense of those terms.

To assess whether these differences in creative flair are legally relevant to the copyrightability of AI-generated output, the next sections will examine what the rationales are to grant copyright protection in the first place (2.3), and the requirements for copyright protection in the four jurisdictions concerned (2.4).

80 See e.g., the European Patent Convention (1973), article 54 [1] – [2].
81 Margaret A. Boden, 'Creativity and Computers,' in Dartnall, *Artificial Intelligence and Creativity* (n 4) 10–11.
82 Ibid.
83 Boden, *The Creative Mind – Myths and Mechanisms* (n 6) 161.

2.3 Copyright rationales

The idea of romantic authorship – the author as a single individual – has changed through time. Copyright systems have accommodated joint author-ship and entrepreneurial works, for instance. As mentioned in the introduction to this Chapter, the question of whether copyright can (or should) be further stretched to include non-human authors such as AI systems (and their crea-tions) is one that necessarily starts with an investigation of what justifies the grant of copyright in the first place. By analysing the justifications for copy-right protection, a conclusion later in this chapter on whether new subjects and/or subject matter should come under copyright protection becomes more grounded.

One of the main rationales for copyright protection is the utilitarian the-ory (which is the dominant theory in some jurisdictions, namely in the US). The utilitarian justification considers that the main goal of copyright is to promote social welfare, which is achieved by granting incentives to creation and supporting the dissemination of intellectual goods to the public.[84] This "incentive" element is not to be confused with the idea of "reward."[85] For utilitarians, copyright is granted having society's interests in mind (see e.g., the US case, where grant of copyright is constitutionally linked to the progress of science[86]). Utilitarianism views copyright as a positive (as opposed to natural) right, which is granted ex ante with the aim of furthering societal goals. In the case of copyright, the societal goal is to encourage the creation of intellectual goods. Put it another way, absent the incentive given by copyright protec-tion, authors might not invest their time, effort, and creativity in generating intellectual goods, because these can be easily and cheaply copied (thus taking away from authors the possibility of deriving income from their works).[87] The downside of granting copyright protection to works is of course that giving authors the right to exclude others from using their works prevents society from benefitting from those creations. Implied in the utilitarian theory is then that the exclusionary powers that copyright affords must be offset by the incen-tive to create more works that giving those exclusionary powers represent.[88]

---

84 William Fisher, 'Theories of Intellectual Property,' in Stephen Munzer (ed.), *New Essays in the Legal and Political Theory of Property* (Cambridge University Press 2001) 168–199, Lucie Guibault, *Copy-right Limitations and Contracts – An Analysis of the Contractual Overridability of Limitations on Copyright* (Kluwer Law International 2002) 10; Estelle Derclaye, *The Legal Protection of Databases – A Compara-tive Analysis* (Edward Elgar 2008) 12.

85 "Reward" is a concept more inherent to natural rights theories, as shall be seen below in this section.

86 The United States Constitution, article I., section 8., clause 8 states that "securing for limited times to authors the exclusive right to their respective writings" will "promote the progress of science." See also Ralph D. Clifford, 'Intellectual Property in the Era of the Creative Computer Program: Will the True Creator Please Stand Up?' (1997) 71 *Tulane Law Review* 1675, 1700–1702.

87 Jeanne C. Fromer, 'Expressive Incentives in Intellectual Property' (2012) 98 *Virginia Law Review* 1745, 1751.

88 Mark Lemley, 'The Economics of Improvement in Intellectual Property Law' (2008) 75 *Texas Law Review* 989, 996–997.

What flows from the utilitarian theory is a system where the rights granted to creators are instrumental to society's interests, causing them to be carefully delineated; the limitation to those rights, conversely, is much less restrained, due to the socially desirable outcome of access to creative works.[89]

Critics of the utilitarian theory point out that it does not (or not always) provide a plausible justification for copyright. This will be the case where authors don't need an incentive to create. For instance, granting copyright protection to home-made videos or personal photos taken with your phone is unlikely to lead to more of those videos or photos being created.[90] This might be because some creators are incentivised by the act of creating itself, independently of any benefit that might derived from the resulting creative output, or because some creative activities (say, home-made videos) have very low costs as compared to others (e.g., producing a blockbuster movie).[91] In that sense, the incentive reasoning, which differs so widely depending on the creator and the creative process at stake, seems ill-fitted to justify a unitary system of copyright where all creators and works are treated equally.[92] An additional example of a case where incentive and protection seem to be at odds are derivative works – arguably, giving an author the right to control derivative works being made from her creation does not necessarily provide an incentive for that author to create the work in the first place.[93]

Another line of rationales for copyright protection concerns the natural rights theories. The natural rights argument equates copyright to a natural right, which implies that laws do not create the right, but merely recognize its existence. From this premise, two main theories of copyright rationales flow: the labour theory and the personality theory.

The labour theory, formulated by the British philosopher John Locke in the 17th century, implies that every man should be the proprietor of the product of his labour. More specifically, the labour theory contends that whoever adds their labour to resources that are either owned by all or not owned by anyone should have a property right in the product of that labour.[94] This is because one has a natural right of property in one's body. Since one owns one's body, then one also owns the labour of it and, consequently, the fruits of that labour.[95]

89 Ana Ramalho, *The Competence of the European Union in Copyright Lawmaking – A Normative Perspective of EU Powers for Copyright Harmonization* (Springer 2016) 5.

90 Stewart E. Sterk, 'Rethoric and Reality in Copyright Law' (1996) 94 *Michigan Law Review* 1197, 1213.

91 Other reasons to create independently of copyright include market incentives, cognitive psychology, social norms, first-mover advantages or path dependency – see Christopher J Sprigman, 'Copyright and Creative Incentives: What We Know (and Don't)' (2017) 55 *Houston Law Review* 451, 468.

92 See also on this point Sprigman (ibid.) 460 ff., and Caterina Sganga, *Propertizing European Copyright. History, Challenges and Opportunities* (Edward Elgar 2018) 27.

93 *Sterk* (n 90) 1215–1216.

94 Locke elaborated on this theory in his book John Locke, *Two Treatises of Civil Government* (first published anonymously in 1689, J.M. Dent & Sons 1962).

95 Ibid., 130.

Locke's theory is relevant to intellectual property in general, and copyright in particular,[96] to the extent that the underlying material of an intellectual property right – an idea or a concept – belongs to the commons. Consequently, if one's intellectual labour contributes to shaping an idea or concept so that it turns into an intellectual good, then one should be entitled to have some kind of proprietary right over the result.[97] The justification for granting a property right over the result of one's labour is, according to Locke's theory, individual merit.[98] The idea of "reward" is suggested here: the intellectual labour invested in creation should be rewarded, creators should be compensated for their intellectual effort.[99] The protection offered results from a sense of justice and the need to ensure individual liberty and autonomy.[100] In sum, under this theory, there is a reason why creative expressions are protected – they are the result of intellectual labour, and the latter should be protected, even if the underlying idea is not. This premise is expressed in case law from several jurisdictions that determine that it is the mind behind the creative process, not the executant, that ultimately is deserving of authorship status.[101] This is significant, as it recognizes the mind as an important element of authorship.

Traces of the need of human authorship can also be found in Locke's work. In 1695, Locke wrote an essay where he criticized a proposal for a law that extended the monopoly granted to the Stationer's Company as the sole printer of literary works.[102] Locke believed that authors, not printers, should have property over their writings[103] one of the reasons being the tenuous link between printers and the authors who created the works.[104]

96 See contra, challenging the use of the labour theory to justify copyright, Carys J. Craig, 'Locke, Labour, and Limiting the Author's Right: A Warning Against a Lockean Approach to Copyright Law' (2012) 28 *Queens Law Journal* <https://papers.ssrn.com/sol3/papers.cfm?abstract_id=2078157> accessed 14 May 2021. The author defends that "the Lockean analysis of copyright forces us to justify as counter-norms the very public policy purposes that lie at the heart of copyright's rationale," as she sees copyright as "an incentive structure with a social policy goal" (pp. 2–3, 60).

97 *Fisher* (n 84) 170.

98 *Sganga* (n 92) 20.

99 *Guibault* (n 84) 8–11.; Justin Hughes, 'The Philosophy of Intellectual Property' (1988) 77 *Georgetown Law Journal* 287, 296ff., discussing the several interpretations of "reward" in the context of the labour theory. Many authors however separate the natural rights justification, on the one hand, and the reward theory, on the other, considering them two different theories – see for example *Fisher* (n 84).

100 *Sganga* (n 92) 21.

101 Jane C. Ginsburg, 'The Concept of Authorship in Comparative Copyright Law' (2003) 52 *DePaul Law Review* 1063, 1072–1074, and case law cited therein.

102 Adam Mossoff, 'Saving Locke from Marx: The Labor Theory of Value in Intellectual Property Theory' (2012) 29 (2) *Social Philosophy & Policy* 283. See also Rebecca S. Curtin, 'Locke's (Own) Literary Property,' in Shubha Ghosh (ed.), *Forgotten Intellectual Property Lore* (Edward Elgar 2020) 4–5.

103 Ibid. The author points out that Locke "proposes an amendment to the 1695 bill in which the precatory clause states "To secure the author's property in his copy, or to his whom he has transferred it." In sum, Locke believes firmly in an "author's property in his copy" – what we now call copyright" (footnotes omitted).

104 *Curtin* (n 102) 10.

Locke's theory comprised two limitations dictated by the need to preserve the commons: the "sufficiency proviso" (where appropriability would be acceptable when "*there is enough and as good left for others*") and the "spoilage proviso" (according to which it is necessary to preserve the integrity of common resources from "*impoverishment and depletion*").[105] One scholar further notes the importance of a "non-waste condition" in the context of Locke's limitations to acquisition of property – this condition would not allow the collection of property to such extent that some of it would be destroyed without being used, since that would imply an "*unjustified diminution of the common stock of potential property*."[106] Underlying Locke's theory and its limitations is the idea of equality: people should be able to reap the fruits of their labour, so long as each individual has an equal opportunity to use the common or unowned resources.[107] This arguably explains copyright's scope and limitations, such as the fact that ideas are not copyrightable, or its limited duration.[108]

The personality rights theory, for which mainly the philosophers Kant and Hegel are responsible, holds that an intellectual work embodies its creator's personality or will. Focusing on piracy in book reprinting in the 18th century, Kant makes a distinction between the physical support and its intellectual content, in the sense that the author should never lose her inalienable paternity right to the latter.[109] His theory conceptualises authors' rights as personality, rather than property, rights.[110] Hegel's theory, more widely used than Kant's in the realm of intellectual property, has freedom as its pivotal element: having freedom as a goal in mind, Hegel holds that property is the first embodiment of freedom and so it is in itself an essential end.[111] The work would be worthy of protection because it is an expression of the personality or self of its creator.[112] According to this conception, property is an extension of personality, providing a means for self-actualization and personal expression.[113] Hegel referred specifically to intellectual objects, mentioning that the products of his mental skill, if alienated indefinitely to others, would be part of someone else's property, with the consequence of the substance of his being and his personality being alienated as well).[114]

---

105 Giovanni B. Ramello, 'Private Appropriability and Sharing of Knowledge: Convergence or Contradiction? The Opposite Tragedy of the Creative Commons,' in Lisa N. Takeyama, Wendy J. Gordon and Ruth Towse (eds.), *Developments in the Economics of Copyright: Research and Analysis* (Edward Elgar 2005) 134–135. See also *Locke* (n 95) 134–135.

106 *Hughes* (n 99) 298 ff.

107 *Sterk* (n 90) 1234.; Wendy J. Gordon, 'A Property Right in Self-Expression: Equality and Individualism in the Natural Law of Intellectual Property' (1993) 102 *Yale Law Journal* 1533, 1563–1564.

108 WJ Gordon, 'A Property Right in Self-expression: Equality and Individualism in the Natural Law of Intellectual Property' 102 *Yale Law Journal* 1993, 1533, 1556–1557.

109 *Sganga* (n 92) 23.

110 Ibid.

111 Georg WF Hegel, *Grundlinien der Philosophie des Rechts* (Intelex Corporation 2003) 107.

112 *Hughes* (n 99) 330 and *Fisher* (n 84).

113 *Hughes* (ibid.)

114 *Hegel* (n 111) 144.

Both natural rights theories focus on the relation between the author and his work, and not on the impact of that relation on society.[115] Many authors consider copyright to be a mix of property and personality interests, being therefore based on both theories.[116]

2.4 Requirements for copyright protection and authorship

The main objective of this section is to investigate whether AI-generated works are eligible for copyright protection in each of the jurisdictions concerned. For that purpose, it analyses the relevant elements for copyright protection in the four jurisdictions selected: the EU, the US, Australia and Japan. The analysis will be based on applicable legislation and case law, but also official documents (such as policy documents or official communications) and existing doctrine, where relevant.

Each subsection will start by examining what each of these jurisdictions considers as protected subject matter. As shall be seen, despite a few differences, the key condition for protection is originality or creativity. The meaning of this condition will be dissected and put in context in relation to AI-generated works. Next, a description of the authorship regime in each of the jurisdictions, and constraints deriving from that regime to the protection of AI-generated works, will be brought to light. The third and last part of each subsection will enquire whether other forms of protection may eventually cover (some) AI-generated output. The legal institutes looked into will include (where available in that particular jurisdiction)[117] rules on derivative works and/or neighbouring rights (because parallel regimes to copyright such as neighbouring rights are not the focus of this book, these will only be briefly mentioned).

2.4.1 The European Union

2.4.1.1 Protected subject matter

Despite extensive harmonisation of member states' copyright laws,[118] the legislative framework in the EU does not harmonise the concept of protected subject

---

115 Linda J. Lacey, 'Of Bread and Roses and Copyrights' (1989) 6 *Duke Law Journal* 1532, 1564 and *Guibault* (n 84) 8.

116 See *Hughes* (n 99) 329–330 and 365–366.; Stef Van Gompel, *Formalities in Copyright Law: An Analysis of Their History, Rationales and Possible Future* (Kluwer Law International 2011) 218 and references cited therein.

117 For instance, unlike the EU and Japan, the US does not have a separate regime for related or neighbouring rights. Instead, some subject matter that in the EU or Japan would be protected under neighbouring rights is covered by the US copyright regime. It is the case of sound recordings, broadcasts and recorded performances (See 17 U.S. Code, section 102).

118 The EU has issued, to date, 14 legal acts (either Directives or Regulations) in the field of copyright, in addition to one Directive on enforcement (Directive 2004/48/EC of the European Parliament

matter.[119] It can however be argued that a protected work in the EU amounts to a literary or artistic work within the meaning of the Berne Convention.[120]

The CJEU has ruled that the concept of "work" has two conditions: it entails an original subject matter that is the author's own intellectual creation; and it requires the expression of that creation.[121] The first of these conditions means that, in order to be protected by copyright, a work must be original. The notion of originality for purposes of copyright protection has its roots on a statutory definition in relation to software, databases and photos, where it was characterised as the "author's own intellectual creation."[122] At the time, it was unclear whether the definition of originality had the same meaning throughout the three Directives where it appeared.[123] However, more recently, scholars

---

and of the Council of 29 April 2004 on the enforcement of intellectual property rights), which is applicable to intellectual property rights in general (thus including copyright).

119 However, certain categories of protected works have been harmonised by specific Directives: it is the case of software, harmonised by Directive 2009/24/EC of the European Parliament and of the Council of 23 April 2009 on the legal protection of computer programs (the "Software Directive"); databases, harmonised by Directive 96/9/EC of the European Parliament and of the Council of 11 March 1996 on the legal protection of databases (the "Database Directive"); and photos, harmonised by Directive 2006/116/EC of the European Parliament and of the Council of 12 December 2006 on the term of protection of copyright and certain related rights (the "Term of Protection Directive").

120 As pointed out by Justine Pila, 'The Authorial Works Protectable by Copyright,' in Eleonora Rosati (ed.), *The Routledge Handbook of EU Copyright Law* (Routledge 2021) 63–81, a few references in the acquis support this conclusion. Examples include Article 1.1. of the Term of Protection Directive, which refers to protected works as "literary or artistic works within the meaning of Article 2 of the Berne Convention," and the Database Directive, which at several points refers to the Berne Convention in the context of authors of databases (see Database Directive, Recitals 28, 35, 37, and article 6.3).

121 See e.g., Case C-833/18 *SI and Brompton Bicycle Ltd. v. Chedech / Get2Get* (Judgment of the Court Fifth Chamber, 11 June 2020) para 22., and Case 683/17 *Cofemel – Sociedade de Vestuario SA v. G-Star Raw CV* (Judgment of the Court third Chamber, 12 September 2019) paras. 29 and 32.

122 See respectively Software Directive, article 1(3).; Database Directive, article 3(1).; Term of Protection Directive, article 6. Arguably, the reason for harmonising the originality threshold only for these three categories of works was the higher risk they represented in terms of internal market fragmentation (because these works were either not part of traditional copyright categories, or because they were already protected according to different standards in national laws) – see Andrea Renda and others, 'The Implementation, Application and Effects of the EU Directive on Copyright in the Information Society' (CEPS Special Report No. 120, November 2015) <http://aei.pitt.edu/69674/1/SR120_0.pdf> accessed 22 May 2021.

123 The Term of Protection Directive, recital 16 states that a work will be its author's own intellectual creation where it reflects her or his personality. This, coupled with the specific rationale of the provision – the need to draw a distinction between original photographs and "mere" photographs – prompted some authors to argue that the EU originality test in relation to photographs is stricter and closer to the traditional continental criterion of originality according to which a work needs to be the "personal expression" of its author – see Bernt Hugenholtz and others, 'The Recasting of Copyright and Related Rights for the Knowledge Economy' Institute for Information Law Research Paper (2006) No. 2012–38, 37 <https://papers.ssrn.com/sol3/papers.cfm?abstract_id=2018238> accessed 22 May 2021.

have noted that it would be strange if the same term ("author's own intellectual creation") would have been chosen to describe different standards.[124]

The assumption regarding the EU originality standard was that it represented a compromise between the different originality thresholds that existed throughout the EU. In fact, the 2000 Commission Report on the Software Directive makes clear that the originality standard in the Software Directive is a compromise between the higher threshold of droit d'auteur countries and the lower one of common law countries such as the UK and Ireland.[125] This seems to be confirmed by Recital 8 of the Software Directive, which excludes any tests as to the qualitative or aesthetic merits of the computer programme: a few commentators have pointed out that this Recital was meant to bar higher thresholds of originality for computer programmes (as adopted by the 1985 *Inkassoprogram* decision of the German Federal Supreme Court),[126] which denotes the compromise inherent to the EU originality threshold. It is arguable that the "author's own intellectual creation" standard in the framework of databases amounts to a compromise between droit d'auteur and common law countries as well.[127]

In 2009, in the *Infopaq* case, the CJEU extended the notion of originality as the "author's own intellectual creation" to subject matter falling within the scope of the Information Society Directive.[128] According to the court, "copyright within the meaning of Article 2(a) of Directive 2001/29 [the Information Society Directive] is liable to apply only in relation to a subject matter which is original in the sense that it is its author's own intellectual creation," which means that "the various parts of a work thus enjoy protection under Article 2(a) of Directive 2001/29, provided that they contain elements which are the expression of the intellectual creation of the author of the work."[129]

Doctrinal views on originality often distinguish between an objective and subjective criterion of originality, where the former requires the work to originate from the author (and thus not copied from anywhere else), while the latter amounts to a personal stamp of the author in his or her work.[130] Some scholars have stated that the EU's definition of originality might be read from either the

---

124 Estelle Derclaye, 'Assessing the Impact and Reception of the Court of Justice of the European Union Case Law on UK Copyright Law: What Does the Future Hold?' (2014) 240 *Revue Internationale du Droit D'Auteur* 5 <https://nottingham.repository.worktribe.com/output/998300/assessing-the-impact-and-reception-of-the-court-of-justice-of-the-european-union-case-law-on-uk-copyright-law-what-does-the-future-hold> accessed 22 May 2021.

125 Ibid., referring to the Report from the Commission to the Council, the European Parliament and the Economic and Social Committee on the Implementation and Effects of Directive 91/250/EEC on the Legal Protection of Computer Programs' (COM 2000) 199 final, 6.

126 Eleonora Rosati, *Originality in EU Copyright: Full Harmonization through Case Law* (Edward Elgar 2013) 64–65, and references cited therein.

127 Ibid., 67.

128 Case C-05/08 *Infopaq International A/S v. Danske Dagblades Forening* [2009] ECR I-6569.

129 Ibid., paras. 37 and 39.

130 Mireille van Eechoud, 'Along the Road to Uniformity – Diverse Readings of the Court of Justice Judgments on Copyright Work' (2012) 3 *JIPITEC* 60, 70.

objective or subjective perspective;[131] the CJEU seemed to embrace both.[132] In the *BSA* case, the Court ruled that the criterion of originality would not be met by components of a graphic user interface which are differentiated only by their technical function.[133] According to the Court, in such situations the author would not be able to "express his creativity in an original manner and achieve a result which is an intellectual creation of that author."[134] The court seemed thus to understand that the work must not only originate from the author, but shall also possess some creativity. In more recent cases, the court veered more towards the subjective perspective of originality, by stating that "it is both necessary and sufficient that the subject matter reflects the personality of its author, as an expression of his free and creative choices."[135]

Importantly, where the work was dictated by technical considerations, rules or other constraints which leave no room for free and creative choices, the subject matter could not therefore be original and eligible for protection.[136] This could in theory be an obstacle to the protection of AI-generated works if "technical considerations, rules or restraints" is interpreted broadly, as any

131 André Lucas and others, *Traité de La Propriété Littéraire et Artistique* (Litec 2006) *apud* Elizabeth F Judge and Daniel J Gervais, 'Of Silos and Constellations: Comparing Notions of Originality in Copyright Law' (2009) 27 *Cardozo Arts & Entertainment Law Journal* 375, 386.

132 This is a contentious issue that divides commentators. Derclaye holds that the criterion adopted by the CJEU is subjective. (*Derclaye,* 'Assessing the Impact and Reception of the Court of Justice of the European Union Case Law' (n 124) 11, citing other authors such as Sirinelli and Michaux). Judge and Gervais (cited above) and Lucas (cited in Derclaye, *op. cit.*), have either different or more nuanced opinions. *Judge and Gervais* (ibid., 386–388) point out that the European lawmaker intended to adopt the objective criterion for computer programmes and databases, as it would provide a "single, low common denominator," but recognise that "it is difficult to draw a single conclusion from [the] analysis of the EU Directives," especially taking into consideration Recital 16 of the Term of Protection Directive. Note however that the Commission's Review of the legal framework in the field of copyright and related rights states that "[o]riginality corresponds to the independent creativity of the author as reflected in his or her literary or artistic creation." 'Commission Staff Working Paper on the Review of the EC Legal Framework in the Field of Copyright and Related Rights' (2004) *European Commission SEC* (2004) 995, 13, where the reference to "*independent* creativity," coupled with its reflection on the creation, appears to include both the objective and subjective tests for originality.

133 Case C-393/09 *Bezpečnostní softwarová asociace – Svaz softwarové ochrany v. Ministerstvo kultury (BSA)* [2010] ECR I-13971, para 48.

134 Ibid., para 50.

135 *Brompton Bicycle* (n 121) para 23, and *Cofemel* (n 121) para 30. See however *European Parliament (Committee on Legal Affairs)* (n 11), stating that "the general trend with regard to that condition [of originality] is towards an objective concept of relative novelty, making it possible to distinguish a protected work from works already created." This view of originality adopted by the Parliament has been criticized by some scholars – see Christian Hartmann and others, 'Trends in Artificial Intelligence – Challenges to the Intellectual Property Rights Framework' (European Commission 2020) 70 <www.ivir.nl/publicaties/download/Trends_and_Developments_in_Artificial_Intelligence-1. pdf> accessed 22 May 2021.

136 *Brompton Bicycle* (n 121) 24; *Cofemel* (n 121) 31; Case C-604/10 *Football Dataco Ltd. and Others v. Yahoo! UK Ltd. and Others* (Judgment of the Court Third Chamber, 1 March 2012) para 39 and case law cited therein.

production by an AI system is ultimately the result of the technical rules inherent to said system. However, even if the realisation of a work has been dictated by technical considerations, such work might still be considered original if "being so dictated has not prevented the author from reflecting his personality in that subject matter, as an expression of free and creative choices."[137]

Moreover, in *Football Dataco*, Advocate General Paolo Mengozzi issued an Opinion where he stated that copyright protection (in that case, for a database) was dependent upon of a finding that the work had a "creative" aspect to it, and that labour and skill would not be enough to qualify the database for copyright protection.[138] Creativity seems thus to be a necessary element in the assessment of a work's originality. In order for a work to be original, the author must be able to "express his creative abilities in the production of the work by making free and creative choices."[139] Creative abilities – as a quality inherent to the author – must be put to good use when he or she is producing the work, through the making of creative choices.[140]

It should also be noted that being able to make choices is not enough for a finding of originality; such choices must be "creative."[141] According to the Court, the free and creative choices can be made at different stages of production of the work.[142] In the *Painer* case, which concerned a portrait photograph, the Court clarified that such choices could be present in the preparation phase (where the photographer could choose, e.g., background and lighting), in the execution phase (where the photographer could exercise his or her creative freedom by choosing the framing, the angle of view or the atmosphere created), or in the final phase (where the photographer could choose a developing technique when selecting the snapshot).[143] The free and creative choices thus made would then give the work the personal touch stamp of its author.[144] The possibility to assess creative choices throughout the creative process means that the scope of relevant acts for a finding of originality is relatively broad, to the advantage of AI-generated works – for example, it could be argued that the preparation phase of training the AI system in the context of machine learning could eventually qualify as a creative choice that would give the work its original character, depending of course on how those choices are expressed in the final result, as there must be a sufficient causal connection between the work

---

137   *Brompton Bicycle* (n 121) para 26.
138   *Football Dataco* (n 136) Opinion of Advocate General Mengozzi, para 35.
139   Case C-145/10 *Eva-Maria Painer v. Standard Verlags GmbH and Others* (Judgment of the Court Third Chamber, March 7, 2013) para 89.
140   This is also in line with the interdisciplinary concept of creativity explored in 2.2., which focuses not only on the creative product (the work), but on the need to have a heuristic process of creation as well.
141   Augustin Waisman, 'Revisiting Originality' (2009) 31 *European Intellectual Property Law* Review 370, 374–375.
142   *Painer* (n 139) para 90.
143   Ibid., para 91.
144   Ibid., para 92.

and the person who created it.[145] Only the elements of a work which reflect the creative choices are part of the concept of (protected) work per se.[146] The need for the author's creative choices to be somewhat visible in the final output in order for the latter to be protected indicates thus that there must be a link between the author's creativity and the work produced.

The Court also seems to admit that there are different levels of creativity worthy of copyright protection, stating that nothing in the EU legislative framework supports the view that the extent of protection should depend on the degree of creative freedom of different works.[147] In other words, both high-level and low-level creative works should qualify for copyright protection.

The CJEU does not elaborate on the concept of creativity itself. It is not clear when a certain choice is creative or not, or when creative abilities are realised in a work. The Advocate General in *Football Dataco* excludes any assessment as to the quality or the 'artistic' nature of the work in the framework of judging whether a work possesses a creative element.[148] The assessment of the quality or artistic nature of the work is also barred by Recital 8 of the Software Directive.[149] This indicates that merit is not part of the concept of creativity[150] (even though it is hard to separate the condition of creativity from an evaluation of a work's cultural value[151]). More recently, the CJEU seems to have

---

145 In the same sense, see *Pila* (n 120) 74: "the requirement of originality ensures that there exists a sufficient causal connection between a given work and the person alleged to have created it in order to justify the subsistence of copyright in the former for the latter's presumptive benefit."

146 *Cofemel* (n 121) para 29: "classification as a work is reserved to the elements that are the expression of [the author's own intellectual] creation." Similarly, see case C-310/17 *Levola Hengelo BV v. Smilde Foods BV* (Judgment of the Court Grand Chamber, 13 November 2018) para 37: "only something which is the expression of the author's own intellectual creation may be classified as a 'work.'"

147 *Painer* (n 139) para 97.

148 *Football Dataco* (n 136) Opinion of Advocate General Mengozzi, para 36.

149 Software Directive, Recital 8 states that "[i]n respect of the criteria to be applied in determining whether or not a computer program is an original work, no tests as to the qualitative or aesthetic merits of the program should be applied."

150 In any case, a few national copyright laws expressly exclude merit as a criterion for protecting a work – see e.g., the French Code of Intellectual Property (1992), article L112–1 ("The provisions of this code protect the rights of authors over all works, independently of their genre, form of expression, *merit* or destination" – emphasis added, own translation), or the Portuguese Code of Copyright and Related Rights (as amended up to Decree-Law No. 100/2017), article 2, paragraph 1 ("Intellectual creations from the literary, scientific and artistic domains, independently of genre, form of expression, *merit*, mode of communication and objective." – emphasis added, own translation).

151 Erlend Lavik and Stef van Gompel, 'On the Prospects of Raising the Originality Requirement in Copyright Law: Perspectives from the Humanities' (2013) 60 *Journal of the Copyright Society of the U.S.A.* 387, 412.; *Waisman* (n 141) 372–373.; Ramon Casas Vallés, 'The Requirement of Originality,' in Estelle Derclaye (ed.), *Research Handbook on the Future of EU Copyright* (Edward Elgar 2009) 114. Caroline Carreau, *Mérite et droit d' auteur* (Librairie Générale de Droit et de Jurisprudence 1981) 235ff., explains that the exclusion of merit in the assessment of originality – i.e., not judging the value or quality of the work – is a principle that is not always followed by judges. In fact, some Court decisions in France have formal references to the merit of the work, while others, although not using the word "merit," resort to equivalent notions such as "high importance,"

confirmed this in relation to copyright protection for designs, by stating in the *Cofemel* case that aesthetic considerations (and, therefore, aesthetic merit) are not necessary to meet the requirement of originality.[152] This also means that if a work generates "an aesthetic effect," that does not immediately qualify it as an original work worthy of protection.[153]

The second condition inherent to the concept of "work" is the expression of the author's own intellectual creation. This condition entails, first and foremost, that the subject matter must be identified with sufficient precision and objectivity.[154] It also implies that there must be a link between the author's creativity and its expression in the work produced, which reinforces the finding mentioned above that the author's creative choices must be reflected in the work produced.[155]

2.4.1.2 Authorship

In principle, the author is the one who creates the work.[156] But the EU acquis does not contain a transversal definition of author or of authorship. In the EU, authorship is only addressed in the Software Directive, the Database Directive, and the Rental and Lending Rights Directive[157] (the latter in relation to cinematographic works, with the corresponding rule repeated in the Satellite and Cable Directive[158] and the Term of Protection Directive). But these legal instruments do not put forth a definition proper; rather, they leave considerable leeway for member states to define the concept of "author" in their national legislations. Namely, the Software and the Database Directives allow member states to define the author of a computer programme or of a database as either

---

"superior artistic value" or "aesthetic value." The author concludes that merit often plays a decisive role when assessing copyright protection for a work (ibid., 413).

152 *Cofemel* (n 121) para 54: "[I]t is admittedly the case that aesthetic considerations play a part in creative activity. Nonetheless, the fact remains that the circumstance that a design may generate an aesthetic effect does not, in itself, make it possible to determine whether that design constitutes an intellectual creation reflecting the freedom of choice and personality of its author, thereby meeting the requirement of originality."

153 Ibid. As expressed by *Hartmann and others* (n 135) 71: "[t]his is an important observation in relation to AI-assisted outputs, many of which are undeniably of aesthetic value."

154 *Brompton Bicycle* (n 121) para 25.; *Cofemel* (n 121) para 32.; *Levola Hengelo* (n 147) para 40.

155 In the same sense, see *Hartmann and others* (n 135) 75 ("This requirement of expression implies a causal link between an author's creative act (the exercising of their creative freedom) and the expression thereof in the form of the work produced").

156 Antoon Quaedvlieg, 'Authorship and Ownership: Authors, Entrepreneurs and Rights,' in Tatiana-Eleni Synodinou, *Codification of European Copyright Law, Challenges and Perspectives* (Kluwer Law International 2012) 198–199.

157 Directive 2006/115/EC of the European Parliament and of the Council of 12 December 2006 on rental right and lending right and on certain rights related to copyright in the field of intellectual property.

158 Council Directive 93/83/EEC of 27 September 1993 on the coordination of certain rules concerning copyright and rights related to copyright applicable to satellite broadcasting and cable retransmission.

the natural person or group of natural persons that created it, or the legal person defined as a right holder under national law.[159] Nevertheless, the *travaux préparatoires* of the Database Directive clarify that the Directive restates the fundamental principle of the Berne Convention, which grants ownership to "the human author who creates the work," even though it is then made clear that, due to the nature of the database industry, national laws that grant ownership to or exercise of rights by a legal person will be allowed.[160] Still, the drafting seems to convey the view that the author will by default be a natural person, while deviations to that rule are merely tolerated.[161]

References to natural persons and moral rights in the original Proposal for a Software Directive lead to the conclusion that not only legal persons were not to be considered as authors, but also that authors were necessarily human beings.[162] Article 2(5) of the Proposed Directive (which did not make the final draft[163]) dealt with computer-generated works and prescribed that the natural or legal person who caused the generation of subsequent programmes would be entitled to exercise all rights in respect of the programs (unless otherwise provided by contract); but authorship was not dealt with per se. However, the Explanatory Memorandum did raise the question of whether authorship of the generated programs should reside with the creator of the first program, or with the user that causes it to generate other works.[164] In connection with this point, the Explanatory Memorandum also touches upon the question of machine versus human author in the following fashion:

> The human input as regards the creation of machine generated programs may be relatively modest, and will be increasingly modest in the future. Nevertheless, a human "author" in the widest sense is always present, and must have the right to claim "authorship" of the program.[165]

Here, too, authorship is considered a human trait.

The fact that the author must necessarily be a human being is also backed up by references to personality and the personal touch stamp of the author in the

---

159 Software Directive, article 2(1) and Database Directive, article 4(1).

160 Commission on the European Communities, 'Proposal for a Council Directive on the Legal Protection of Databases-Explanatory Memorandum' (COM (92) 24 final, 1992) 44.

161 *Quaedvlieg* (n 156) 207.

162 See Commission on the European Communities, 'Proposal for a Software Directive-Explanatory Memorandum' (COM (88) 816 final, 1989) 20: "[i]n common with all literary works, the question of authorship of the program is to be resolved in favour of the natural person or group of persons who have created the work. Although the right to exercise exclusive rights may be assigned to another, the author will retain at least the unalienable rights to claim paternity of his work."

163 Article 2(5) was judged too premature and was deleted following a vote by the European Parliament – see Thomas Dreier, 'The Council Directive of 14 May 1991 on the Legal Protection of Computer Programs' (1991) 13 *European Intellectual Property Review* 319, 321.

164 'Proposal for a Software Directive-Explanatory Memorandum' (n 165) 21.

165 Ibid.

case law of the CJEU. Recent case law seems to indicate that the existence of an author who created the work is a condition inherent to originality – e.g., in *Brompton Bicycle*, as mentioned, the CJEU ruled that the subject matter must reflect the personality of its author to be considered original.[166] Likewise, in *Painer*, the CJEU makes reference to stamping the work with the author's "personal touch.[167] Also in *Painer*, upon interpretation of the first sentence of Article 6 of Directive 93/98 (the original Term of Protection Directive), which states that "Photographs which are original in the sense that they are the author's own intellectual creation shall be protected," Advocate General Trstenjak also stated that "only human creations are therefore protected, which can also include those for which the person employs a technical aid, such as a camera."[168]

Other cases of the CJEU confirm the human nature of authorship and its connection to originality as a protection requirement. In the *Luksan* case,[169] for instance, the CJEU has made a clear link between Article 17(2) of the Charter of Fundamental Rights of the EU (which states that "intellectual property shall be protected") and the protection of the author of a copyright protected work (in that case, the principal director of a cinematographic work, thus a natural person). The Court reasoned that the principal director of a cinematographic work was, as an author, entitled to exploitation rights to that work.[170] Because the national law at stake did not allocate such exploitation rights to the principal director, the Court considered that it was in breach of Article 17(2) of the Charter.[171]

In *Phil Collins/EMI Electrola*,[172] the Court established that the specific subject matter of copyright and related rights is "to ensure the protection of the moral and economic rights of their holders."[173] The reference to moral rights conveys the message that it is the creator (who is also the original copyright holder) that is at the forefront of the Court's reasoning. The goal of protecting authors and their interests in their works is thus at the core of the notion of "specific subject matter,"[174] and is consequently inherent to the very nature of copyright protection. In a similar way, the General Court also put the emphasis of copyright on the individual creator by stating that the "essential function" of copyright is to "protect the moral rights in the work and ensure a reward for creative effort."[175]

---

166 See *Brompton Bicycle* (n 121) para 23.
167 *Painer* (n 139) para 92.
168 Ibid., Opinion of the Advocate General Trstenjak, para 121.
169 Case C-277/10 *Martin Luksan v. Petrus van der Let* (Judgment of the Court Third Chamber, 9 February 2012).
170 Ibid., paras. 44–53.
171 Ibid., paras. 68–70.
172 Joined cases C-92/92 and C-326/92, *Phil Collins v. Imtrat Handelsgesellschaft mbH and Patricia Im – und Export Verwaltungsgesellschaft mbH and Leif Emanuel Kraul v. EMI Electrola GmbH* [1993] ECR I-5145.
173 Ibid., para 20.
174 See also Ulrich Loewenheim, 'Intellectual Property Before the European Court of Justice' (1995) 26 *International Review of Intellectual Property and Competition Law* 829, 841.
175 Case T-76/89 *Independent Television Publications Ltd. v. Commission of the European Communities* [1991] ECR II-575, para 56.

This definition presupposes the existence of a natural person and clearly reports back to the concept of original creator (while at the same time connecting authorship and creativity).

2.4.1.3 Other forms of protection

If in the EU the author as creator of the work must necessarily be a human being, and his or her creative choices should be reflected in the work, the same cannot be said about related or neighbouring rights, which protect subject matter that is somewhat related to, but does not consist of, literary and artistic works (such as phonograms or broadcasts). One of the main characteristics of related or neighbouring rights is the lack of "authorial creativity."[176] The subject matter of neighbouring rights is not the result of an author's creativity, and thus there is no direct link between such subject matter and a human author that creates it. Another characteristic is the lack of a minimum threshold of protection – these are rights that, for the most part, have investment as a rationale, but there is no protection requirement linked to a certain minimum of investment, for example.[177] At the EU level, the harmonized neighbouring rights are the rights of performers, phonogram producers, broadcasters and film producers,[178] as well as, more recently, press publishers.[179] It is possible to conceive that some of the output produced by an AI could in theory amount to subject matter protected by a neighbouring right – e.g., the film producer's right can afford protection to video content generated by AI systems, such as drone footage or content automatically generated for media channels.[180] This protection assumes however that the AI is used as a tool by the related rights holder, be that holder a natural or legal person (for instance, in the example

---

176 Paul Goldstein and Bernt Hugenholtz, *International Copyright: Principles, Law and Practice* (Oxford University Press 2010) 230.

177 Bernt Hugenholtz, 'Neighbouring Rights are Obsolete' (2019) 50 *International Review of Intellectual Property and Competition Law* 1006, 1008–1009: "According to the letter of the law, every first recording of sounds automatically leads to a phonographic right, even if no significant investment or effort whatsoever is involved. (For example, a recording of street noise on a smartphone.) Apparently, the Rome neighbouring rights were premised on the idea that the technical costs of recording or broadcasting posed a de facto investment threshold." (footnotes omitted) See also e.g., Rental and Lending Rights Directive, recital 5: "the investments required particularly for the production of phonograms and films are especially high and risky."

178 Directive 2006/115/EC of the European Parliament and of the council of 12 December 2006 on rental right and lending right and on certain rights related to copyright in the field of intellectual property (the "Rental and Lending Rights Directive"), and Directive 2001/29/EC of the European Parliament and of the Council of 22 May 2001 on the harmonisation of certain aspects of copyright and related rights in the information society (the "Information Society Directive") jointly grant several rights to these four categories of rights holders, such as the reproduction right and the right of communication to the public.

179 Directive (EU) 2019/790 of the European Parliament and of the Council of 17 April 2019 on copyright and related rights in the Digital Single Market and amending Directives 96/9/EC and 2001/29/EC (the Directive on Copyright in the Digital Single Market), article 15.

180 1 *Hartmann and others* (n 135) 91.

given above, the film producer's right in the drone footage would probably be owned by the human user of the drone).

Moreover, next to these related rights, the EU acquis also includes a sui generis right for database makers.[181] The sui generis right is granted to database makers that have made a qualitatively or quantitatively substantial investment in either obtaining, verifying or presenting the contents of a database. A database maker is, according to Recital 41 of the Database Directive, "the *person* who takes the initiative and the risk of investing," who furthermore must be a national of an EU member state or have their habitual residence in the EU territory (article 11(1) of the Database Directive). Article 11(2) of the Directive further clarifies that paragraph 1 "applies to companies and firms formed in accordance with the law of a member state and having their registered office, central administration or principal place of business within the Community." Like other related rights, it seems thus that the database maker must be either a natural or legal person (which leaves aside the possibility of having the AI system itself as the "maker" of the database). It is however possible that a natural or legal person makes a substantial investment in AI systems and tools that automate, e.g., the gathering of data or the verification of the contents of a database, in which case such database – which is at least partially generated by an AI – could qualify for sui generis right protection.[182] This possibility stems in particular from Recital 7, which refers to the "investment of considerable human, technical and financial resources", and from Recital 12, which mentions the "investment in modern information storage and processing systems." In other words, the holder of the sui generis right in a database that is – partially or fully – generated by an AI system would be the natural or legal person who made it possible for that database to be generated in the first place, through their substantial investment, e.g., in the AI system.

2.4.2 The United States

2.4.2.1 Protected subject matter

In the US, copyright protection is granted to original works of authorship fixed in any tangible medium of expression.[183] For a work to qualify for copyright

---

181 Database Directive, article 7. Some authors include the sui generis or database right in the plethora of neighbouring rights – see e.g., Derclaye, *The Legal Protection of Databases* (n 84) 53–54. For the purposes of this book, the sui generis right is treated separately because, unlike the related rights mentioned in the text, it requires a substantial investment, i.e., a minimum threshold for protection (see also in the same sense *Hartmann and others* (n 135) 92–93).

182 See *Hartmann and others* (n 135) 93, stating that substantial investment "might include expenditure in AI systems or technology used to produce a database. For example, if a producer of a legal database would use AI technology to automatically create cross-references between documents and cases, the database producer's costs of procuring and implementing this technology would undoubtedly count towards (quantitative) investment."

183 17 U.S. Code (the Copyright Act), section 102(a): "Copyright protection subsists, in accordance with this title, in original works of authorship fixed in any tangible medium of expression, now

protection, it must be "original to the author," i.e., it must be independently created by that author and display a minimal level of creativity.[184] The first condition – that the work be independently created by the author – means that it is not copied from another work,[185] although it may contain references to other works or include ideas or suggestions from others.[186] The second condition requires that the work possess a modicum of creativity in order to be original. The creativity threshold is admittedly low; according to the Supreme Court in *Feist*, it is enough that the work has a "creative spark" (no matter how crude, humble or obvious).[187] However, *some* creativity is necessary: only works that have more than a *de minimis* quantum of creativity can qualify for copyright protection.[188] The creativity in *Feist* was reflected in the choices of the author (as to the selection and arrangement of materials), just as many years before the case *Burrow-Giles* focused on the creative choices of the author too (in that case, in relation to a photograph).[189] Creativity thus entails not only the potential creative freedom that the author has, but also how he or she exercises that freedom.[190]

The court hasn't defined what is meant by "creativity" or "creative spark," but it has been pointed out that, based on the court's case law, random, arbitrary or insufficient selection will not pass the bar; and that, where choices are constrained by functionality, efficiency or standards – just as many choices made by machines are – then such choices are not creative.[191]

2.4.2.2 Authorship

US law appears to imply that the author will necessarily be a natural person, even though no definition of authorship is found in the law.[192] Section 101 of Title

---

known or later developed, from which they can be perceived, reproduced, or otherwise communicated, either directly or with the aid of a machine or device."

184 *Feist Publications, Inc. v. Rural Telephone Service Co.*, 499 U.S. 340, 345 (1991).

185 Ibid., see also *Acuff-Rose Music, Inc. v. Jostens, Inc*, 155 F.3d 140, 143–144 (2nd Cir. 1998), where the Court decided that a sentence over which the plaintiff claimed copyright had already been used several times by others, which made it unlikely that the plaintiff had independently created it.

186 William Patry, *Patry on Copyright* (West Thomson Reuters 2021) section 3:28.

187 Ibid.

188 *Feist Publications* (n 184) 363.

189 In *Burrow-Giles Litographic Co. v. Sarony*, 111 U.S. 53, 60 (1884) the Court held that the author "gave visible form [to his original mental conception]by posing the said Oscar Wilde in front of the camera, selecting and arranging the costume, draperies, and other various accessories in said photograph, arranging the subject so as to present graceful outlines, arranging and disposing the light and shade, suggesting and evoking the desired expression, and from such disposition, arrangement, or representation, made entirely by plaintiff, he produced the picture in suit." Highlighting the similarity between *Feist* and *Burrow-Giles* in relation to the concept of "creative choices, see Daniel Gervais, 'The Machine as Author' (2020) 105 *Iowa Law Review* 2053, 2089.

190 *Patry* (n 186) section 3:34: "the trier of fact must examine the potential amount of creativity available as well as the amount of creativity actually exercised."

191 *Gervais* (n 189) 2091–2092, and references cited therein.

192 Note that at its origin American copyright law identified originality as a defining trait of the author, fusing the two concepts together – see Oren Bracha, *Owning Ideas: The Intellectual Origins of American Intellectual Property, 1790–1909* (Cambridge University Press 2016) 64–65 and 89.

17 of the US Code (the Copyright Act) defines anonymous works as the ones where no natural person is identified as an author, which seems to presume that an author is necessarily a human being. Moreover, in *Feist*, the Court quotes the case *Burrow-Giles* and states that "an author who claims infringement must prove 'the existence of . . . intellectual production, of thought, and conception'" – which entails an intention or a purpose to create.[193] In another case, *Community for Creative Non-Violence v. Reid*, the Supreme Court clarified that the author is a *"person* who translates an idea into a fixed, tangible expression"[194] (emphasis added). The reference to a "person" who has an idea clearly refers to a human being. In a rather exotic case about authorship by celestial beings, the Ninth Circuit had the opportunity to analyse the validity of claims on non-human authorship and ruled that "some element of human creativity" must be present in order for a work to qualify for copyright protection, and very bluntly established that "a work is copyrightable if copyrightability is claimed by the first human beings who compiled, selected, coordinated, and arranged" the work.[195] In other words, independently of the beliefs of the party regarding the non-human contribution to the creation of the work, what must be assessed is, according to the Court, the *human* intervention in that creation. In the case *Naruto v. Slater (Monkey Selfie)*, decided on 28 January 2016 by the Northern District Court of California, the court denied authorship to an animal (a macaque), adding that "the Supreme Court and Ninth Circuit have repeatedly referred to "persons" or "human beings" when analysing authorship under the Act."[196]

This human-centric view of authorship is concomitant with early American copyright that put the author at the centre of its justification.[197] A current human-centric view of authorship is also reinforced by the *Compendium of US Copyright Office Practices*, an administrative manual of the Register of Copyrights which, while not having the force or effect of law, does nevertheless provide guidance and explain the legal rationale and determinations of the Office.[198] The compendium clearly states that it is necessary for the work to be created by a human being for it to be registered, as copyright law only protects the product of a creative mind and intellectual labour.[199] The office can thus refuse to register a work if it determines that a human being did not create the work.[200]

---

193 Annemarie Bridy, 'Coding Creativity: Copyright and the Artificially Intelligent Author' (2012) 5 *Stanford Technology Law Review* 8.
194 *Community for Creative Non-Violence v. Reid*, 490 U.S. 730, 737 (1989).
195 *Urantia Foundation v. Maaherra*, 114 F.3d 955, 958 (9th Circ 1997).
196 *Naruto and others v. David John Slater and others*, Case No. 15-cv-04324-WHO (N.D. Cal. Jan. 28, 2016) 5.
197 *Gervais* (n 189) 2081–2083, and references cited therein.
198 See United States Copyright Office, 'Compendium of U.S. Copyright Office Practices' (3rd ed., United States Copyright Office 2021) Introduction <www.copyright.gov/comp3/docs/compendium.pdf> accessed 22 May 2021. As noted there, courts have often cited the Compendium in copyright cases.
199 Ibid., section 306 <www.copyright.gov/comp3/chap300/ch300-copyrightable-authorship.pdf> accessed 22 May 2021.
200 Ibid.

Section 313.2 of the compendium further elaborates on this point and emphasizes the intertwinement of authorship with requirements for protection. After quoting Section 102(a) of the Copyright Act, which states that copyright protects original works of authorship, the Compendium expressly declares that "to qualify as a work of 'authorship', a work must be created by a human being." The statement is backed with a reference to the case *Burrow-Giles*, where the Supreme Court expressed the following view: "We entertain no doubt that the Constitution is broad enough to cover an act authorizing copyright of photographs, *so far as they are representatives of original intellectual conceptions of the author*"[201] (emphasis added).

What the court is implying here is that a given subject matter may be copyright protected if, and only if, they consist of "original intellectual conceptions" of its author – meaning, authorship is embedded by its own nature in the requirements for copyright protection.

Further on under the same section, the compendium adds that the Copyright Office will not register works produced by nature animals, plants, and neither by "machines or mere mechanical processes that operate randomly or automatically without any creative input or intervention from a human author." The office will thus refuse to register works that lack human authorship.[202] Therefore, while it is arguable that the current drafting does not seem to contemplate a future where machines will create works nonrandomly or automatically, the requirement of a human author is clear and unescapable.

The reference to both intellectual conceptions and to creative input or intervention from the author seems to endorse some doctrinal views according to which human authorship requires at least that a human being was involved in the conception of the work *and* in the control or supervision of the execution of the work.[203] Conception of the work implies that the author formulated an entire creative plan for the work; that plan does not need to be directly connected to key aesthetic elements of the work such as contents or form, so long as "those expressive elements flowed directly from the author's creative plan or conception."[204]

To what extent more sophisticated AI systems such as deep learning require a human author being involved in the conception or supervision of the execution of the work can be disputed. Is programming and/or providing input data to an AI enough of an authorial activity for the human being performing both or any of those activities to be considered an author? To date, there is no case

201 *Burrow-Giles v. Sarony* (n 189) 58.

202 See *Compendium* (n 198), section 608 <www.copyright.gov/comp3/chap600/ch600-examination-practices.pdf> accessed 22 May 2021.

203 *Ginsburg* (n 101) 1072. See also *Ginsburg and Budiardjo* (n 10) 401: "The idea that a machine could be an "author" of a work must rest on the assumption that a machine is capable of carrying out the required elements of authorship: conception and execution."

204 *Ginsburg and Budiardjo* (n 10) 414.

law that can provide a clear answer to this question, although a few academic studies have discussed it.[205]

A relevant point to this discussion is that, similarly to a few other jurisdictions, the US includes in its copyright law a legal fiction according to which an entity, rather than a natural person, is deemed to be the author of a work: the regime of works made for hire, where the employer or another person for whom the work was prepared is considered both the author and the owner.[206] This legal fiction finds its roots in the notion of control and agency.[207] It is the aspect of controlling the production of the work (be it through an employment link or in certain cases of commissioned works) that affords the status of "author" to an employer or a commissioning party; where the creator (a human being) is a mere agent of someone else (who can be a legal person), then the latter should be given authorship.[208] It is often the employer that initiates the creative process, which means that, were it not for its actions, many creative works would not be produced.[209] Another reason for attributing authorship to the employer is a practical one: it is easier for purposes of exploitation, and it facilitates investment.[210]

It has been argued by some authors that the regime of works made for hire could accommodate copyright protection for AI-generated works.[211] The

---

205 Ibid. contending these activities are enough for a finding of authorship: "Thus, the designers of fully-generative machines, such as AARON, which create works without further intervention or input from their users, can be the authors of the resulting outputs. These designers fully formulate a creative plan, manifested in the machines' algorithms and processes, which will directly lead to the creation of expressive content. . . . The designer of the fully-generative machine thus meets the 'conception' requirement of authorship. And as long as those designers, by designing the tool's algorithms, or training a 'learning' generative model to produce outputs, control the inner workings of the system, they have also executed the resulting works." See contra Russ Pearlman, 'Recognizing Artificial Intelligence (AI) as Authors and Investors under US Intellectual Property Law' (2018) 24 *Richmond Journal of Law & Technology* 1, 28: "Certainly, it was the programmer who invested the time, energy, and creativity to create the AI tool. However, this point of view makes the same false assumptions that some critics have made in arguing against any AI ownership of IP: it assumes that the programmer explicitly programmed the AI with step-by-step instructions."

206 Copyright Act, sections 101 and 201.

207 Jacqueline Seignette, *Challenges to the Creator Doctrine: Authorship, Copyright Ownership and the Exploitation of Creative Works in the Netherlands, Germany and the United States* (Kluwer Law and Taxation Publishers 1994) 136ff.

208 Peter Jaszi, 'Toward a Theory of Copyright: The Metamorphoses of "Authorship"' (1991) Duke Law Journal 455, 489–490 and decisions cited therein.

209 Matthew R. Harris, 'Copyright, Computer Software, and Work Made for Hire' (1990) 89 *Michigan Law Review* 661, 662.

210 *Ginsburg* (n 101) 1088–1089.

211 See e.g., Kalin Hristov, 'Artificial Intelligence and the Copyright Dilemma' (2017) 57 *IDEA – The Journal of the Franklin Pierce Center for Intellectual Property* 431. See also Shlomit Yanisky-Ravid, 'Generating Rembrandt: Artificial Intelligence, Copyright, and Accountability in the 3A Era – The Human-Like Authors are Already Here – A New Model' (2017) 4 *Michigan State Law Review* 659, who, although not considering that the current works made for hire regime can be applicable to AI-generated works, suggests creating a new category of works made for hire that covers "AI systems as independent contractors or employees and thus imposes ownership and accountability in regard to the works on the human users of such machines."

attractiveness of applying the regime to AI-generated works is in fact under-standable, as its basic premises – authorship vested not in the actual creator of the work, but in a legal person – could at first sight apply to the displacement of authorship from a machine (the "creator") to a human being (who by way of legal fiction would be considered the author and owner of the work).

However, the regime of works made for hire cannot accommodate AI creations: they do not necessarily fall under the exhaustive list of catego-ries of commissioned works (for the case of works not done in the course of employment),[212] and in addition the relationship between the creator of the AI and the AI does not fit the characterization as commissioner-creator or employer-employee. Some authors have suggested adopting a more flexible interpretation of the concepts of "employer" and "employee," so as to reflect new social changes and accommodate the reality of AI-generated works.[213] However, the difficulties in applying the work for hire regime to AI-generated works go beyond a mere inadequacy of the terms "employer" and "employee" to encompass the relationship between human beings and machines that create. For example, the employee or agent has legal rights and duties by agreement with the employer/commissioner, which seems ill-fitted to the relationship machine-human.[214] More importantly, works made for hire also do not escape the inevitable lack of human authorship of AI-generated works. In fact, under the doctrine, a legal person might be the author of a copyright work that a *natural* person (i.e., a human being) created. While the legal fiction permits a non-human to be considered as the author of a copyright work, the act of crea-tion itself is human, and has an inextricable connection to humanness.

2.4.2.3 *Other forms of protection*

Some authors have argued that the regime of derivative works could be appli-cable to AI-generated works, since such works are produced only following the ingestion, by the AI, of great amounts of materials.[215] In the US, a work will be considered a derivative work when it is "based upon one or more preexisting works," which it recasts, transforms or adapts.[216] The right to prepare derivative works belongs to the author of the copyright work(s) upon which the deriva-tive work is based.[217]

Courts have interpreted the provision as meaning that the derivative work must contain a substantial amount of material from the pre-existing

---

212 These categories are listed in the Copyright Act, section 101(2): contribution to a collective work, part of a motion picture or other audio-visual work, translation, supplementary work, compilation, instructional text, test, answer material for a test, atlas.

213 *Hristov* (n 211) 446.

214 *Bridy*, 'Coding Creativity' (n 193) 26–27.; Timothy L. Butler, 'Can a Computer Be an Author? Copyright Aspects of Artificial Intelligence' (1981–1982) 4 *Comm/Ent L.S.* 707, 741.

215 See *Gervais* (n 189) 2096 ff and references cited therein.

216 Copyright Act, section 101.

217 Ibid., section 106(2).

work.[218] Conversely, if the new work is merely based on ideas from, or incorporates insubstantial amounts of, pre-existing works, it will not be deemed a derivative work.[219] In the same fashion, the work will not be considered derivative where it "sufficiently transforms the expression of the original work such that the two works cease to be substantially similar."[220]

Two possibilities are at stake here. The first one would be to consider that AI-generated works are derivative works based upon the works that were used to train the AI. Copyright in derivative works, however, "extends only to the material contributed by the author of such work, as distinguished from the pre-existing material employed in the work."[221] This scenario thus leads to a dead-end, as it is still necessary that the AI-generated work is in part authored by the AI (which, as seen above, is not possible, since authorship requires the existence of a human being). This is also made clear in the Compendium of US Copyright Office Practices, which clarifies that derivative works contain two authorships: that in the pre-existing work(s) upon which the derivative work is based, and the one in the derivative work itself.[222] Inherent to the definition of "derivative work" are a recast, a transformation or an adaptation, *authored* by whoever creates the derivative work. That is, the derivative work must also amount to an original work of authorship.

The second possibility would be to argue that AI-generated works are derivative works that are based upon the protected software that enabled the AI to produce them in the first place. However, as pointed out by Bridy, AI-generated works do not incorporate the code that produces them – a necessary requirement for derivative works, which must contain material taken from pre-existing work.[223] And, in any case, treating AI creations as derivative works in this sense would bring about another problem: the owner of the software/AI would not automatically be the owner of the AI creation, since even though

218 *Patry* (n 186) sections 3:47 and 12, esp. 12:12 and 12:13.; Omri Rachum-Twaig, *Copyright Law and Derivative Works – Regulating Creativity* (Routledge 2019) 130. For case law on derivative works (including cases judging that a derivative work infringes where it is *substantially similar* to a pre-existing work), see e.g., *Architettura, Inc. v. DBSI Cumberland at Granbury LP*, 652 F. Supp. 2d 775 (N.D. Tex. 2009).; *Warner Brothers Entertainment, Inc. v. RDR Books*, 575 F. Supp. 2d 513 (S.D.N.Y. 2008); *Peter Lettersee and Associates, Inc. v. World Institute of Scientology Enterprises, International*, 533 F.3d 1287 (11th Cir. 2008); *Ritah Mulcahy v. Cheetah Learning LLC and Jeff Schurrer*, 386 F.3d 849 (8th Cir. 2004) (all referenced in *Patry* (n 186) chapter 12).
219 *Patry* (n 186) section 3:47, and case law cited therein (namely *Service & Training, Inc. v. Data General Corp.*, 963 F.2d, 680 (4th Cir. 1992), where a computer programme that contained 1,200 files, with 200 being substantially reworked from an earlier version, was not considered to be a derivative work).
220 *Castle Rock Entertainment, Inc. v. Carol Publishing Group, Inc.*, 150 F.3d 132, 143 (2d Cir. 1998).
221 Copyright Act, section 103(b).
222 *Compendium* (n 198), section 507.1: the authorship in the derivative work is defined as a "new authorship involved in recasting, transforming, or adapting the preexisting work(s)." On this point see also *Patry* (n 186) sections 3:47 and 12:21.
223 Bridy, 'Coding Creativity' (n 193) 25–26. See also, along the same lines, Robert Yu, 'The Machine Author: What Level of Copyright Protection is Appropriate for Fully Independent Computer Generated Works?' (2017) 165 *University of Pennsylvania Law Review* 1245, 1258.

the right to produce a derivate work belongs to the original copyright owner, derivative works can be independently copyrightable.[224]

2.4.3 Australia

2.4.3.1 Protected subject matter

The Australian Copyright Act (ACA)[225] distinguishes between original literary, dramatic, musical and artistic works (Part III), and "copyright in subject-matter other than works" (Part IV), which are entrepreneurial works such as broadcasts, sound recordings or films. The two categories differ in many aspects. One of such aspects is the requirement that literary, dramatic, musical and artistic works be original (Section 32 ACA), while entrepreneurial works need only not to be copied.

The originality threshold in Australia was rather low, being dependent only on the author having exercised labour, skill and effort in producing the work.[226] For a work to be protected, it was sufficient that the work originated from an author in the sense that said work was the result of the author's skill and labour. So, for instance, exam papers of mathematics[227] and phone directories like the Yellow Pages[228] were both deemed original for purposes of copyright protection.

More recent cases however seem to deviate from this approach. In the case of *IceTV v. Nine Network Australia*,[229] the court considered that IceTV had not infringed the copyright of Nine Network Australia in weekly schedules of TV programmes by taking part of the data therein (time and title information) and including it in its own guide. Subsistence of copyright was not being considered – IceTV had conceded originality – so the discussion revolved around whether the level of skill and labour required to express the time and title information was sufficient for a finding of infringement, because of amounting to a reproduction of a substantial part of the work. The court concluded that the skill and labour employed in producing the weekly schedules "was not directed to the originality of the particular form of expression of the time and title information."[230] However, the Court still made a few observations concerning originality in the context of copyright subsistence. It stated that originality required the work to originate with the author and to not be merely copied from another work.[231] But also originality meant, according to the Court, that the creation of the work involved some "independent intellectual effort."[232]

224 *Bridy*, 'Coding Creativity' (n 193).
225 The Australian Copyright Act (1968) ('ACA').
226 See *Sands & McDougall Pty. Ltd. v. Robinson* [1917] 23 CLR 49.
227 *University of London Press Ltd. v. University Tutorial Press Ltd.* [1916] 2 Ch 601.
228 *Telstra Corporation Ltd. V. Desktop Marketing Systems Pty. Ltd* [2002] FCA 112.
229 *IceTV Pty. Ltd. v. Nine Network Australia Pty. Ltd.* [2009] 239 CLR 458.
230 Ibid. [54].
231 Ibid. [33] (French CJ, Crennan J and Kiefel J).
232 Ibid. As a consequence of this threshold, it has been pointed out that "[t]he transformation of copyright law effected by IceTV moves Australian law towards a civil law, 'authors' rights' model,

2.4.3.2 Authorship

In a subsequent case – *Telstra Corporation Ltd. v. Phone Directories Co. Pty*[233] – when discussing more in-depth the concept of originality in relation to white pages and yellow pages (telephone directories), the Federal Court of Australia drew some conclusions on authorship. The Court stated that the author with whom the work originated had to be an actual person (as, amongst other reasons, the determination of copyright duration was made by reference to the author's life).[234] It is that person – the author – that must deploy "independent intellectual effort" in creating the work.[235] In this case, significant human activity was involved at some point in the process of collecting the information that ended up in the directories, namely by maintaining, updating and editing a database with customer details. However, human beings merely oversaw the creation of the material form of the directories, giving high level instructions about the main parameters of the directories, while the directories themselves were produced by a computer programme – the human beings thus did not have any substantive input into that form. It followed that the Court had to analyse whether the human contribution at the stage of collecting the information – i.e., prior to the creation of the work proper – was relevant for a finding of originality. Perram J was of the view that it was not, remarking that there must be a connection between the author and the reduction of the work to its material form, since skill and hard work in that preparatory stage are not what copyright protects.[236] Importantly, the creation of the material form of the directories, because it was done by a computer, could not be considered original either. Or, to put it differently, the human contribution at that stage was not relevant because it did not display sufficient independent intellectual effort (Perram J recognised that intellectual effort went into the operation of the software by human beings, but "that effort was not directed to the incarnation of the material form of the directories").[237]

The *Acohs* case further confirmed the importance of human authorship.[238] The suit concerned the question of copyright in relation to electronic datasheets and certain underlying works. Acohs had a large relational database that stored the data necessary to generate the datasheets. When access to a particular

---

and away from the common law tradition." See David Lindsay, 'Protection of Compilations and Databases after ICETV: Authorship, Originality and the Transformation of Australian Copyright Law' (2012) 38 *Monash University Law Review* 17, 58.

233   *Telstra Corporation Ltd. v. Phone Directories Co. Pty.* [2010] FCAFC 149.
234   Ibid. [100] (Perram J).
235   Ibid.
236   Ibid., [105–106]: "Whatever else might be said of the kind of efforts required of an author, they must be efforts which result in the material form of the work. . . . Much skill and hard work – "sweat of the brow" – may be involved in the steps preparatory to the making of the material form of a work but those labours are not what is protected by copyright and are relevant only to show that the work is not copied."
237   Ibid., [117].
238   *Acohs Pty. Ltd. v. Ucorp Pty* [2012] FCAFC 16.

sheet was required, a computer programme would call up the data and other necessary elements from the database, compile the relevant HTML source code, and send that code to a user's computer, which would cause the datasheet to appear on the user's screen.[239] Relevant for the purposes of this book is the finding by the full court of the federal court that the HTML source code that was generated autonomously by the software hadn't emanated from authors, and could not be "an original work in the copyright sense."[240]

The ruling confirms the primary judge's findings that no copyright subsisted in the source code, because it had not been authored by a human being ("a fundamental requirement of copyright law," according to the judge).[241] Importantly, to Acohs's argument that the computer programme was merely a tool in the hands of human authors (the computer programmers), the primary judge sentenced that

> it would be artificial to regard the programmers as involved in the task of writing the source code for thousands of [datasheets] yet to take a material form merely because they wrote, and amended, the program which, when prompted, would put together a selection of the fragments of source code which they did write with other fragments later contributed by the authors and transcribers.[242]

As for authors and transcribers, they were responsible for some of the data that ended up in the source code since they entered data into the database; but because they were not programmers, and there was "no suggestion that they either understood source code or ever had a perception of the body of source code which was relevant to the [datasheets] on which they worked," the primary judge considered that they were not the authors of the source code either.

As is apparent from this string of cases, authorship is expressly connected to originality. As the Court in *IceTV* remarked, there was a "long held assumption in copyright law that "authorship" and "original work" are correlatives."[243] A work is original if it can be traced back to the author with whom that work originated. Originality thus requires that an author has personally put some mental/intellectual effort in the work, and that such mental effort, even if it is low, is directed to the particular form of expression of that work.[244] A work

239 Ibid. [15–16].
240 Ibid. [57].
241 Ibid. [48].
242 Ibid. [53].
243 *IceTV Pty.* (n 229) 34.
244 *McCutcheon* (n 9) 936–942; Sam Ricketson, 'The Need for Human Authorship – Australian Developments: *Telstra Corp Ltd. v. Phone Directories Co. Pty. Ltd.*' (2012) 34 *European Intellectual Property Review* 54, 57, quoting Perram J in the Phone Directories case: "So long as the person controlling the program can be seen as directing or fashioning the material form of the work there is no particular danger in viewing that person as the work's author. But there will be cases where the person operating the program is not controlling the nature of the material form produced by it

might comprise several stages of production where originality can be identified, but it is necessary that such originality is reflected in the final product,
i.e., that it influences its material form. In this sense, skill and labour used in
the preparatory stage of creation of a work are not relevant for a finding of
originality (and therefore protectability) of the work.

As for statutory law, the ACA establishes that the author shall be a qualified
person (Section 32(1)), which means that s/he will be an Australian citizen or a
person resident in Australia (Section 32(4)) – and seemingly a human being.[245]
Moreover, while the requirement of humanness is unescapable under Australian law, the fact that skill and labour exercised at the preparatory stage of a work
don't seem to count towards a finding of originality is relevant in the AI realm
as well: if the human intervention in the production of a work is made mostly
at the preparatory stage of an AI-generated work (for example, by training the
AI through feeding it with data or other works), that contribution would likely
not qualify as enough for a finding of originality either.

In 2013, the Australian Law Reform Commission issued a report that may at
first sight seem incompatible with these findings. The Commission cautioned
that " '[a]uthorship' is not to be interpreted in a manner that is too narrow or
culturally specific. It needs to be noted that the concept of the author is specifically left undefined in the Copyright Act, allowing for an enormous range of
expressive and pedestrian works to be encompassed."[246] However, this should
not be taken to mean that the concept of 'author' can encompass AI authorship.
The rulings in *IceTV*, *Phone Directories* and *Acohs* all underline that authorship
is a key element when assessing whether a work is protected by copyright (and
all refuse to grant copyright to products that were computer generated and
lacked – completely or a great part of – human input). Previous decisions to
those go as far as to assert that "the word 'original' connotes the 'authorship',"
emphasizing the dependency of copyright protection on (human) authorship.[247] It is therefore doubtful that the flexibility of the concept of authorship
advocated by the Australian Law Reform Commission can accommodate non-
human authorship.

Like other jurisdictions, Australia has a special regime for works created by
employees, whereby first ownership of a literary, dramatic, artistic or musical
work created in the course of employment vests in the employer.[248] The ACA
also provides that, in case of a photograph, portrait or engraving done for a
private or domestic purposes, it is the commissioner – not the author – that is

and in those cases that person will not contribute sufficient independent intellectual effort . . . to
constitute that person as its author."

245 *McCutcheon* (n 9) 936–942.
246 Australia Law Reform Commission, 'Copyright and the Digital Economy' (ALRC Report 122,
     Australian Government 2013), para. 2.11. <www.alrc.gov.au/publication/copyright-and-the-
     digital-economy-alrc-report-122/2-framing-principles-for-reform-2/principle-1-acknowledging-
     and-respecting-authorship-and-creation-2/> accessed 26 May 2021.
247 *Sands & McDougall* (n 226), as explained in *McCutcheon* (n 9) 935.
248 ACA (1968), section 35.6.

entitled to first ownership of the work. However, the same objections in relation to considering, under US law, AI-generated works as works-for-hire apply here, most notably the difficulties in qualifying the relationship of a human being with an AI as akin to that of commissioner-creator or employer-employee.[249]

2.4.3.3 Other forms of protection

Like other jurisdictions, Australia has a specific regime for derivative works. It does not seem however that said regime can be used to protect AI-generated works. In Australia, authors of literary and musical works have limited and exhaustive adaptation rights (authors of artistic works do not have any adaptation rights at all[250]). The author of a dramatic literary work has the right to make it into a non-dramatic literary work (and vice-versa); to translate it; and to make a version of the work in which the story or action is conveyed solely or mainly through pictures.[251] If the literary work is a computer programme, adaptation is taken to mean any version of it that is not a reproduction.[252] In relation to musical works, adaptation amounts to an arrangement or transcription of the work.[253] The author of the original work has the same rights in relation to the adapted work that she has in relation to that original work.[254] For the most part, it is apparent that the legal provisions could only be applied to AI-generated works in a number of limited circumstances – for example, in theory, a computer programme automatically generated by an AI could eventually be considered an adaptation of the code that was used to train the AI; just like images produced by an AI system through the conversion of natural language text descriptions could be considered an adaptation of the latter. However, even in these cases, the requirement of authorship is unsurmountable: if the output or adapted work is autonomously generated by the AI, then one cannot say that the author of the original work(s) that was/were used to train the AI has a claim over the adapted work, as she did not create them; and as the AI cannot be considered an author as explained above, the AI-generated adapted work would be authorless and therefore unprotectable.

Could AI-generated output be protected under Part IV of the ACA, i.e., "copyright in subject-matter other than works?" Differently from original literary, dramatic, musical and artistic works, initial ownership of copyright in subject matter other than works – such as film, sound recordings, broadcasts or

---

249 Ibid., section 2.4.2.2.
250 Note however that the reproduction right granted to authors of artistic works is rather broad, and includes e.g., producing a version of a two-dimensional work in a three-dimensional form (ACA (1968), section 31.3a).
251 ACA (1968), sections 10a, b and c, and 31.1a(vi).
252 Ibid., section 10ba, and 31.1a(vi).
253 Ibid., section 10d and 31.1a(vi).
254 Ibid., section 31.1a(vii).

published editions – may vest in either a person or a corporation (section 84 et seq.). Cautiously, in this part of the Act, the word "author" is avoided: it is the "maker" (of films, sound recordings and broadcasts)[255] or the "publisher" (of the published edition)[256] who are deemed the owners of the respective subject matter. Subject matter other than works need not be original to be protected, it being only necessary that it is not copied from another film, sound recording, broadcast or published edition.[257] The lower threshold of protection is offset by a narrower scope of protection though, as the set of rights given to owners of subject matter other than works is more limited than the one granted to authors and owners of Part III works.[258]

Because the list of subject matter other than works is exhaustive, Part IV of the ACA would not be able to accommodate AI-generated works in general, such as paintings or books. In relation to subject matter that is already included in Part IV, such as films, sound recordings or published editions, even though there is no "author," a "maker" or "publisher" owns the respective subject matter. If an output produced by an AI amounted to said subject matter, then protection could arise (however, similarly to what was mentioned in relation to EU neighbouring rights, the AI in this scenario would be a tool used by the respective right holder, i.e., the maker or publisher).

Interestingly, as early as 1995, the Copyright Law Review Committee, upon making a distinction between machine-assisted and machine-generated outputs, recommended that the latter not be included in Part III of the ACA – as they have no human author – and be instead inserted in Part IV.[259] For this, the Committee suggested creating a new category in Part IV, to be named "computer-generated material," the owner of which would be the person by whom the arrangements necessary for the creation of the material are undertaken (according to the Committee, this ought to be the investor or owner of the computer/computer programme).[260] This recommendation was however never adopted.

255 Ibid., sections 97–99.

256 Ibid., section 100.

257 Mark J. Davison and others, *Australian Intellectual Property Law* (4th ed., Cambridge University Press 2020) chapter 3.5.2. See also ACA (1968), sections 89–92.

258 The owner of copyright in a sound recording or a film has the exclusive right to make a copy of the recording; cause the recording to be seen or heard in public; or communicate the recording or film to the public. The owner of copyright in a sound recording has in addition the right of commercial rental. The owner of copyright in a broadcast has the rights of rebroadcast and communication to the public (owners of copyright in television broadcasts have the additional right of making a cinematograph film of the broadcast, or a copy of such a film, insofar as the broadcast consists of visual images). The owner of copyright in a published edition has the right to make a facsimile copy of the edition. See ACA (1968), sections 85–88.

259 Copyright Law Review Committee, 'Report on Computer Software Protection' (ID 221 445, Parliament of Australia 1995), paras. 13–03–13.22 and rec. 2.42.

260 Ibid. Note that the "person by whom the arrangements necessary for the creation of the material" is an expression close to that found in existing regimes of protection of computer generated-works, present, most notably, in the United Kingdom. See on this infra. 2.5.2.1.

2.4.4 Japan

2.4.4.1 *Protected subject matter*

Under Article 2(1)(i) of the Japanese Copyright Act (JCA),[261] the subject matter of copyright in Japan are works that amount to a creatively produced expression of thoughts or feelings, falling within the literary, scientific, artistic or musical domains.[262] The notion of "work" under Japanese Copyright Law is open-ended. This is confirmed by Article 10(1) JCA, which gives a Berne-like list of examples of the term "work."

The definition in Article 2(1)(i) encapsulates a three-pronged test: first, it is necessary that the work expresses thoughts or feelings; second, the thoughts or feelings must be expressed in a creative way; third, the work must fall within the literary, scientific, artistic or musical domain.[263] It could be argued that the threshold for copyrightability is higher in Japan than in other jurisdictions, and that the social trade-offs of Article 1 JCA – referring specifically to the rationale of copyright law – take place at that stage (instead of being effected through a broad fair use clause, for instance).[264]

Japanese law sets creativity as the key requirement for copyrightability.[265] A "creatively produced" expression will be one which is original and which is not a mere copy of someone else's work.[266] Courts have stressed that the term "creatively" does not necessarily require creativity in the sense of novelty; it is enough that the author's personality is imprinted on the work through his or her particular style of expression of thoughts and feelings.[267] In other words, the required expression of thoughts and feelings means that it is personal to the author and that it goes beyond mere facts[268] because, for instance,

---

261 Copyright Act (Law No. 48, promulgated on May 6, 1970)

262 The Japanese Copyright Act ('JCA'), article 2(1)(i).

263 Dennis S. Karjala and Keiji Sugiyama, 'Fundamental Concepts in Japanese and American Copyright Law' (1988) 36 *American Journal of Comparative Law* 613, 617–623. Article 1 JCA states expressly that the purpose of the law is to ensure the protection of authors and other rights holders, while taking into account a fair exploitation of the cultural products they generate, and thereby contributing to cultural development.

264 Ibid.

265 Keiji Sugiyama, 'Japanese Copyright Law Development' (2002) 7 *International Intellectual Property Law and Policy* 48–2.

266 Masayasu Ishida, 'Outline of the Japanese Copyright Law' (2008) 19–20 <www.jpo.go.jp/e/news/kokusai/developing/training/textbook/document/index/Copyright_Law.pdf> accessed 21 May 2021; Peter Ganea, 'Protected Works', in Peter Ganea and others (eds.), *Japanese Copyright Law: Writings in Honour of Gerhard Schricker* (Kluwer Law International 2005) 19.

267 See e.g., "SMAP Interview Article" unreported case (Tokyo District Court 46th Civil Division, No.19455 (Wa) 1995, October 29, 1998). See also Ryosuke Kojima, 'Japan', in Reto M. Hilty and Sylvie Nerisson (eds.), *Balancing Copyright – A Survey of National Approaches* (Springer 2012) 571. Note however that a few decisions have mentioned 'novelty' as a characteristic of creative expression – see e.g., Case (unreported) 2014 (Ne) 10059, Intellectual Property High Court 1st Division, No. 10059 (Ne) 2014, April 27, 2016), and, for older cases, see *Karjala and Sugiyama* (n 264) 630–633.

268 *Ganea* (n 266).

the thoughts and feelings are drawn from the author's personal experience.[269] Thus, an expression that is ordinary or commonplace cannot be considered creative.[270] Expressions selected from a limited range of choices have been considered "commonplace."[271]

2.4.4.2 Authorship

Japan follows an author's right – Continental European – approach and generally shows the ways of thinking behind this approach – namely, by placing the individual author at the centre of protection.[272] Even though not expressly mentioned, authors point out that the thoughts and feelings expressed in the work must be ascribed to a human being.[273] Likewise, the expression "falling within the literary, academic, artistic or musical domains" amounts to the result of intellectual or cultural activities of the human mind.[274]

It is arguable that the JCA places significant emphasis on the author as a person (which would in turn be detrimental to holding that a machine could ever be an author in the eyes of copyright law). The JCA defines the author as the person who creates the work (Article 2(1)(ii)), enjoying both moral and economic rights (Article 17(1)). The reference to moral rights hints that "person" here is understood to be a natural person. Furthermore, the specific regime of moral rights in the JCA also denotes the intention to place the author at the centre of copyright law. To start with, the moral rights available to authors are more than those prescribed by the Berne Convention. The JCA also grants authors the moral right of disclosure (Article 18 JCA). Further, the scope of moral rights is, in some instances, broader than in Berne: according to Article 20(1) JCA, the integrity right gives authors the possibility to object to any alteration or modification of the work that is contrary to the author's *intention*.

---

269 Case (unreported) Tokyo District Court 46th Civil Division, No. 37117 (Wa), 2017, January 30, 2018.

270 "Architectural Design" unreported case (Intellectual Property High Court 1st Division, No. 10130 (Ne) 2014, May 25, 2015).; "TRIPP TRAPPII" unreported case (Intellectual Property High Court 2nd Division, No. 10063 (Ne) 2014, April 14, 2015).; "Fashion Show" unreported case (Intellectual Property High Court 3rd Division, No. 10068 (Ne) 2013, August 28, 2014).

271 Case (unreported) Tokyo District Court 29th Division, No. 22400 (Wa) 2014. The case concerned a play on words, where the author linked certain translated English words or phrases to Japanese words or phrases.

272 Hiroshi Saitô and Shinichi Isa, 'General Introduction', in *Ganea and others* (n 266) 11–13. Japanese Copyright Law in particular was initially modelled after German Copyright Law – Mira T. Sundara Rajan, *Moral Rights: Principles, Practice and New Technology* (Oxford University Press 2011) 182. On the differences between author's rights systems and common law systems, see Ramalho, *The Competence of the European Union in Copyright Lawmaking* (n 89) 6–9, and references cited therein.

273 *Ganea* (n 266) referring in turn to the example given by Mamoru Kato in *Commentary About the Copyright Act* (2003) about a work created by a chimpanzee, which would not be protected even though it could express the animal's feelings. See also the "SMAP Interview Article" case (n 267) where it was ruled that "thoughts and feelings" refers to human mental activities.

274 As decided in the *"SMAP Interview Article"* case (n 267).

Theoretically, this means that even modifications that enhance the value of a work can be barred by the author.[275]

Another evidence of a strong moral rights regime is Article 113(7) JCA, which states that "the exploitation of a work in a way that is prejudicial to the honour or reputation of the author is deemed to constitute an infringement of the authors' moral rights." Article 113(7) is a catch-all provision that does not necessarily imply modifying the work; it could include e.g., the placement of a work in a context prejudicial to the author's honour or reputation.[276] The rationale for this approach to moral rights by the JCA is the close connection between authors and their progeny[277] – an additional argument to justify attributing authorship to natural persons, but not machines.

The lack of protection of works that are autonomously generated by AI was also underlined by the Report "Intellectual Property Strategic Program 2017," issued by the Intellectual Property Strategy Headquarters (conversely, if there would be a creative contribution from a human along the creative process that involves AI, the latter would be considered as a tool and copyright protection could arise).[278]

To be considered an author, the person has to actively be involved in creating the work; merely providing ideas and topics, or only playing a supportive role in the creative process – by, e.g., providing the materials to create the work – does not afford authorship.[279] Moreover, a person who requests the creation of a work, much like a person who merely gives abstract ideas and materials for another to create a work, is not considered an author under Japanese copyright law.[280] So, for instance, in the case of a literary work, the author would be the one who used his or her creativity to prepare a text and produce the expressions used in that text.[281] If such literary work was based on oral statements, the person making the oral statements could only be considered an author of the literary work if the oral statements were directly turned into text unchanged, or if the person making the oral statements would make edits to the text.[282] In cases of works that combine the intervention of AI systems and human beings, it would then be necessary to ascertain whether the latter were actively involved in the sense required by Japanese law. For instance, since providing materials to create the work is not considered enough for an authorship claim, it is unclear

---

275 Tatsuhiro Ueno, 'Moral Rights,' in *Ganea and others* (n 266) 46. Note however that the second paragraph of Article 20 then sets forth several exceptions to the right of integrity, namely that the modification is found unavoidable in light of the nature of the work and the purpose and circumstances of its exploitation.

276 *Saitô and Isa* (n 272) 12.

277 *Sundara Rajan* (n 272) 184.

278 Intellectual Property Strategy Headquarters, 'Intellectual Property Strategic Program 2017' (May 2017) 17 <www.kantei.go.jp/jp/singi/titeki2/kettei/chizaikeikaku20170516_e.pdf> accessed 12 May 2021).

279 *"SMAP Interview Article" case* (n 267).

280 Shigeki Chaen, 'Copyright Ownership,' in *Ganea and others* (n 266) 32.

281 *"SMAP Interview Article" case* (n 267).

282 Ibid.

whether the preparatory stage of training the AI system could be considered relevant for purposes of authorship.

As in other jurisdictions, questions could also be raised as to whether the regime of authorship of legal persons may apply by analogy to AI-generated works. Authorship of legal persons is possible in the context of an employment relationship, and provided certain requirements are met: it is necessary that the work was created by an employee in the course of her duties, at the initiative of the legal person, and made public under the name of the legal person (unless agreed otherwise).[283] Authorship of legal persons is grounded inter alia on the fact that it facilitates the exploitation (and therefore dissemination) of works, as well as on the need to give incentives to legal persons for the production of creative works within the corporate world.[284] The "initiative of the legal person" should be understood broadly. It covers cases where the employee is akin to a tool in the process of making a work (e.g., following precise instructions from the legal person), but also situations where employees produce something that they are supposed or expected to make in the course of their duties, independently of specific instructions or even consent or awareness from the legal person.[285] Thus, the "initiative of the legal person" does not necessarily translate into a specific order, but can rather result from an "indirect intention" of the legal person (which can be objectively assessed based on the employment relationship and/or on whether the employee performs his duties in accordance with the business plan of the legal person).[286] The "duties" of the employee involve all that is expected from the employee considering factors such as his position, the type and content of his duties, and the type and content of the work created by him.[287]

The term "employee" is also construed broadly: it includes of course someone who is in an employment relationship, but also anyone who is in a position to follow instructions from the legal person for the production of the work, under the agreement that the corporation shall have the initial copyright ownership of the work.[288] The employment relationship is to be evaluated substantively, i.e., by investigating whether the person concerned is actually providing labour under the supervision of the legal person, and whether the money paid to the person providing labour can be considered as compensation for that labour.[289]

283 JCA, article 15(1).

284 Case (unreported) Tokyo District Court 29th Division, No. 33577 (Wa) 2007.

285 "FOMA" unreported case (Intellectual Property High Court 4th division, No. 10029 (Ne) 2010, March 28, 2016).; *MTG Co., Ltd. v. Five Stars Co. Ltd.* unreported case (Intellectual Property High Court 1st division, No. 10003 (Ne) 2006, June 7, 2020).; "Device for separating and removing foreign matter on war laver" unreported case (Tokyo District Court 29th Division, No. 27552 (Wa) 2000, October 26, 2000).

286 *Case No. 33577* (n 284).; *MTG Co., Ltd. v. Five Stars Co. Ltd.* (n 285).

287 *Case No. 33577* (n 284).

288 "*SMAP Interview Article*" case (n 267).

289 Judgment of July 13, 2004 in Keishu 58(5) (Sup. Ct. No. 216 (JU) 2001)

Despite the broad scope of several elements in this regime, it is doubtful that the concept of authorship of legal persons could be applied by analogy to the owner of the AI system. Legal persons as authors is the exception rather than the rule.[290] More importantly, just like other jurisdictions and as explained in other subsections of this chapter, the construction employer-employee implies that the latter is a natural person, who has entered into a labour contract with the former. Machines are – at least for now – unable to conclude contracts. Even if the term "employee" is construed broadly, as explained above, it implies that the person has entered into some sort of agreement with the employer (i.e., the owner of the AI), whereby the latter is granted initial copyright ownership of the work. In other words, even if under Japanese law no labour contract is needed, there would have to be an underlying agreement, and machines are not able to conclude agreements.

An argument that could speak towards having legal persons as the authors of AI-generated works under the regime of employment is the fact that employers enjoy authorship just like natural persons, and this includes having moral rights. However, despite the (few) instances where legal persons enjoy moral rights, moral rights are considered to protect the character and personality of the author.[291] They are inextricably connected to the author as a person: they are inalienable (Article 59 JCA) and its protection is extended after the author's death through Article 60 JCA, which stipulates that it is forbidden to engage in conduct that would be prejudicial to the moral rights of the author if he were alive.[292] The grant of moral rights to legal persons can be attributed to the employment culture in Japan, which emphasizes the loyalty between employer and employee, rather than an approximation to the Anglo-Saxon approach to copyright.[293] Seen in this light, the grant of moral rights to companies is thus more of a way to emphasize the concepts of honour and loyalty – which are central to Japanese culture –, and less an evidence of a depersonalization of moral rights.[294] Moreover, in practical terms, granting moral rights to companies is also a means to facilitate the exploitation of works.[295]

2.4.4.3 Other forms of protection

Like other jurisdictions, Japan has a regime of derivative works that may at first sight be considered an option to protect AI-generated works, given the *modus operandi* of AI systems that produce creative output (the AI-generated

290 *Ishida* (n 266) 18–19.
291 Ibid., 26.
292 Note however, for the sake of completion, the second part of the provision: "provided, however, that this does not apply if that conduct is found not to contravene the will of the author in light of the nature and extent of the conduct as well as changes in social circumstances and other conditions."
293 *Saitô and Isa* (n 272) 13.
294 Similarly, see *Sundara Rajan* (n 272) 186.
295 *Chaen* (n 280) 36. This point was also emphasized by the Tokyo District Court in *Case No. 33577* (n 284).

output could be seen as a derivative work vis-à-vis the works that the AI system ingested). In Japanese law, derivative works are defined as works "created by translating, arranging musically, transforming, or dramatizing, cinematizing or otherwise adapting a pre-existing work" (Article 2(1)(xi) JCA). A derivative work has the creative elements of the original work, while adding new creative elements to it.[296] Derivative works are copyright protected works themselves, provided of course that the respective requirements for protection are met. Only the parts of a derivative work that are creative and newly introduced will be copyright protected; the parts in the derivative work that are identical in substance to the original work will not be granted protection as a separate work.[297]

However, Article 28 JCA prescribes that the author of the pre-existing work has the same rights of exploitation of the derivative work as the *author* of said work.[298] Since, as seen above, the definition of "author" presupposes by default a natural person, it does not seem to be possible to qualify AI-generated works as derivative works.

Also as with other jurisdictions – namely, the EU – the JCA features an independent neighbouring rights protection for certain beneficiaries (performers, phonogram producers, broadcasters and "wire diffusion organisations," which are cable radio and TV broadcasters).[299] The protection granted to these categories of rights holders is based on interpretative or entrepreneurial efforts, rather than creative.[300] Like the EU, it is conceivable that some of the output produced by an AI system might be protected by a neighbouring right (also here assuming that the AI is used as a tool by the related rights holder).

2.5 Conclusions and recommendations

2.5.1 Conclusions

Technological advancements in AI (including its computational power) have made its application increasingly common in music, the visual arts, literature and other fields, and its operation is becoming gradually independent from human beings. AI still lacks the so-called "general intelligence," or "common

---

296 *Ganea* (n 266) 27.

297 "Popeye" unreported case (Supreme Court of Japan, 1443 (O) 1992, July 17, 1997). *Ganea* (n 266) 27, points out in addition that the subject matter underlying a derivative work must amount to a work in itself, and gives the example of translation of non-copyrightable subject matter (which would be ineligible for copyright protection).

298 Arguably, the purpose of Article 28 is to give the author control over secondary works which are derived from his own work – Simone Schroff, 'How Japanese Law Facilitates Access to Art for Persons with a Visual Impairment,' in Jani McCutcheon and Ana Ramalho (eds.), *International Perspectives on Copyright Law and the Visual Arts: Feeling Art* (Routledge 2020) 222.

299 See JCA, chapter IV. See also *Saitô and Isa* (n 272) 14., and Shu Masuyama, 'Neigbouring Rights', in *Ganea and others* (n 266) 91ff.

300 Ibid.

sense reasoning,"[301] but as explained in section 2.2, AI systems are able to produce musical, artistic or literary works that resemble the ones created by humans. Against this background, it is important to bear in mind the spectrum of autonomy of AI systems when producing works: at the lower end of the spectrum, AI systems are a tool in the hands of a human creator, while the higher end of the spectrum would see AI as a completely autonomous system. The more recent AI systems produce output that is high in the spectrum of autonomy, but a human being is still present at some point in the creative process – namely, at a preparatory stage where the AI system needs to be trained.

All jurisdictions examined require – albeit some more expressly than others – a human being to be involved in creating the work in order for it to be eligible for copyright protection. That human being must make certain creative choices – see e.g., *Burrow-Giles* (US) and *Painer* (EU), both cases about photographs, where the creative choices of the photographer were highlighted as key to assessing copyrightability. Arguably, those choices can be made at different stages of the production of the work, such as its preparation/composition, execution or final stage (where the latter might amount to e.g., adding finishing touches, selecting the work among several attempts or drafts, etc). However, the jurisdictions examined in this book approach the issue of creative choices differently from one another. Namely, the primary judge in the Australian case *Acohs* (2010) hinted that intention or at least perception (at the preparatory stage) was necessary for a finding of authorship. This is in line with another Australian decision, the *Telstra* case, which requires that the choices made in the preparatory stage amount to an independent intellectual effort that needs to be reflected in the final product. That is, in Australia the need for a connection between the author and the reduction of the work to its material form seems more apparent (none of the other jurisdictions refer so specifically to a similar requirement). In any case, in one way or another, all the jurisdictions examined intertwine authorship with requirements for protection such that the former appears to be embedded in the latter. Where there is no human author, a work cannot be original; and without originality, a work cannot be protected by copyright.[302]

In none of the jurisdictions is the lack of a human in the creative process able to be remedied through specific regimes such as works made in the course of employment or for hire; nor is it possible to protect AI-generated creations through the legal institute of derivative works. As demonstrated in the relevant

301 See on this specific point *Pavón and González-Espejo* (n 12) 18: "Although AI is solving new categories of problems with great success, it still faces relevant limitations as it lacks an intrinsically human capacity: common sense reasoning. Although AI systems can manage relationships among the objects they manipulate, they do not have a real understanding of the meaning of what they do."

302 See also Séverine Dussolier, 'Scoping Study on Copyright and Related Rights and the Public Domain' (CDIP/7/INF/2, World Intellectual Property Organization – Committee on Development and Intellectual Property 2011) 24 <www.wipo.int/edocs/mdocs/mdocs/en/cdip_7/cdip_7_inf_2.pdf> accessed 27 May 2021: "the entrance to the copyright building is conditioned of finding of some degree of originality in the work."

subsections of 2.4, these norms are ill-suited to regulate a possible attribution of copyright to AI-generated works.

The positive law thus examined leads to the need to find a human being throughout the creative process when a work is generated by an AI system. This book has rejected the idea of a fixed number of categories of AI-generated content (e.g., "AI-assisted" versus "AI-fully generated" content), and has rather opted for the idea of a spectrum of autonomy, which is more flexible (and therefore deemed more adaptable to different configurations of AI systems). This approach allows for directly looking for a human intervention worthy of an authorship claim, instead of relying on a pre-established categorization of an AI-generated output as "assisted by AI" or "fully-generated by AI."

The quest to find a human being that might have an authorship claim to an AI-generated output starts with tracing the human intervention in the creative process, which can be identified at the different stages of producing a work (namely, the preparation, execution, or final stage).

The second step is to assess whether that intervention is enough of an original contribution to merit copyright protection. That is, human intervention should be more than *de minimis*.[303] In that sense, this second step is no different from assessing the degree of originality for purposes of protection of a fully human-produced work – if there is enough of a human input in creating an original work, then copyright protection will be available. The problem regarding AI-generated works is that it might be problematic to trace and gauge human intervention, and to determine to what extent there is (copyright protected) human input in the act of creation of works that blend contributions from both human and machine. Another difficulty regarding tracing and evaluating human intervention is that not all courts look at the work and trace back the process of creation to its origin; in some jurisdictions, courts tend to focus on the work and not on who created it for purposes of assessing originality.[304]

---

303 A "more-than-*de minimis*" human intervention would be in line with the copyrightability tests of some jurisdictions, in so far as they require, in one way or another, a substantiality test for copyright subsistence that mandates a certain level of originality or creativity – see e.g., in the US, *Feist Publications* (n 184) 363 ("As a constitutional matter, copyright protects only those constituent elements of a work that possess more than a *de minimis* quantum of creativity."); and in Japan, see "Architectural Design" case ("the work is required to express a certain level of distinctiveness of the creator"[emphasis added]. Note however that the de minimis threshold is not applied everywhere – e.g., arguably, in Australia, it is not yet clear whether there is a de minimis threshold of originality (see *Davison and others* (n 257), section 3.5.1: "It is unclear . . . whether there is a *de minimis* level of creativity needed to establish originality. There is no guidance as to exactly how much skill, labour or effort is required for a creation to be considered an original work.")

304 Stef van Gompel, 'Creativity, Autonomy and Personal Touch: A Critical Appraisal of the CJEU's Originality Test for Copyright,' in Mireille van Eechoud (ed.), *The Work of Authorship* (Amsterdam University Press 2014) 128 (giving the example of Dutch courts). The European Parliament seems to endorse a similar approach by pointing out that the focus is shifting from the creative process to the creative product – see 'Report on Intellectual Property Rights for the Development of Artificial Intelligence Technologies' (n 135) 13: "At a time when artistic creation by AI is becoming more common . . . we seem to be moving towards an acknowledgement that an AI-generated creation could

Different court practices, grouped with the fact that some works merge indistinctly human and machine contributions, may prove to be a hurdle.

Here is where a third step should be adopted. The third step draws inspiration from Australian case law (which requires that input during the creative process should be reflected in the final work), and from EU case law (which seems to recently have adopted a similar line of reasoning).[305] In fact, what Bringsjord and Ferrucci called "creative distance," i.e., the difference between a program's initial data (or input) and the product it generates (or output),[306] is fundamental for assessing whether authorship of an AI-generated work can be ascribed to a human being. The creativity of the author, the expression of his or her ideas, should be reflected in the final work produced. Not all creative choices need to be reflected in the work, but the latter must still contain some expressive elements deriving from the author's intellectual conception. This link between creative input and the final work is connected to something that I have argued before, which is how authorship relates to the intention or purpose to create.[307] While, of course, the intention to create might not yield the exact result that the author is expecting, there must be a flow of creation between the author's contribution towards the creative process and what ends up being the final creative product.[308] It should also be noted that the creative input of a human author is not necessarily provided only at the preparatory stage (e.g., through the choices made when training the AI system, namely in selecting and curating data), but also at other stages of production, namely at a final stage of post-production where human choices might be present in, for instance, editing the work.[309] The crux of the matter is again assessing whether the human intervention is worthy of copyright protection due to its creative proximity to the final version of the work, regardless of the stage of the creative process where it takes place.

How would these rules fare when applied to current AI systems that produce creative content? Taking the example of the Computoser, which involves human contributions of both the programmer and the user, it is submitted that

---

be deemed to constitute a work of art on the basis of the creative result rather than the creative process."

305 See *Cofemel* (n 121) para 29: "classification as a work is reserved to the elements that are the expression of [the author's own intellectual] creation." Similarly, *Levola Hengelo* (n 147) para 37: "only something which is the expression of the author's own intellectual creation may be classified as a 'work.'"

306 *Bringsjord and Ferrucci* (n 47) 161.

307 Ramalho, 'Will Robots Rule the (Artistic) World?' (n 8) 15. Along the same lines and specifically in relation to US law see *Bridy*, 'Coding Creativity' (n 193) 8. More recently, see in the context of EU law, see *Hartmann and others* (n 135) 75: "[I]t is fair to assume that the concept of a work as "the author's own intellectual creation" not merely requires human agency or intervention, but also some degree of authorial intent." See however *Ginsburg and Budiardjo* (n 10) 403: "We do not endorse the view that authorship requires the putative author to claim that she had the 'purpose to create.'"

308 Similarly see *Hartmann and others* (n 135) 75: "[W]hat is probably enough is general authorial intent. That is to say, it is sufficient that the author has a general conception of the work before it is expressed, while leaving room for unintended expressive features."

309 Ibid. 80.

the contribution of the programmer is reflected in the algorithm itself and its architecture, but the creative distance between the input from the programmer and the music track generated by the algorithm is too great to consider that the programmer has any authorship claim on said music track. The programmer set the rules by which the generation of music abides. Those rules are, in his own words, "loosely defined"[310] – a strong indication that the programmer does not envisage or intend to create whatever result is produced by the Computoser. The creativity of the programmer stopped at the moment of conception and creation of the algorithm. As for the contribution of the user to the generated music track, he or she can influence it by choosing its mood, tempo, accompaniment, instrument, scale, drums, dissonance, or whether they want a more classical or electronic-like track. However, it does not seem that such intervention by the user is enough for an authorship claim either. The parameters chosen by the user are abstract rules that shape the final result, but they don't amount to the substance of that result. In other words, the choice of a particular instrument or tempo, for instance, does not dictate the musical notes of the particular melody that the Computoser generates; while being an element of the AI-generated track, the use of a particular instrument or tempo does not constitute the creative core of that track. The parameters are also limited in number, which means that the range of choices at the user's disposal is quite narrow and constrained (thus giving the user little room to exercise his or her own creativity).

By the same token, more modern AIs such as neural networks are likely to represent a challenge to authorship claims as well, since the creative distance between the input of the programmer/developer and the output or work might be too great[311] – unless of course there is significant human contribution at the final stage (e.g., substantially editing a text that was automatically generated by a neural network).[312]

The need to evaluate whether human contribution is original enough to merit copyright protection, and the subsequent assessment of the creative distance between the human being's input and the AI-generated work, highlight a central problem in AI-generated works: traceability. More modern AI systems such as neural networks are quite opaque – the way they work and the reasons that underlie a certain result are not always apparent (the so-called "black box problem").[313] This might make it hard to identify the human contribution and

---

310   *Bozhanov* (n 53) 5.

311   See however *Hartmann and others* (n 135) 82–83: "Due to the 'black box' characteristic of ML systems, the human author in charge of designing the production at the conception phase will not be able to precisely predict or explain the outcome of the execution phase. This, however, need not present an obstacle to the "work" status of the final output, assuming that such output stays within the ambit of the author's general authorial intent."

312   In the same sense, *Hartmann and others* (n 135) 83: "[E]ven completely unpredicted, non-explainable, quasi-random AI-assisted output might still be converted into a protected "work" at the redaction phase."

313   See e.g., Carlos Zednik, 'Solving the Black Box Problem: A Normative Framework for Explainable Artificial Intelligence' (arXiv 2019) <https://arxiv.org/pdf/1903.04361.pdf> accessed 23 May 2021.

to assess how that contribution is reflected in the final output.[314] Deep learning in particular often depends on trial and error, which makes the final result difficult to explain without going through the previous iterations.[315] It has also been pointed out that "developers in machine learning exert limited influence on the way in which the relevant problems are solved."[316] In fact, as the Computoser example shows, while developers must make certain choices with regard to the architecture of the system, the learning algorithm used and the learning environment, their influence does not extend to the particular workings of the learning parameters used, and therefore they cannot understand and/or predict how a given input is used by the AI to generated a certain output.[317]

If a human author cannot be traced throughout the creative process in the terms just mentioned (or if one simply does not exist), the consequence is that the output generated by the AI system cannot be protected by copyright, being thus in the public domain (which is traditionally defined as encompassing intellectual elements not protected by copyright or whose protection has elapsed).[318] This is without prejudice to it eventually being protected by neighbouring rights or similar regimes (such as the Australian copyright for subject matter other than works), assuming of course that the AI-output corresponds to eligible subject matter (e.g., films or sound recordings).[319]

---

314 Note however that some AI applications allow for tracing individual examples in the training process, which prove useful for explaining predictions in terms of training examples – see Frederick Liu & Garima Pruthi, 'TracIn – A Simple Method to Estimate Training Data Influence' (February 2021) <https://ai.googleblog.com/2021/02/tracin-simple-method-to-estimate.html> accessed 3 June 2021.

315 Vincent Aravantinos and Frederik Diehl, 'Traceability of Deep Neural Networks' (*arXiv* 2018) <https://arxiv.org/pdf/1812.06744.pdf> accessed 23 May 2021.

316 *Zednik* (n 313) 3.

317 Ibid., 3–4: "Of course, ML developers must decide on basic architectural principles such as whether the system takes the form of a deep neural network, a support vector machine, a decision tree, or some other kind of system with a particular set of learnable parameters. Moreover, they must choose an appropriate learning algorithm, and must identify a suitable learning environment, in which the learnable parameters can obtain values with which to solve the problem at hand. Nevertheless, ML developers do not typically decide on the particular values these parameters eventually obtain (e.g., the weights of individual network connections), and in this sense, do not wholly determine the way in which the problem is actually solved . . . even if individual parameter values are known, the fact that they might interact nonlinearly as well as recurrently means that it is almost impossible to understand, predict, or systematically intervene on the way in which a particular input is transformed so as to generate a particular output."

318 Definition advanced by *Dussolier* (n 302) 6–7. See also WIPO Intergovernmental Committee on Intellectual Property and Genetic Resources, Traditional Knowledge and Folklore, '*Note on the Meanings of the Term 'Public Domain' in the Intellectual Property System with Special Reference to the Protection of Traditional Knowledge and Traditional Cultural Expressions/Expressions of Folklore*' (WIPO/GRTKF/IC/17/INF/8, World Intellectual Property Organization 2010) annex 4 [4], [22]. <www.wipo.int/edocs/mdocs/tk/en/wipo_grtkf_ic_17/wipo_grtkf_ic_17_inf_8.pdf> accessed 22 May 2021.

319 However, if no neighbouring rights (or similar) regime applies, the complete lack of subjective rights and the possibility to access AI creations could lead to the unencumbered creation of new knowledge and to free or low cost access to information – see on these characteristics of the public

Another question is whether determining that authorless works are in the public domain ensures internal consistency in copyright. On the one hand, maintaining internal consistency in copyright implies accepting that copyright must keep definite limits.[320] On the other hand, it is necessary to assess whether those limits are adequate. Beyond stating that under positive law authorless works cannot be protected, it is opportune to discuss whether they should. This will be done in the next Section.

2.5.2 Recommendations

In order to assess whether AI-generated works lacking a human author should be protected, this section will first evaluate regimes in other jurisdictions that aim at protecting such works (2.5.2.1), and then analyse if protecting these works would be compatible with copyright's rationales (2.5.2.2). The last section will suggest that, while copyright should not protect authorless works, an eventual neighbouring right might be enough to balance the interests at stake (2.5.2.3).

2.5.2.1 Existing solutions in specific jurisdictions

A few common law jurisdictions – New Zealand, United Kingdom, Ireland, Hong Kong, South Africa and India – have a special regime for computer-generated works, i.e., a work that is generated by a computer "such that there is no human author,"[321] or in relation to which the author "is not an individual."[322] Authorship in computer-generated works is given to the person by whom the arrangements necessary for the creation of the work are undertaken,[323] or to the person who causes the work to be created,[324] depending on the jurisdiction. The term of protection for computer-generated works is counted from the date of production (e.g., in the UK, that term is set at 50 years from the date the work was made).[325]

---

domain Alexander Peukert, '*A Doctrine of the Public Domain*' (2016) Goethe University Frankfurt in Josef Drexl (ed.), *The Innovation Society and Intellectual Property* (Edward Elgar Publishing 2019) para 16ff <https://papers.ssrn.com/sol3/papers2.cfm?abstract_id=2713757> accessed 22 May 2021. See WIPO, '*Note on the Meanings of the Term 'Public Domain'* (ibid) 29.

320 Ralph S. Brown, 'Eligibility for Copyright Protection: A Search for Principled Standards' (1986) 70 *Minnesota Law Review* 579, 608, pointing out the importance of maintaining internal consistency in copyright, quotes the statement that L. Ray Petterson, Law Professor, made in relation to copyright protection for semi-conductor chips: "while consistency for its own sake is a virtue of small consequence, consistent principles for a body of law are essential for integrity in the interpretation and administration of that law." The same line of thought could be applicable here – it is necessary to seek consistency in copyright principles, in order to ensure integrity of this body of law when applied to new realities.

321 United Kingdom Copyright, Designs and Patents Act (1988) ('CDPA'), section 178.

322 Irish Copyright and Related Rights Act (2000), section 2(1).

323 CDPA (1988), section 9(3).

324 Indian Copyright Act (1957), section 2(d)(vi).

325 CDPA (1988), section 12(7).

The rule on authorship for computer-generated works is a legal fiction that derogates from the general rule that defines the author as the one who creates the work.[326] As such, the link between authorship and conditions for protection is rekindled, as the originality requirement will have to be self-standing and independent of authorship – not linked to the person responsible for the arrangements (as s/he is the author only due to the legal fiction and has no direct connection to the work), but also not linked to the computer.[327]

Central to this regime is the interpretation of the term "arrangements," and the person responsible for them, who might include the user, the programmer, the person who sells or produces the software, or an investor;[328] but also, more broadly, the person instructing or training the programmer or the person customizing the software;[329] or even a combination of them, depending on the specific work at issue (and on whether the interpreter agrees that the word "person"[by whom arrangements are undertaken] can include more than one person, which is debatable). All these options are possible, because the term "arrangements" amounts to preparing or organizing something so that the work may be created (considering that, without such preparation or organization, the work could not have been produced, which is indicated by the expression "*necessary* arrangements").[330] The person responsible for the arrangements will depend on the factors weighed in, which can include inter alia the initiative to create the work, the proximity to the final act of creation (the closer to the final creation, the more likely to be in charge of the arrangements to create the work), or the extent to which the arrangements are responsible for the creation of the work (which would put the emphasis on the operation of the software).[331]

In a British case concerning the frame images generated when the user plays the game, the person by whom arrangements were undertaken was considered to be the person who programmed and designed the game.[332] The Court expressly refused to confer that status to the user, as the latter's input was not artistic in nature, nor had he undertaken the arrangements necessary to create the frame images.[333] However, other situations might not be as straightforward, especially taking into account the increasingly relevant and active role of users in certain types of creative output (such as computer games). The uncertainty regarding the person by whom arrangements are undertaken, who will have to

---

326 See e.g., CDPA (1988), section 9(1).

327 Jani McCutcheon, 'Curing the Authorless Void: Protecting Computer Generated Works following Ice TV and Phone Directories' (2013) 37 *Melbourne University Law Review* 46, 51: "it seems that the criterion of originality would be applied on a hypothetical basis: if the work had been authored by a human, or if that human could be identified, would it be original?"

328 See Lionel Bently and Brad Sherman, *Intellectual Property Law* (3rd ed., Oxford University Press 2009) 122.

329 *McCutcheon*, 'Curing the Authorless Void' (n 327) 54.

330 Ibid., 53.

331 Ibid., 55–56.

332 *Nova Productions Ltd. v. Mazooma Games Ltd* [2006] RPC 379.

333 Ibid., 399.

be identified on a case-by-case basis, does not favour legal certainty and speaks against extending this legal fiction to other jurisdictions.[334]

In addition, "the person by whom arrangements are undertaken" presupposes human intervention at some point. Current legal regimes that recognise computer-generated works as such still trace back authorship to human intervention (the person that makes the arrangements and that therefore is considered to ultimately have produced the work). In that sense, the regime of computer-generated works is similar to what was suggested in the previous section – using a sufficient human link to establish (human) authorship. In both cases, the computers are, to a certain extent, still tools. The difference here is that the traceability to a human being is expressly established by law, and there is no assessment as to the sufficiency of that link. That is, the author will be "the person by whom arrangements are undertaken," independently of the creative distance between that person and the work, and regardless of the true weight or influence that that person's actions had in the final product (although the creative distance or influence of the person who undertakes the arrangements might presumably be taken into account when assessing authorship on a case-by-case basis).

In short, it seems unnecessary and disadvantageous to transplant the regime of computer-generated works to other jurisdictions. Unnecessary, because it still forces the interpreter to look for a human being in the context of the creative process (something that must be done in any case in jurisdictions that do not have this regime). Disadvantageous, because the human being that the interpreter must trace – the person who undertakes arrangements – is not inevitably the one who is closer to the creative essence of the work, which puts into question the compatibility of the regime with copyright's internal consistency. Moreover, in (future) cases of a completely autonomous AI, it might even be hard to discern a human being who would be responsible for the arrangements further up the chain of creation.

2.5.2.2 *Protection of AI-generated works in light of copyright's rationales*

Copyright rationales provide a sound basis for the evaluation as to whether authorless, AI-generated works ought to be protected. Since copyright rationales are the foundation that justifies current copyright laws, those same

---

334 Interestingly, similar cases in the US concerning (copyright protected) displays in videogames have had the same outcome, with courts ruling that it is immaterial whether the displays are generated autonomously by the machine or through the actions of the player – copyright belongs, in both cases, to the owner of the copyright in the game code (see *Bridy*, 'Coding Creativity' (n 193) 24., citing *Stern Electronics, Inc. v. Harold Kaufman*, 'Scramble" 669 F.2d 852 (2nd Circ. 1982), *Atari, Inc. v. North American Philips Consumer Electronics Corp.*, "Pacman" 672 F.2d 607 (7th Circ. 1982) and *Williams Electronics, Inc. v. Artic International, Inc.*, "Defender" 1981 WL 1287 (D.N.J. 1981)). This raises legitimate doubts as to the usefulness of the regime for computer-generated works and their quest for authorship, at least in cases where the user does not perform that relevant a role in computer games.

rationales should be used as a yardstick against which to analyse whether new paradigms should be accommodated by said laws. As clarified in section 2.3, the rationales for copyright protection can be divided into two main theories: the utilitarian theory and natural rights theories.

The utilitarian theory is premised on incentives to create. This constitutes a fundamental obstacle to defend that AI-generated works ought to be protected by copyright, since, if there is no human being behind the creation, then the incentive does not have an addressee. AI systems do not need an incentive to create (at least not for now, as they lack consciousness), not to mention that they have no means of reaping the economic benefits deriving from copyright protection (which dictated that protection in the first place).[335] Here, the criticisms to the utilitarian theory – namely, the feeble link between incentive and certain forms of creation, such as amateur or derivative works[336] – gain prominence and could be brought to the fore to show the inadequacy of the utilitarian theory to justify the protection of authorless, AI-generated works. Yet, the alternative reasons to create highlighted by critics of the utilitarian theory are heavily human-dependent as well. For instance, the incentive derived by the act of creation itself, or the choice of one creative activity over another because of its lower costs, are judgements and intention states that are foreign to machines.

Some authors point out that developers of AI systems need the incentive to create and improve them, and that granting some sort of protection to AI-generated works could provide that incentive.[337] However, the AI systems themselves may be protected by copyright or patents, depending on the case.[338] Arguably, that protection is the one that better correlates with the incentive that needs to be given to developers of AI systems. Using copyright to protect the output of those systems would be a "meta incentive," which would not be efficient to motivate people whose creative distance from the work dictated the absence of a human author under copyright laws in the first place. Granting protection to AI-generated output in those terms would lead to a double reward of the creator of the AI (who would then be able to derive income not only from the creation of the AI but from all its output).[339] It should also be recalled that developers have the so-called first-mover advantage, as they can be the first ones to sell the works produced by the AI system, regardless of the copyright status

---

335 Pamela Samuelson, 'Allocating Ownership Rights in Computer Generated Works' (1985) 47 *University of Pittsburgh Law Review* 1185, 1199.

336 Ibid. section 2.3.

337 *Hristov* (n 211) 439.

338 AI systems may rely on patent protection for e.g., the architecture of training models, or for the implementation of an algorithm – cf. Jean-Marc Deltorn, 'Disentangling Deep Learning and Copyrights' (2018) 5 *AMI* 172, 177 (see for a concrete example the case of DABUS and the Creativity Machine, both "creative robots" that are in themselves patented, in chapter 3.2ff); and copyright protection may arise for a computer's source or object code (see TRIPS Agreement (1995), article 10(1) and WIPO Copyright Treaty (1996), article 4).

339 Terry Dartnall, 'Introduction: On Having a Mind of Your Own,' in Dartnall, *Artificial Intelligence and Creativity* (n 4) 36.

of said works. In fact, the first-mover advantage can be enough of an economic incentive and it is independent of any copyright protection.[340] In any case, the developer (or the user of the AI more generally) can always use AI-generated output as a springboard to create copyrightable "derivative" works.[341]

Excluding others from using AI-generated works through copyright comes as a cost for society, and there is no perceived advantage from it since that exclusionary right is not an incentive for the production of more works. Because an implied principle of the utilitarian theory is the balance between advantages and costs to society that come from granting copyright protection to works, it does not seem that granting copyright protection to AI-generated works where no human author can be found complies with the utilitarian justification.

As for natural rights justifications, both the labour theory and the personality theory have at their core the relationship of the author with his work, which constitutes a hurdle for granting copyright protection to authorless, AI-generated works: it is doubtful that, at least for now, AI systems can engage in any type of relation with their work, for that entails deeper emotional connections. The labour theory implies a reward for effort, and machines do not respond to such rewards (again, at least at the current time, where there is no such thing as machine consciousness and emotions). Although it can be argued that humans don't always make a conscious effort to create, it is a fact that at least for the most part they can articulate their creative process and explain their creative choices. As has been pointed out by others, the idea of labour as a plausible justification for intellectual property involves purposiveness – labour is a human activity that is connected to the capacity to control one's life according to one's goals and values.[342] Machines, on the other hand, are unaware of its processes.[343] They are deprived of intention states such as desire (unlike the "higher human intelligence"), and therefore the reward mechanism speaks little to them.

Moreover, works that are autonomously generated by AI systems also call into question the true meaning of "creativity." As concluded in section 2.2., "creativity" should be taken as a holistic term that encompasses both product and process, intuition and rationality. A strict interpretation of this definition of creativity would thus lead to a conclusion that machines cannot truly be creative, and that therefore no reward should be considered.

The personality theory as a justification for the grant of copyright seems even less applicable, as "personality" implies a person, with intention states that, as observed, are for now inexistent in AI systems.

---

340 *Yu* (n 223) 1264–1265.

341 Ibid.

342 Bryan Cwik, 'Labor as the Basis for Intellectual Property Rights' (2014) 17 *Ethical Theory and Moral Practice* 681, 686; Wendy J. Gordon, 'A Property Right in Self-Expression: Equality and Individualism in the Natural Law of Intellectual Property' (1993) 102 *Yale Law Journal* 1533, 1547. In that regard, it is interesting to note that Locke believed that authors (as opposed to printers) should have property over their own writings, inter alia because of the tenuous link between printers and the authors who created the works – see on this point section 2.3. *supra.*

343 *Dartnall* (n 339) 36.

Ultimately, an autonomous, juridical will – i.e., an intentional state that legal systems use to operationalize legal agency[344] – is lacking in AI systems. Absent any justification for copyright protection, and even if AI systems could be given legal personhood for purposes of holding rights, there is no argument to support the grant of copyright in case of AI-generated works that bear no intervention of a human being (or where the human intervention is not enough to succeed in an authorship claim).

2.5.2.3 Possible solution: a neighbouring right or similar regime

Since neighbouring rights' protection (and the regime of copyright for subject matter other than works, in Australia) has mostly a commercial or technical nature, an option to protect authorless, AI-generated works would be to establish a regime akin to the protection of producers or broadcasters.[345] It is also possible to consider the grant of a sui generis right in AI-generated works, much like the EU legislature decided to do for makers of databases.[346] The common rationale here is the protection of investment.[347]

A neighbouring right for AI-generated works where no human author can be traced is not necessarily incompatible with their public domain status. "Public domain" does not mean that free access is ensured; free access and free use are not interchangeable notions.[348] AI systems as creators don't need an incentive to create, nor does it make sense to protect works as an extension of its (non-existing) personality, or to award it a reward for its (non-existing) effort to create. It is however possible that someone who disseminates AI creations (thus bringing them to the public) needs to be incentivized or rewarded for doing so, much like the publishers of e.g., books in the public domain expect users to pay for copies of the book. In other words, a distinction must be made between incentives or rewards for creation – which are not needed – and incentives or rewards for dissemination – which might be.

---

344 Catherine M. Brölmann, 'Capturing the Juridical Will of International Organizations' (2019) Amsterdam Law School Research Paper No. 2019–09, 5 <https://privpapers.ssrn.com/sol3/papers.cfm?abstract_id=3341457> accessed 27 May 2021.

345 Note that the US does not have neighbouring rights. An eventual regime of protection for AI-generated works would have to come under copyright, similarly to e.g., sound recordings or broadcasts.

346 See Database Directive.

347 Mireille van Eechoud and others, *Harmonizing European Copyright Law: The Challenges of Better Lawmaking* (Kluwer Law International 2009) 191.; Paul Torremans, *Holyoak and Torremans Intellectual Property Law* (5th ed., Oxford University Press 2008) 192–193 (in relation to entrepreneurial works).; Derclaye, *The Legal Protection of Databases* (n 84) 45 (in relation to databases). See also recently, in relation to phonogram producers, case C-476/17 *Pelham GmbH and Others v. Ralf Hütter and Florian Schneider-Esleben* (Judgment of the Court Grand Chamber, 29 July 2019) [30]: "the specific objective of the exclusive right of the phonogram producer, referred to in recital 10 [of the Information Society Directive], . . . is to protect a phonogram producer's investment."

348 *Dussolier* (n 302) 7–9.

A similar regime to the publisher's right in the publication of previously unpublished works, prescribed by the EU's Term of Protection Directive, provides a good example of a possible solution. Article 4 of the Term of Protection Directive gives publishers a 25-year protection equivalent to the economic rights of the author for the first lawful publication or communication of a previously unpublished work after the expiry of copyright protection. The sentence "after the expiry of copyright protection" does not mean that the work must have been protected by copyright at some time in the past; some member states, such as Spain, have explicitly extended the right to works that were never protected by copyright.[349] This right is exactly intended to stimulate publication of works.[350]

However, the introduction of a new right in the legal order – be it in the form of a neighbouring right, sui generis right, or a new category under copyright – should be carefully reflected upon, and its impact on other policy areas should be mapped and studied thoroughly. It would also be essential to conduct empirical studies to assess whether incentives to dissemination are necessary (i.e., absent a "disseminator's right," would these AI-generated works not be made available or commercialised?).[351] It should be borne in mind that rights that do not have a minimum threshold for protection, such as neighbouring rights, run the risk of leading to overprotection and being unbalanced,[352] thus possibly impairing the production of follow-on creations and easier access to information.

Even sui generis rights that do have a minimum threshold – such as the sui generis right for databases, which only arises in case of substantial investment – are not a sure recipe for success. The First Evaluation Report of the Database Directive admitted that the economic impact of the sui generis right on database protection is unproven, and that the sui generis provisions have caused "considerable legal uncertainty."[353] The Second Evaluation Report reinforced that the sui generis right had no proven impact on the production of databases,

---

349 Christina Angelopoulos, 'The Myth of European Term Harmonisation – 27 Public Domains for 27 Member States' (2012) 43 *International Review of Intellectual Property and Competition Law* 567, 592.

350 David Bradshaw, 'The EC Copyright Duration Directive: Its Main Highlights and Some of its Ramifications for Businesses in the UK Entertainment Industry' (1995) 6 *Entertainment Law Review* 171, 174.

351 An assessment (although with a view to granting copyright, not neighbouring rights) is also proposed in the Explanatory Statement to the *'Report on Intellectual Property Rights for the Development of Artificial Intelligence Technologies'* (n 135) 13: "it is proposed that an assessment should be undertaken of the advisability of granting copyright to such a 'creative work' to the natural person who prepares and publishes it lawfully, provided that the designer(s) of the underlying technology has/have not opposed such use."

352 *Hugenholtz*, 'Neighbouring Rights are Obsolete' (n 177) 1006–1011.

353 Commission of the European Communities, 'DG Internal Market and Services Working Paper – First Evaluation of Directive 96/9/EC on the Legal Protection of Databases' (December 2005) <https://ec.europa.eu/digital-single-market/en/news/staff-working-document-and-executive-summary-evaluation-directive-969ec-legal-protection> accessed 2 June 2021.

and concluded that the right was not used as a licensing tool, which would suggest that it does not fulfil a strong investment role.[354]

Finally, how feasible it is to introduce a right across different jurisdictions is yet another question that should be addressed. Given the different copyright systems, creating a new right that does not come under "classic" copyright would prove challenging. Importantly, in light of increasing globalisation (especially in the field of AI), the formation of legislative silos with different regimes for protecting (or not) AI-generated works seems counter-productive.

References

Primary sources

17 U.S. Code (1976)

Acohs Pty Ltd v. Ucorp Pty [2012] FCAFC 16

Acuff-Rose Music, Inc. v. Jostens, Inc, 155 F.3d 140 (2nd Cir. 1998)

Architettura, Inc. v. DBSI Cumberland at Granbury LP, 652 F. Supp. 2d 775 (N.D. Tex. 2009) *Warner Brothers Entertainment, Inc. v. RDR Books*, 575 F. Supp. 2d 513 (S.D.N.Y. 2008)

"Architectural Design" unreported case (Intellectual Property High Court 1st Division, No. 10130 (Ne) 2014, May 25, 2015)

Australia Law Reform Commission, 'Copyright and the Digital Economy' (ALRC Report 122, Australian Government 2013) <www.alrc.gov.au/publication/copyright-and-the-digital-economy-alrc-report-122/2-framing-principles-for-reform-2/principle-1-acknowledging-and-respecting-authorship-and-creation-2/> accessed 26 May 2021

Burrow-Giles Litographic Co. v. Sarony, 111 U.S. 53, 60 (1884)

Case 683/17 *Cofemel – Socedade de Vestuario SA v. G-Star Raw CV* (Judgment of the Court third Chamber, September 12, 2019)

Case C-05/08 *Infopaq International A/S v Danske Dagblades Forening* [2009] ECR I-6569

Case C-145/10 *Eva-Maria Painer v Standard Verlags GmbH and Others* (Judgment of the Court Third Chamber, March 7, 2013)

Case C-277/10 *Martin Luksan v Petrus van der Let* (Judgment of the Court Third Chamber, February 9, 2012)

Case C-310/17 *Levola Hengelo BV v. Smilde Foods BV* (Judgment of the Court Grand Chamber, November 13, 2018)

Case C-393/09 *Bezpečnostní softwarová asociace – Svaz softwarové ochrany v Ministerstvo kultury (BSA)* [2010] ECR I-13971

Case C-604/10 *Football Dataco Ltd and Others v. Yahoo! UK Ltd and Others* (Judgment of the Court Third Chamber, March 1, 2012)

Case C-476/17 *Pelham GmbH and Others v Ralf Hütter and Florian Schneider-Esleben* (Judgment of the Court Grand Chamber, July 29, 2019)

Case C-604/10 *Football Dataco Ltd and Others v. Yahoo! UK Ltd and Others* (Judgment of the Court Third Chamber, March 1, 2012), Opinion of Advocate General Mengozzi

---

354 European Commission, 'Commission Staff Working Document: Evaluation of Directive 96/9/EC on the Legal Protection of Databases' (SWD (2018) 147 final, April 2018) 17–19 <https://ec.europa.eu/digital-single-market/en/news/staff-working-document-and-executive-summary-evaluation-directive-969ec-legal-protection> accessed 2 June 2021.

Case C-833/18 *SI and Brompton Bicycle Ltd v. Chedech/Get2Get* (Judgment of the Court Fifth Chamber, June 11, 2020)

Case T-76/89 *Independent Television Publications Ltd v. Commission of the European Communities* [1991] ECR II-575

Case unreported Tokyo District Court 29th Division, No. 33577 (Wa) 2007.

Case (unreported) 2014 (Ne) 10059, Intellectual Property High Court 1st Division, No. 10059 (Ne) 2014, April 27, 2016

Case (unreported) Tokyo District Court 29th Division, No. 22400 (Wa) 2014

Case (unreported) Tokyo District Court 29th Division, No. 33577 (Wa) 2007.

Case (unreported) Tokyo District Court 46th Civil Division, No. 37117 (Wa), 2017, January 30, 2018.

Case (unreported) Tokyo District Court 46th Civil Division, No. 37117 (Wa), 2017, January 30, 2018.

Castle Rock Entertainment, Inc. v. Carol Publishing Group, Inc., 150 F.3d 132, 143 (2d Cir.1998)

Code of Copyright and Related Rights as amended up to Decree-Law No. 100/2017

Commission of the European Communities, 'DG Internal Market and Services Working Paper – First Evaluation of Directive 96/9/EC on the Legal Protection of Databases' (December 2005) <https://ec.europa.eu/digital-single-market/en/news/staff-working-document-and-executive-summary-evaluation-directive-969ec-legal-protection> accessed 2 June 2021

Commission on the European Communities, 'Proposal for a Software Directive-Explanatory Memorandum' (COM (88) 816 final, 1989)

Commission on the European Communities, 'The Proposal for a Council Directive on the Legal Protection of Databases-Explanatory Memorandum' (COM (92) 24 final, 1992)

Community for Creative Non-Violence v. Reid, 490 U.S. 730 (1989)

Copyright Act (1957)

Copyright and Related Rights Act (2000)

Copyright, Designs and Patents Act (1988)

Copyright Law Review Committee, '*Report on Computer Software Protection*' (ID 221 445, Parliament of Australia 1995)

Council Directive 93/83/EEC of 27 September 1993 on the coordination of certain rules concerning copyright and rights related to copyright applicable to satellite broadcasting and cable retransmission

"Device for Separating and Removing Foreign Matter on War Laver" unreported case (Tokyo District Court 29th Division, No. 27552 (Wa) 2000, October 26, 2000)

Directive 2001/29/EC of the European Parliament and of the Council of 22 May 2001 on the harmonisation of certain aspects of copyright and related rights in the information society

Directive 2004/48/EC of the European Parliament and of the Council of 29 April 2004 on the enforcement of intellectual property rights

Directive 2006/115/EC of the European Parliament and of the Council of 12 December 2006 on rental right and lending right and on certain rights related to copyright in the field of intellectual property

Directive 2006/116/EC of the European Parliament and of the Council of 12 December 2006 on the term of protection of copyright and certain related rights

Directive 2009/24/EC of the European Parliament and of the Council of 23 April 2009 on the legal protection of computer programs

Directive 96/9/EC of the European Parliament and of the Council of 11 March 1996 on the legal protection of databases

European Commission, 'Commission Staff Working Document: Evaluation of Directive 96/9/EC on the legal protection of databases' (SWD(2018) 147 final, April 2018)

<https://ec.europa.eu/digital-single-market/en/news/staff-working-document-and-executive-summary-evaluation-directive-969ec-legal-protection> accessed 2 June 2021

European Commission, 'Commission Staff Working Paper on the Review of the EC Legal Framework in the Field of Copyright and Related Rights' SEC (2004) 995

European Commission, 'Report from the Commission to the Council, the European Parliament and the Economic and Social Committee on the Implementation and Effects of Directive 91/250/EEC on the Legal Protection of Computer Programs' (COM(2000) 199 final

European Parliament (Committee on Legal Affairs), 'Report on Intellectual Property Rights for the Development of Artificial Intelligence Technologies' (2020/2015(INI), European Parliament 2020) <www.europarl.europa.eu/doceo/document/A-9-2020-0176_EN.pdf> accessed 22 May 2021

European Parliament, 'Resolution of 16 February 2017 with Recommendations to the Commission on Civil Law Rules on Robotics' (2015/2103(INL) <www.europarl.europa.eu/sides/getDoc.do?type=TA&language=EN&reference=P8-TA-2017-0051> accessed 7 May 2021

"Fashion Show" unreported case (Intellectual Property High Court 3rd Division, No. 10068 (Ne) 2013, August 28, 2014)

Feist Publications, Inc. v. Rural Telephone Service Co., 499 U.S. 340 (1991)

"FOMA" unreported case (Intellectual Property High Court 4th division, No. 10029 (Ne) 2010, March 28, 2016)

IceTV Pty Ltd v. Nine Network Australia Pty Ltd [2009] 239 CLR 458

Indian Copyright Act (1957)

Judgment of July 13, 2004 in Keishu 58(5) (Sup. Ct. No. 216 (JU) 2001)

MTG Co., Ltd. V. Five Stars Co. Ltd. unreported case (Intellectual Property High Court 1st division, No. 10003 (Ne) 2006, June 7, 2020)

Naruto and others v. David John Slater and others, Case No. 15-cv-04324-WHO (N.D. Cal. January 28, 2016)

Nova Productions Ltd v. Mazooma Games Ltd [2006] RPC 379

Peter Lettersee and Associates, Inc. v. World Institute of Scientology Enterprises, International, 533 F.3d 1287 (11th Cir. 2008)

"Popeye" unreported case (Supreme Court of Japan, 1443 (O) 1992, July 17, 1997

Ritah Mulcahy v. Cheetah Learning LLC and Jeff Schurrer, 386 F.3d 849 (8th Cir. 2004)

Sands & McDougall Pty Ltd v. Robinson [1917] 23 CLR 49

Service & Training, Inc. v. Data General Corp., 963 F.2d, 680 (4th Cir. 1992)

"SMAP interview article" unreported case (Tokyo District Court 46th Civil Division, No. 19455 (Wa) 1995, October 29, 1998)

Telstra Corporation Ltd v. Desktop Marketing Systems Pty Ltd [2002] FCA 112

Telstra Corporation Ltd v. Phone Directories Co Pty [2010] FCAFC 149

The Australian Copyright Act (1968)

The Berne Convention for the Protection of Literary and Artistic Works (1886)

The Copyright, Designs and Patents Act (1988)

The European Patent Convention (1973)

The French Code of Intellectual Property

The Irish Copyright and Related Rights Act (2000)

The Japanese Copyright Act (1970)

"TRIPP TRAPPII" unreported case (Intellectual Property High Court 2nd Division, No. 10063 (Ne) 2014, April 14, 2015)

TRIPS Agreement (1994)

University of London Press Ltd v. University Tutorial Press Ltd [1916] 2 Ch 601

Urantia Foundation v. Maaherra, 114 F.3d 955, 958 (9th Circ 1997)

WIPO Copyright Treaty (1996)

Secondary sources

Abbott R, *The Reasonable Robot – Artificial Intelligence and the Law* (Cambridge University Press 2020)

Amabile TM, *Creativity in Context* (Westview Press 1996)

Angelopoulos C, 'The Myth of European Term Harmonisation – 27 Public Domains for 27 Member States' (2012) 43 *International Review of Intellectual Property and Competition Law* 567

Aravantinos V and Diehl F, 'Traceability of Deep Neural Networks' (*arXiv* 2018) <https://arxiv.org/pdf/1812.06744.pdf> accessed 23 May 2021

Bently L and Sherman B, *Intellectual Property Law* (3rd ed., Oxford University Press 2009)

Boden M, 'Creativity: How Does It Work?,' in Michael Krausz, Denis Dutton D and Karen Bardsley (eds.), *The Idea of Creativity* (Brill 2009)

———— 'Creativity and Computers,' in Terry Dartnall (ed.), *Artificial Intelligence and Creativity – An Interdisciplinary Approach* (Springer 1994)

———— 'Foreword,' in Tarek R Besold and others (eds.), *Computational Creativity Research: Towards Creative Machines* (Atlantis Press 2015)

———— *The Creative Mind – Myths and Mechanisms* (2nd ed., Taylor & Francis Group 2004)

Bozhanov B, 'Computoser – Rule-Based, Probability-Driven Algorithmic Music Composition' (*arXiv* 2014) <https://arxiv.org/abs/1412.3079> accessed 22 May 2021

Bracha O, *Owning Ideas: The Intellectual Origins of American Intellectual Property, 1790–1909* (Cambridge University Press 2016)

Bradshaw D, 'The EC Copyright Duration Directive: Its Main Highlights and Some of its Ramifications for Businesses in the UK Entertainment Industry' (1995) 6 *Entertainment Law Review* 171

Bridy A, 'Coding Creativity: Copyright and the Artificially Intelligent Author' (2012) 5 *Stanford Technology Law Review*

———— 'The Evolution of Authorship: Works Made by Code' (2016) 39 *Columbia Journal of Law and the Arts* 395

Bringsjord S and Ferrucci DA, *Artificial Intelligence and Literary Creativity: Inside the Mind of Brutus, A Storytelling Machine* (Lawrence Erlbaum Associates 2000)

Brölmann CM, 'Capturing the Juridical Will of International Organizations' (2019) Amsterdam Law School Research Paper No. 2019–09 <https://privpapers.ssrn.com/sol3/papers.cfm?abstract_id=3341457> accessed 27 May 2021

Brown RS, 'Eligibility for Copyright Protection: A Search for Principled Standards' (1986) 70 *Minnesota Law Review* 579

Brown TB and others, 'Language Models are Few – Shot Learners' (May 2020) <https://arxiv.org/abs/2005.14165> accessed 28 May 2021

Butler TL, 'Can a Computer Be an Author? Copyright Aspects of Artificial Intelligence' (1981–1982) 4 *Comm/Ent L.S.* 707

Câmara Pereira F, *Creativity and Artificial Intelligence – A Conceptual Blending Approach* (Mouton de Gruyter 2007)

Carreau C, *Mérite et droit d' auteur* (Librairie Générale de Droit et de Jurisprudence 1981)

Chaen S, 'Copyright Ownership,' in Peter Ganea and others (eds.), *Japanese Copyright Law: Writings in Honour of Gerhard Schricker* (Kluwer Law International 2005)

Clifford RD, 'Intellectual Property in the Era of the Creative Computer Program: Will the True Creator Please Stand Up?' (1997) 71 *Tulane Law Review* 1675

Cohen H, 'The Further Exploits of AARON, Painter' (1995) 4 *SEHR*

'Computoser' <http://computoser.com> accessed 22 May 2021

Copeland JB, 'What is Artificial Intelligence?' (*Alan Turing*, May 2000) <www.alanturing. net/turing_archive/pages/Reference%20Articles/What%20is%20AI.html> accessed 5 May 2021

Copyright Clearance Center, 'Written Comments to the Content of WIPO Conversation on Intellectual Property and Artificial Intelligence (Second Session)' (Draft Issues Paper on Intellectual Property and Artificial Intelligence, World Intellectual Property Office 2020) <www.wipo.int/export/sites/www/about-ip/en/artificial_intelligence/call_for_ comments/pdf/org_ccc.pdf> accessed 28 May 2021

Craig CJ, 'Locke, Labour, and Limiting the Author's Right: A Warning Against a Lockean Approach to Copyright Law' (2012) 28 *Queens Law Journal* <https://papers.ssrn.com/ sol3/papers.cfm?abstract_id=2078157> accessed 14 May 2021

Curtin RS, 'Locke's (Own) Literary Property,' in Shubha Ghosh (ed.), *Forgotten Intellectual Property Lore* (Edward Elgar 2020)

Cwik B, 'Labor as the Basis for Intellectual Property Rights' (2014) 17 *Ethical Theory and Moral Practice* 681

Dartnall T, 'Introduction: On Having a Mind of Your Own,' in Terry Dartnall (ed.), *Artificial Intelligence and Creativity* (Springer 1994)

Davison, Mark J and others, *Australian Intellectual Property Law* (4th ed., Cambridge University Press 2020)

De Cock Buning M, 'Autonomous Intelligence Systems as Creative Agents Under the EU Framework for Intellectual Property' (2016) 7 *European Journal of Risk Regulation* 310

Deltorn JM, 'Disentangling Deep Learning and Copyrights' (2018) 5 *AMI* 172

Derclaye E, 'Assessing the Impact and Reception of the Court of Justice of the European Union Case Law on UK Copyright Law: What Does the Future Hold?' (2014) 240 *Revue Internationale du Droit D' Auteur* <https://nottingham-repository.worktribe.com/out-put/998300/assessing-the-impact-and-reception-of-the-court-of-justice-of-the-european-union-case-law-on-uk-copyright-law-what-does-the-future-hold> accessed 22 May 2021

———*The Legal Protection of Databases – A Comparative Analysis* (Edward Elgar 2008)

Dreier T, 'The Council Directive of 14 May 1991 on the Legal Protection of Computer Programs' (1991) 13 *European Intellectual Property Review* 319

Drexl J and others, 'Comments of the Max Planck Institute for Innovation and Competition of 11 February 2020 on the Draft Issues Paper of the World Intellectual Property Organization on Intellectual Property Policy and Artificial Intelligence' (Max Planck Institute for Innovation and Competition 2020) <https://pure.mpg.de/rest/items/item_3193085_1/ component/file_3193086/content> accessed 22 May 2021

———'Technical Aspects of Artificial Intelligence: An Understanding from an Intellectual Property Law Perspective' (October 2019) Max Planck Institute for Innovation and Competition Research Paper No. 19–13, version 1.0 <https://ssrn.com/abstract=3465577> accessed 21 May 2020

Dussolier S, '*Scoping Study on Copyright and Related Rights and the Public Domain*' (CDIP/7/ INF/2, World Intellectual Property Organization – Committee on Development and Intellectual Property 2011)

Elgammal A and others, 'CAN: Creative Adversarial Networks Generating – "Art" by Learning About Styles and Deviating from Style Norms" (*arXiv* 2017) <https://arxiv. org/abs/1706.07068> accessed 28 May 2021

European Commission Independent High-Level Expert Group on Artificial Intelligence, 'A Definition of AI: Main Capabilities and Disciplines' (European Commission April 8, 2019) <https://ec.europa.eu/digital-single-market/en/news/definition-artificial-intelligence-main-capabilities-and-scientific-disciplines> accessed 22 May 2021

European Group on Ethics in Science and New Technologies, *Statement on Artificial Intelligence, Robotics and 'Autonomous Systems'* (Publication Office of the EU March 2018) <https://op.europa.eu/en/publication-detail/-/publication/dfebe62e-4ce9-11e8-be1d-01aa75ed71a1> accessed 25 May 2021

Fisher W, 'Theories of Intellectual Property,' in Stephen Munzer (ed.), *New Essays in the Legal and Political Theory of Property* (Cambridge University Press 2001)

Fromer JC, 'Expressive Incentives in Intellectual Property' (2012) 98 *Virginia Law Review* 1745

Ganea P, 'Protected Works,' in Peter Ganea and others (eds.), *Japanese Copyright Law: Writings in Honour of Gerhard Schricker* (Kluwer Law International 2005)

Garcia C, 'Harold Cohen and AARON – A 40-year Collaboration' (*Computer History*, August 23, 2016) <https://computerhistory.org/blog/harold-cohen-and-aaron-a-40-year-collaboration/> accessed 18 May 2021

Gaut B, 'Creativity and Skill,' in Michael Krausz, Denis Dutton D and Karen Bardsley (eds.), *The Idea of Creativity* (Brill 2009)

Gervais D, 'The Machine as Author' (2020) 105 *Iowa Law Review* 2053

Ginsburg JC, 'The Concept of Authorship in Comparative Copyright Law' (2003) 52 *DePaul Law Review* 1063

Ginsburg JC and Budiardjo LA, 'Authors and Machines' (2019) 34 *Berkeley Technology Law Journal*

Goldstein P and Hugenholtz B, *International Copyright: Principles, Law and Practice* (Oxford University Press 2010)

Goodfellow I and others, 'Generative Adversarial Nets,' in Zoubin Ghahramani and others (eds.), *Advances in Neural Information Processing Systems* (NIPS 2014) 2672–2680

Gordon WJ, 'A Property Right in Self-Expression: Equality and Individualism in the Natural Law of Intellectual Property' (1993) 102 *Yale Law Journal* 1533

Guibault L, *Copyright Limitations and Contracts – An Analysis of the Contractual Overridability of Limitations on Copyright* (Kluwer Law International 2002)

Harris MR, 'Copyright, Computer Software, and Work Made for Hire' (1990) 89 *Michigan Law Review* 661

Hartmann C and others, 'Trends in Artificial Intelligence – Challenges to the Intellectual Property Rights Framework' (European Commission 2020) <www.ivir.nl/publicaties/download/Trends_and_Developments_in_Artificial_Intelligence-1.pdf> accessed 22 May 2021

Hausman CR, 'Criteria of Creativity,' in Michael Krausz, Denis Dutton D and Karen Bardsley (eds.), *The Idea of Creativity* (Brill 2009)

Heaven WD, 'Open AI's New Language Generator GPT-3 is Shockingly Good – and Completely Mindless' (*MIT Technology Review*, July 20, 2020) <www.technologyreview.com/2020/07/20/1005454/openai-machine-learning-language-generator-gpt-3-nlp/> accessed 28 May 2021

Hegel GWF, *Grundlinien der Philosophie des Rechts* (Intelex Corporation 2003)

Hennessey BA and Amabile TM, 'Creativity' (2010) 61 *Annual Review of Psychology* 569

Hristov K, 'Artificial Intelligence and the Copyright Dilemma' (2017) 57 *IDEA – The Journal of the Franklin Pierce Center for Intellectual Property* 431

Hugenholtz B and others, 'The Recasting of Copyright and Related Rights for the Knowledge Economy' Institute for Information Law Research Paper (2006) No. 2012–38, 37 <https://papers.ssrn.com/sol3/papers.cfm?abstract_id=2018238> accessed 22 May 2021

Hughes J, 'The Philosophy of Intellectual Property' (1988) 77 *Georgetown Law Journal* 287

Intellectual Property Strategy Headquarters, 'Intellectual Property Strategic Program 2017' (May 2017) <www.kantei.go.jp/jp/singi/titeki2/kettei/chizaikeikaku20170516_e.pdf> accessed 12 May 2021

Ishida M, 'Outline of the Japanese Copyright Law' (2008) 19–20 <www.jpo.go.jp/e/news/kokusai/developing/training/textbook/document/index/Copyright_Law.pdf > accessed 21 May 2021

Jaszi P, 'Toward a Theory of Copyright: The Metamorphoses of "Authorship"' (1991) *Duke Law Journal* 455

Kampylis PG and Valtanen J, 'Redefining Creativity – Analysing Definitions, Collocations, and Consequences' (2010) 44 *Journal of Creative Behaviour* 191

Karjala DS and Sugiyama K, 'Fundamental Concepts in Japanese and American Copyright Law' (1988) 36 *American Journal of Comparative Law* 613

Koestler A, 'The Three Domains of Creativity,' in Michael Krausz, Denis Dutton and Karen Bardsley (eds.), *The Idea of Creativity* (Brill 2009)

Kojima R, 'Japan', in Reto M Hilty and Sylvie Nerisson (eds.), *Balancing Copyright – A Survey of National Approaches* (Springer 2012)

Lacey LJ, 'Of Bread and Roses and Copyrights' (1989) 6 *Duke Law Journal* 1532

Lavik E and Van Gompel S, 'On the Prospects of Raising the Originality Requirement in Copyright Law: Perspectives from the Humanities' (2013) 60 *Journal of the Copyright Society of the U.S.A.* 387

Lemley M, 'The Economics of Improvement in Intellectual Property Law' (2008) 75 *Texas Law Review* 989

Levendowski A, 'How Copyright Law Can Fix Artificial Intelligence's Implicit Bias Problem' (2018) 93 *Washington Law Review* 579

Levy D, *Robots Unlimited – Life in a Virtual Age* (Taylor & Francis 2005)

Lindsay D, 'Protection of Compilations and Databases after ICETV: Authorship, Originality and the Transformation of Australian Copyright Law' (2012) 38 *Monash University Law Review* 17

Liu, Frederick and Pruthi, Garima, 'TracIn – A Simple Method to Estimate Training Data Influence' (February 2021) <https://ai.googleblog.com/2021/02/tracin-simple-method-to-estimate.html> accessed 3 June 2021

Locke J, *Two Treatises of Civil Government* (first published anonymously in 1689, J.M. Dent & Sons 1962)

Loewenheim U, 'Intellectual Property Before the European Court of Justice' (1995) 26 *International Review of Intellectual Property and Competition Law* 829

Lucas A and others, *Traité de La Propriété Littéraire et Artistique* (Litec 2006) *apud* Judge, Elizabeth F and Gervais, Daniel J, 'Of Silos and Constellations: Comparing Notions of Originality in Copyright Law' (2009) 27 *Cardozo Arts & Entertainment Law Journal* 375

Mandel GN, 'Left-Brain versus Right-Brain: Competing Conceptions of Creativity in Intellectual Property Law' (2010) 44 *UC Davis Law Review* 283

Masuyama S, 'Neigbouring Rights,' in Peter Ganea and others (eds.), *Japanese Copyright Law: Writings in Honour of Gerhard Schricker* (Kluwer Law International 2005)

McCorduck P, *Aaron's Code: Meta-Art, Artificial Intelligence, and the Work of Harold Cohen* (W.H. Freeman & Company 1991)

——— *Machines Who Think. A Personal Inquiry into the History and Prospects of Artificial Intelligence* (A K Peters 2004)

McCutcheon J, 'Curing the Authorless Void: Protecting Computer Generated Works following Ice TV and Phone Directories' (2013) 37 *Melbourne University Law Review* 46

——— 'The Vanishing Author in Computer-generated Works: A Critical Analysis of Recent Australian Case Law' (2013) 36 *Melbourne University Law Review* 915

McDonough R, 'Machine Predictability versus Human Creativity', in Terry Dartnall (ed.), *Artificial Intelligence and Creativity – An Interdisciplinary Approach* (Springer 1994)

McLaughlin M, 'Computer Generated Inventions' (2018) American University Washington College of Law <https://papers.ssrn.com/sol3/papers.cfm?abstract_id=3097822> accessed 22 May 2021

Mordvintsev A and others, 'Inceptionism: Going Deeper into Neural Networks' (Google AI Blog, June 17, 2015) <https://ai.googleblog.com/2015/06/inceptionism-going-deeper-into-neural.html> accessed 28 May 2021

Moss R, 'Creative AI: The Robots that Would be Painters' (*New Atlas*, February 16, 2015) <http://newatlas.com/creative-ai-algorithmic-art-painting-fool-aaron/36106/> accessed 18 May 2021

Mossoff A, 'Saving Locke from Marx: The Labor Theory of Value in Intellectual Property Theory' (2012) 29 *Social Philosophy & Policy* 283

'Next Rembrandt' <www.nextrembrandt.com> accessed 28 May 2021

Patry W, *Patry on Copyright* (West Thomson Reuters 2021)

Pavón J and González-Espejo MJ, 'Fundamentals of Artificial Intelligence,' in María J González-Espejo and Juan Pavón (eds.), *An Introductory Guide to Artificial Intelligence for Legal Professionals* (Kluwer Law International 2020)

Pearlman R, 'Recognizing Artificial Intelligence (AI) as Authors and Investors under US Intellectual Property Law' (2018) 24 *Richmond Journal of Law & Technology* 1

Peukert A, '*A Doctrine of the Public Domain*' (2016) Goethe University Frankfurt forthcoming in Josef Drexl (ed.), *The Innovation Society and Intellectual Property* (Edward Elgar Publishing 2019) <https://papers.ssrn.com/sol3/papers2.cfm?abstract_id=2713757> accessed 22 May 2021

Pila J, 'The Authorial Works Protectable by Copyright,' in Eleonora Rosati (ed.), *The Routledge Handbook of EU Copyright Law* (Routledge 2021)

Public Views on Artificial Intelligence and Intellectual Property Policy (United States Patent and Trademark Office October 2020) <www.uspto.gov/sites/default/files/documents/USPTO_AI-Report_2020-10-07.pdf> accessed 20 May 2021

Quaedvlieg A, 'Authorship and Ownership: Authors, Entrepreneurs and Rights,' in E Tatiana-Synodinou (ed.), *Codification of European Copyright Law, Challenges and Perspectives* (Kluwer Law International 2012)

Rachum-Twaig O, *Copyright Law and Derivative Works – Regulating Creativity* (Routledge 2019)

Ramalho A, 'Will Robots Rule the (Artistic) World? A Proposed Model for the Legal Status of Creations by Artificial Intelligence Systems' (2017) 21 *Journal of Internet Law*

———— *The Competence of the European Union in Copyright Lawmaking – A Normative Perspective of EU Powers for Copyright Harmonization* (Springer 2016)

Ramello GB, 'Private Appropriability and Sharing of Knowledge: Convergence or Contradiction? The Opposite Tragedy of the Creative Commons,' in Lisa N Takeyama, Wendy J. Gordon and Ruth Towse (eds.), *Developments in the Economics of Copyright: Research and Analysis* (Edward Elgar 2005)

Renda A and others, 'The Implementation, Application and Effects of the EU Directive on Copyright in the Information Society' (CEPS Special Report No.120, November 2015) <http://aei.pitt.edu/69674/1/SR120_0.pdf> accessed 22 May 2021

Ricketson S, 'The Need for Human Authorship – Australian Developments: *Telstra Corp Ltd v Phone Directories Co Pty Ltd*.' (2012) 34 *EIPR* 54

Rosati E, *Originality in EU Copyright: Full Harmonization through Case Law* (Edward Elgar 2013)

Rothkegel T and Taylor M, 'What Characterises Artificial Intelligence and How Does It Work?' (2016) 22 *Computer and Telecommunications Law Review* 98

Runco MA, *Creativity: Theories and Themes: Research, Development, and Practice* (2nd ed., Elsevier 2007)

Russell S and Norvig P, *Artificial Intelligence – A Modern Approach* (3rd ed., Pearson 2014)

Saitô H and Isa S, 'General Introduction,' in Peter Ganea and others (eds.), *Japanese Copyright Law: Writings in Honour of Gerhard Schricker* (Kluwer Law International 2005)

Samuelson P, 'Allocating Ownership Rights in Computer Generated Works' (1985) 47 *University of Pittsburgh Law Review* 1185

Schroff S, 'How Japanese Law Facilitates Access to Art for Persons with a Visual Impairment,' in Jani McCutcheon and Ana Ramalho (eds.), *International Perspectives on Copyright Law and the Visual Arts: Feeling Art* (Routledge 2020)

Seignette J, *Challenges to the Creator Doctrine: Authorship, Copyright Ownership and the Exploitation of Creative Works in the Netherlands, Germany and the United States* (Kluwer Law and Taxation Publishers 1994)

Sganga C, *Propertizing European Copyright. History, Challenges and Opportunities* (Edward Elgar 2018)

Sprigman CJ, 'Copyright and Creative Incentives: What We Know (and Don't)' (2017) 55 *Houston Law Review* 451

Sterk SE, 'Rethoric and Reality in Copyright Law' (1996) 94 *Michigan Law Review* 1197

Sugiyama K, 'Japanese Copyright Law Development' (2002) 7 *International Intellectual Property Law and Policy* 48–2

Sundara Rajan MS, *Moral Rights: Principles, Practice and New Technology* (Oxford University Press 2011) 182

Surden H, 'Machine Learning and Law' (2014) 89 *Washington Law Review* 87

Tatsuhiro Ueno, 'Moral Rights,' in Peter Ganea and others (eds.), *Japanese Copyright Law: Writings in Honour of Gerhard Schricker* (Kluwer Law International 2005)

'Tensor Flow Tutorial on DeepDream' <www.tensorflow.org/tutorials/generative/deepdream> accessed 28 September 2020

The Royal Academy of Engineering, *Autonomous Systems: Social, Legal and Ethical Issues* (The Royal Academy of Engineering August 2009) <www.raeng.org.uk/publications/reports/autonomous-systems-report> accessed 5 May 2021

Torremans P, *Holyoak and Torremans Intellectual Property Law* (5th ed., Oxford University Press 2008)

United States Copyright Office, 'Compendium of U.S. Copyright Office Practices' (3rd ed., United States Copyright Office 2021) Introduction <www.copyright.gov/comp3/docs/compendium.pdf> accessed 22 May 2021

United States Copyright Office, 'Compendium of U.S. Copyright Office Practices' (3rd ed., United States Copyright Office 2021) Section 608 <www.copyright.gov/comp3/chap600/ch600-examination-practices.pdf> accessed 22 May 2021

United States Copyright Office, 'Compendium of U.S. Copyright Office Practices' (3rd ed., United States Copyright Office 2021) Section 306 <www.copyright.gov/comp3/chap300/ch300-copyrightable-authorship.pdf> accessed 22 May 2021.

Vallés RC, 'The Requirement of Originality,' in Estelle Derclaye E (ed.), *Research Handbook on the Future of EU Copyright* (Edward Elgar 2009)

Van Eechoud M, 'Along the Road to Uniformity – Diverse Readings of the Court of Justice Judgments on Copyright Work' (2012) 3 *JIPITEC* 60

Van Eechoud M and others, *Harmonizing European Copyright Law: The Challenges of Better Lawmaking* (Kluwer Law International 2009)

Van Gompel S, 'Creativity, Autonomy and Personal Touch: A Critical Appraisal of the CJEU's Originality Test for Copyright,' in Mireille van Eechoud (ed.), *The Work of Authorship* (Amsterdam University Press 2014)

——— *Formalities in Copyright Law: An Analysis of Their History, Rationales and Possible Future* (Kluwer Law International 2011)

Vincent J, 'Open AI's Latest Breakthrough is Astonishingly Powerful, but Still Fighting its Flaws' (*The Verge*, July 30, 2020) <www.theverge.com/21346343/gpt-3-explainer-openai-examples-errors-agi-potential> accessed 28 May 2021

Waisman A, 'Revisiting Originality' (2009) 31 *European Intellectual Property Law Review* 370

Wilks Y, *Artificial Intelligence – Modern Magic or Dangerous Future?* (Icon Books 2019)

WIPO Intergovernmental Committee on Intellectual Property and Genetic Resources, Traditional Knowledge and Folklore, '*Note on the Meanings of the Term 'Public Domain' in the Intellectual Property System with Special Reference to the Protection of Traditional Knowledge and Traditional Cultural Expressions/Expressions of Folklore*' (WIPO/GRTKF/IC/17/INF/8, World Intellectual Property Organization 2010) <www.wipo.int/edocs/mdocs/tk/en/wipo_grtkf_ic_17/wipo_grtkf_ic_17_inf_8.pdf> accessed 22 May 2021

Yang LC and others, 'MidiNet: A Convolutional Generative Adversarial Network for Symbolic-Domain Music Generation' (*arXiv* 2017) <https://arxiv.org/abs/1703.10847> accessed 28 May 2021

Yanisky-Ravid S, 'Generating Rembrandt: Artificial Intelligence, Copyright, and Accountability in the 3A Era – The Human-Like Authors are Already Here – A New Model' (2017) 4 *Michigan State Law Review* 659

Yu R, 'The Machine Author: What Level of Copyright Protection is Appropriate for Fully Independent Computer Generated Works?' (2017) 165 *University of Pennsylvania Law Review* 1245

Yu-Liu M and others, 'Unsupervised Image-to-Image Translation Networks,' in Isabelle Guyon and others (eds.), *Advances in Neural Information Processing Systems* (NIPS 2017)

Zednik C, 'Solving the Black Box Problem: A Normative Framework for Explainable Artificial Intelligence' (*arXiv* 2019) <https://arxiv.org/pdf/1903.04361.pdf> accessed 23 May 2021

3 AI and patent protection

3.1 Introduction

As with what happens in relation to artistic creations, AI systems are progressively capable of substituting human ingenuity in the inventing process, thus generating inventions that have less human input. Unlike artistic creations, however, technical creations such as the ones protected by patents have long needed technical tools throughout the inventing process, and certain AI techniques such as artificial neural networks and evolutionary algorithms have (for decades) been used in the inventing process in fields ranging from life sciences to civil engineering.[1] This has led some authors to defend that it is likely that patent offices have in practice granted patents that were at least partially generated by an AI – it just so happens that the AI contribution was not disclosed in the patent application.[2] In other words, the use of AI in the inventing system seems to be incremental – with AI systems being increasingly used in said process – rather than disruptive.

This is not to say, however, that the increased use of AI systems in the inventing process does not have an impact on patent law. For instance, artificial neural networks can autonomously carry out problem-solving and generate ideas that constitute solutions to technical problems. Therefore, where an AI is involved, odds are that inventing becomes quicker, and possibly cheaper. The easiness of inventing brought by AI may lead to an increase of patenting activity, which might in turn lead to low quality patents, patent flooding and patent trolling (i.e., the activity carried out by entities that patent inventions not to

---

1 Daria Kim, '"AI-generated Inventions": Time to Get the Record Straight?' (2020) 69 (5) *GRUR International* 443, 446. The author defines artificial neural networks as comprising "a variety of computational models with biologically motivated structures and form a subfield of machine learning," while according to her evolutionary algorithms "generate and evolve a set of candidate solutions . . . through reiterative modifications – mutation, recombination, selection – and reach the 'best-scoring' solution based on the principle of natural evolution that the fittest survives (451–452, footnotes omitted).
2 Ryan Abbott, *The Reasonable Robot – Artificial Intelligence and the Law* (Cambridge University Press 2020) 10.

DOI: 10.4324/9780367823290-3

practice or make the invention, but instead to make money by building patent portfolios and finding practitioners that may be infringing their patents).[3]

If AI systems can autonomously or semi-autonomously generate a large number of inventions at a relatively low cost, patent policies may need to be recalibrated. The fundamental interests in patent law might need to be considered and rebalanced. For that purpose, it is necessary to analyse patent rationales, as well as the relevant elements of the patent regimes in the chosen jurisdictions, following a similar methodology to the previous chapter. Thus, this chapter will start by describing how AI systems are able to generate inventions and their role in the inventing process, resorting to some real-life examples (section 3.2). It is important to note in that regard that, throughout this chapter, the expression "AI-generated inventions" will be used for convenience, but that this does not convey a decision on the merits of whether an invention is in fact *autonomously* generated by an AI (i.e., without the intervention or contribution of a human being). In fact, as section 3.2 will demonstrate, a human being is still very much needed in the inventing process.

Section 3.3 follows to provide an overview of patent rationales, some of which overlap with the copyright rationales already explored in the previous chapter. Where this is the case, the main arguments of each theory will be recalled, and put into context in the framework of patent law.

Section 3.4 analyses elements of the patent systems that were deemed the most relevant for the topic of this book. This will be done in relation to the four jurisdictions concerned (Europe, the United States, Australia, Japan), in a similar fashion to the previous chapter. The first element selected was the definition of patentable subject matter, since the concept varies slightly from one jurisdiction to another and it is necessary to ascertain whether such differences have an impact on a judgement of patentability of AI-generated inventions. Next, the patentability requirements should be considered. Most patent laws require that inventions be new, capable of industrial application, and involve an inventive step or be non-obvious in order to be granted a patent. The latter requirement is central to defining an invention, and it is of utmost importance in instances where society and technology are rapidly changing.[4] Moreover, specifically when it comes to AI-generated inventions and their treatment under patent law, it is in this latter requirement that most problems lie.[5] While an invention

---

3 On the definition of patent trolls, see Christoph Ann, 'Patent Trolls – Menace or Myth?,' in Wolrad P. zu Waldeck und Pyrmont et al. (eds.), *Patents and Technological Progress in a Globalized World* (Springer Science and Business Media 2009) 356.

4 John F. Duffy, 'Inventing Invention: A Case Study of Legal Innovation' (2007) 86 *Texas Law Review* 2.: According to Ove Granstrand, 'Patents and Policies for Innovations and Entrepreneurship', in Toshiko Takenaka (ed.), *Research Handbook on Patent Law and Theory* (2nd ed., Edward Elgar 2019) 89, inventive step or non-obviousness is also the most difficult patentability requirement to assess, both in theory and in practice – which makes its in-depth analysis a necessary step for shedding some light into its application to AI-generated innovations.

5 Some impact may be seen on the novelty requirement, in the sense that patent offices may use AI systems to perform a novelty assessment, thus being able to review relevant prior art faster. This

might be non-obvious to a skilled person, that same invention might become obvious when seen through the lenses of a skilled person who can use a similar AI system to generate it. An example of this would be an AI that is able to process tests in millions of prototypes in a fraction of the time that it takes a human being to perform the same operation, and arguably with less flaws (since an AI system is not limited by human prejudices and might thus arrive at more effective solutions).[6] Therefore, the inventive step requirement is analysed in-depth for each of the jurisdictions. Moreover, because the use of AI in the inventing process might impact the assessment of the inventive step, it is also critical to examine the requirement of enablement or disclosure. Enablement or disclosure essentially means that the invention must be described in sufficient detail to allow someone else to reproduce the invention. It is thus necessary to analyse whether the requirement of enablement or disclosure mandates patent applicants to reveal the use of AI systems in the inventing process. In addition, and similarly to copyright, where the regime of authorship was analysed for each of the jurisdictions, inventorship rules are going to be examined. The main angle adopted in relation to the inventorship analysis will be whether current inventorship rules can accommodate non-human inventors. Finally, some jurisdictions protect innovations that have a lower level of inventive step through utility models or similar regimes. Given that the use of AI systems in the inventing process might have an impact on an inventive step assessment, section 3.4. will also briefly explore existing regimes of utility models.

Section 3.5 is the last section of this chapter and will offer a few conclusions and recommendations, drawing on a comparative analysis enabled by section 3.4. The analysis will highlight the extent to which the patent laws of the four jurisdictions are harmonised, and the recommendations will be made from the perspective of a future harmonisation of patent laws, policies and/or practices, rather than on a per jurisdiction basis. This is because harmonisation saves costs and increases legal certainty, thereby improving the patent system.[7] International harmonization may also increase the effectiveness of the patent system at a global level. This was recognized e.g., in the joint statement of the JPO, EPO and USPTO, issued at the 35th Trilateral Conference in Seville,

---

impact is however marginal for the purposes of this book and will therefore not be analysed any further. See Christian Hartmann and others, *Trends and Developments in Artificial Intelligence. Challenges to the Intellectual Property Rights Framework* (2020) 106 <www.ivir.nl/publicaties/download/Trends_and_Developments_in_Artificial_Intelligence-1.pdf> accessed 22 May 2021.

6 Cody S.D. Wamsley, 'Flashes of Genius, Toiled Experimentation, and Now Artificial Creation: A Case for Inventive Process Disclosures' (Master of Laws, The George Washington University Law School, 2011) <https://scholarspace.library.gwu.edu/concern/gw_etds/rf55z7888?locale=en> accessed 26 April 2021.; Erica Fraser, 'Computers as Inventors – Legal and Policy Implications of Artificial Intelligence on Patent Law' (2016) 13 *SCRIPTed* 305.

7 See also Joseph Straus and Nina-Sophie Klunker, 'Harmonization of International Patent Law' (2017) 38 *International Review of Intellectual Property and Competition Law* 919.: "In order to reduce the costs for global patent protection, to encourage cooperation between the offices and to secure the quality of the patents, it is absolutely indispensable to harmonise patentability requirements."

Spain (30 March 2017).[8] Moreover, patent quality, or how to ensure that patents are granted on truly innovative inventions, is now an international concern[9] – it thus makes sense to fashion pan-international recommendations to a problem which is jurisdiction agnostic.

3.2 Artificial intelligence systems as inventors

3.2.1 Setting the stage

As mentioned in Chapter 2 (section 2.2), the term "artificial intelligence" presupposes intelligence and autonomy. In this part of the book, the main question is what type of human intelligence might an AI system emulate that is relevant to patent law. Human intelligence can translate into using creativity to produce artistic works, but it can also amount to using logic and reasoning to find a solution to a problem. At the heart of patent law is the need to find a solution to a problem, so a more specific question is whether an AI system is capable of using logic and reasoning to find a solution to a problem. In this context, it should be noted that the inventing process implies identifying a problem to be solved, creating a solution to solve the problem, and applying the technical teachings of that solution to the problem. At least for now, a human being is necessary for identifying the problem to be solved in the first place. In that sense, there is not a machine that produces inventions "autonomously" in the same way as in copyright.

This is not to say that AI systems cannot produce ideas; they can, and they do so in different technical fields, from mechanics to chemistry (where in addition creating inventions needs experimentation and trial-and-error – and the AI can perform trial-and-error testing much more rapidly and flawlessly than a human). However, it is in principle a human being who is behind (at least) the first step of producing ideas, i.e., it is the human being who will define the problem that those ideas are supposed to solve.[10] This is connected to the question

---

8 1 '35th Trilateral Conference – European Patent Office, Japan Patent Office and United States and Trademark Office' (Seville, March 2017) <www.trilateral.net/conferences/35conference.pdf> accessed 22 May 2021.

9 Tomoko Miyamoto, 'International Treaties and Patent Law Harmonization: Today and Beyond,' in *Takenaka* (n 4) 42.

10 Josef Drexl and others, 'Artificial Intelligence and Intellectual Property Law: Position Statement of the Max Planck Institute for Innovation and Competition of 9 April 2021 on the current debate' (2021) Max Planck Institute for Innovation and Competition Research Paper No. 21–10, 23 <www.ip.mpg.de/fileadmin/ipmpg/content/stellungnahmen/MPI_PositionPaper__SSRN_21-10.pdf> accessed 2 May 2021, points out even more functions for a human being in the inventive process where an AI system is involved: "[t]he contention that AI generates inventions in an autonomous way, whereby a human only states the final goal without providing instructions as to how it should be achieved, is not defendable in light of the technological state of the art. AI techniques, including ANN and evolutionary algorithms, have been applied in solving optimisation problems in technical design and engineering for decades. However, the use of such techniques in research and development still considerably relies on the decision-making of human designers and engineers applying them to a problem at hand. This includes the analysis and formal representation of a problem so that

of whether current forms of AI are that much different from previously used tools used in the inventing process (and if so, to what extent). As mentioned in the introduction, AI techniques such as artificial neural networks and evolutionary algorithms have, for quite some time, been used for producing output that could potentially be qualified as inventions. The difference here, it is submitted, is exactly the degree of autonomy of the AI system used in the inventing process.

In fact, as also explored in Chapter 2 (section 2.2), in addition to some form of intelligence, AI presupposes a measure of autonomy. Autonomy works on a scale rather than on a binary definition of autonomous/non-autonomous, with the lower end of the scale representing machines that are mere tools, and the higher end amounting to AI systems that can produce output with little to no human input – which means that, even though AI might in some cases be no different from other tools in terms of the impact it has on the inventing process, in other instances it might autonomise that process to such an extent that it becomes difficult to discern a contribution of the human inventor that goes beyond identifying the problem to be solved.

Crucially, the tendency is for the autonomy of AI systems to increase over time. A relevant question in this regard is therefore how autonomous an AI-system can be in patent law (and whether that degree of autonomy has – or should have – consequences for the protection of AI-produced output by patent law, which is going to be discussed in the next chapters). It should be recalled that, unlike other tools that were traditionally used to invent, AI systems enhance human inventing capabilities and skills in a way that had not been seen before. Even though they cannot produce inventive concepts across every field of technology, they autonomously provide, test and select technical solutions (and in that sense AI goes beyond tools that merely perform pre-defined tasks).[11] Thus, current AI systems stand somewhere between the traditional tools used by humans to invent, and a completely autonomous being that is able to autonomously carry out the inventing process from beginning till end.[12] Like copyright law, scholars in the field of patent law also distinguish between AI-assisted and AI-generated content.[13] The observations made in relation to copyright in

---

it can be solvable by means of computational modelling, the selection of input data, the definition of an objective function . . . the design of a new algorithm or the adjustment of an existing algorithm, the interpretation of computational outcomes, etc."

11 Peter Hendrik Blok, 'The Inventor's New Tool: Artificial Intelligence – How Does it Fit the European Patent System?' (2017) 39 *European Intellectual Property Review* 69, 70.

12 Still, note that some of the tasks performed by an AI during an inventive process could result in an entitlement to the invention, had they been performed by a human being: "[A]rtificial intelligence systems have become capable of delivering input in the inventive process that, if it was performed by a human inventor, would be rewarded with an entitlement to the resulting invention, or at least a partial entitlement." ibid.

13 See Chapter 2, section 2.2. Scholars in the field of patent law who have referred to this classification include *Kim* (n 1) 445; *Drexl and others* (n 10) distinguishing three types of AI output ("WIPO could consider distinguishing three categories: (i) AI-generated inventions (where AI acts autonomously without human intervention), (ii) AI-assisted inventions (where humans use AI as a tool to invent) and (iii) AI-implemented inventions (where AI is implemented as part of the invention).").

Chapter 2 (section 2.2) are valid here too: while it is helpful to conceptualise AI-generated works in different categories according to the degree of autonomy of the AI, it is less advantageous to do so in a binary fashion, or in a way that establishes a limited, fixed number of categories. Also in the field of patent law, AI systems can blend human and machine contributions to many different degrees, and that is why using autonomy as a spectrum is the approach used here.

Likewise, the remarks in Chapter 2 (section 2.2) regarding machine learning are also valid here: AI intervention in the creation of potentially patentable output will often imply a previous stage of machine learning, i.e., an automated process that finds patterns in data and applies such patterns to new data. That learning can be done in a supervised or unsupervised way (depending on whether that data used for the learning is labelled or unlabelled), or still following a system of reinforced learning (where the AI makes its decisions freely, and a human being provides a reward signal in relation to each decision indicating whether the AI decision is good or bad). All three types of machine learning involve, in some way or another, a human being (be it because e.g., it is necessary to label the data – in the case of supervised learning – or because a human must interpret the AI output, especially in unsupervised learning).[14] The relevant question in this regard is whether that human contribution at the level of machine learning has consequences in the realm of patent law.

3.2.2 AI and their inventions

One field that has proven particularly fertile for the use of AI systems in the inventing process is drug discovery. Making use of deep learning, scientists are now able to take advantage of large datasets available from a variety of sources for e.g., the design of new molecules, the calculation of compound properties, or the planning of new chemical syntheses.[15] AI systems in drug discovery can automate a large part of the inventing process by automatically developing and testing hypotheses that relate to previous observations, as well as interpreting the results to amend their hypotheses after running experiments, and repeating

---

Another qualification has been put forward by the President of the European Patent Office in the report "Update of legal aspects of artificial intelligence and patents," cit., p. 4: "From the perspective of inventorship, three possible types of inventions using AI technologies can be considered: 1) human-made inventions using AI for the verification of the outcome, 2) inventions in which a human identifies a problem and uses AI to find a solution, 3) AI-made inventions, in which AI identifies a problem and proposes a solution without human intervention"; Hartmann and others (n 5) 102, distinguish three categories: (1) inventions that are produced by human inventors, the development of which is supported by AI technology; (2) inventions where the "inventive activity" was co-produced by humans and machine; (3) inventions generated autonomously by AI, where no natural person can qualify as an inventor.

14 See Chapter 2 (section 2.2).

15 Nathan Brown, 'Introduction,' in Nathan Brown (ed.), *Artificial Intelligence in Drug Discovery* (Royal Society of Chemistry 2021) 2–6.; H.C. Stephan Chan and others, 'Advancing Drug Discovery via Artificial Intelligence' (2017) 40 *Trends in Pharmaceutical Sciences* 592, 604.

the cycle as many times over as needed.[16] Examples of using AI in the field of drug discovery abound. For instance, IBM's Watson enables scientists to find hidden patterns and develop predictive models from unstructured data sources "at a scale and speed that is beyond what humans can do today."[17] Another example is the AI Eve, which first uses a smart screening system to learn from early successes, and then statistics and machine learning to select compounds and/or predict new structures that have a higher probability of working against the condition or disease targeted by a certain drug. [18]

The use of AI in the field of drug discovery also highlights the most common paradigm of AI use in the inventing process – a sophisticated, semi-autonomous system that nevertheless still needs human contribution somewhere along the way. Another concrete AI use illustrates this: the Benevolent Platform, owned by the company BenevolentAI, ingests and analyses biomedical information sourced from research papers, patents, and patient records, the representation of which is composed of more than one billion relationships (known or inferred) between biological elements such as genes, symptoms, diseases, proteins, species and candidate drugs.[19] From this wealth of data and through the use of deep learning, it is possible to produce knowledge graphs of, for instance, a disease, the genes that are associated with it, and/or the substances that affect it.[20] The graphs are "therapeutic area agnostic," which enables links and synergies across the entire spectrum of drug discovery and development process.[21] Using the Benevolent Platform, the company queried the system about new ways to treat amyotrophic lateral sclerosis (ALS), which returned the result of about 100 existing compounds that had potential.[22] Out of these, (human) scientists

---

16 University of Cambridge, 'Artificially Intelligent Robot Scientist "Eve" Could Boost Search for New Drugs' (*Phys Org*, February 3, 2015) <https://phys.org/news/2015-02-artificially-intelligent-robot-scientist-eve.html> accessed 15 May 2021

17 '5737-B19 IBM Watson for Drug Discovery' (2009) IBM United States Sales Manual <https://www-01.ibm.com/common/ssi/ShowDoc.wss?docURL=/common/ssi/rep_sm/9/897/ENUS5737-B19/index.html&lang=en&request_locale=en> accessed 14 May 2021. Watson for drug discovery was however discontinued in 2020. Arguably this was because of a low return on investment. see Conor Hale, 'IBM to wind down Watson's Work in AI-based Drug Discovery: Report' (*Fierce Biotech*, April 19, 2019) <www.fiercebiotech.com/medtech/ibm-to-wind-down-watson-s-work-ai-based-drug-discovery-report> accessed 14 May 2021. However, more critical voices indicate that Watson did not deliver to all its promises, as it could not e.g., make sense of patient files recorded in confusing handwriting and containing ambiguous information. see Maddie Iribarren, 'IBM's Watson for Drug Discovery Program No Longer Taking New Clients' (*Voicebot*, April 22, 2019) <https://voicebot.ai/2019/04/22/ibms-watson-for-drug-discovery-program-no-longer-taking-new-clients/> accessed 14 May 2021.

18 For example, through Eve it was possible to discover that a compound previously investigated as an anti-cancer drug also inhibit a molecule in the malaria parasite – see *University of Cambridge* (n 16).

19 Nic Fleming, 'How Artificial Intelligence is Changing Drug Discovery' (*Nature*, May 30, 2018) <www.nature.com/articles/d41586-018-05267-x> accessed 15 May 2021.

20 Ibid.

21 'What We Do: Finding New Ways to Treat Disease' (*Benevolent AI*) <www.benevolent.com/what-we-do> accessed 15 May 2021.

22 *Fleming* (n 19).

chose five for further testing, and from that research it was possible to find out that four of them were promising, and one of them had successful results in mice.[23] From this example alone, it is possible to identify points in the inventive process where the involvement of a human being was necessary: it was a human who had to set the question to be answered in the first place, to select the most promising results, and to choose the compounds for further testing.

Other types of AI systems used in other fields confirm the need for a human being to contribute to the inventive process. For instance, one famous inventing AI is the Creativity Machine, an artificial neural network that autonomously generates designs, music, discovery and problem-solving. The Creativity Machine, invented by Stephen Thaler, was composed of at least two neural nets connected into a neural architecture, where one (the generator) would create ideas that were increasingly useful or valuable because they built on the feedback given by the other net (the critic or discriminator).[24] In a layperson's terms, this would be as if the machine carries out a brainstorming process with itself.

A couple of patent applications were filed (and granted) in relation to the Creativity Machine. US patent 5659666 concerns a device for the autonomous generation of useful information, which simulates human creativity by making use of said generator and critic nets.[25] US patent 7454388B2 was granted to an invention employing a neural network that generated novel output, and a critic network that learned to associate that novel output with their utility while triggering reinforcement learning of the more useful or valuable outputs (i.e., a memorization of sorts).[26]

The Creativity Machine came up with the idea of crossing the bristles of a toothbrush for optimal cleaning, which became the famous Oral-B CrossAction toothbrush.[27] But it was the inventor of the Creativity Machine, Stephen Thaler, that fed it information about the characteristics of existing toothbrushes (such as the angle and stiffness of the bristles), in a total of 80 parameters, after being

---

23　Ibid.

24　On this type of neural network, see Chapter 2 (section 2.2). On the Creativity machine in particular, see 'IEI's Patented Creativity Machine Paradigm' (*Imagination Engines Incorporated*) <http://imagination-engines.com/iei_cm.php> accessed 25 March 2021.

25　Stephen L. Thaler, 1997, *Device for the Autonomous Generation of Useful Information*, U.S. patent No. 5,659,666, filed October 13, 1994 and issued August 19, 1997 <www.google.com/patents/US5659666> accessed 13 May 2021. The abstract states in particular that the simulation of human creativity is achieved by "employing a neural network trained to produce input-output maps within some predetermined knowledge domain, an apparatus for subjecting the neural network to perturbations that produce changes in the predetermined knowledge domain, the neural network having an optional output for feeding the outputs of the neural network to a second neural network that evaluates and selects outputs based on training within the second neural network."

26　The invention underlying Stephen L. Thaler, 2005, U.S. patent No. 7,454,388B2, filed May 8, 2006 and issued November 18, 2008 <https://patents.google.com/patent/US7454388B2/en> is tellingly named "Device for the autonomous bootstrapping of useful information."

27　Robert Plotkin, *The Genie in the Machine: How Computer-Automated Inventing is Revolutionizing Law and Business* (Stanford University Press 2009) 51–54. The Creativity Machine is itself a patented invention. Thaler, *Device for the Autonomous Generation of Useful Information* (n 25).

asked by Gillette (the parent company of Oral-B) to design its "next-generation toothbrush".[28] The Creativity Machine was also fed information on the performance of the existing toothbrushes (which were used by robots to brush fake teeth covered in dye). The information on the performance concerned two parameters: amount of dye removed and depth of penetration.[29] From this, the Creativity Machine autonomously identified patterns, learned which parameters made for more efficient toothbrushes, and produced around 2000 possible designs of toothbrushes.[30] Gillette then chose the design amongst those 2000 designs, many of which had crossed bristles. [31] In other words, humans, not the machine, defined the objective to be accomplished/problem to be solved; set the current parameters of toothbrush design; and identified the best solution.[32]

More recently, in August 2019, an international team of patent attorneys filed patent applications for inventions autonomously generated by an AI named DABUS – itself a patented invention[33] – which was named in the patent applications as the inventor. [34]

DABUS was also created by Thaler, who insisted that DABUS was not a mere tool aiding in the design of the products (which included a food container[35] and devices and methods for attracting enhanced attention[36]), but rather the originator of the ideas (Thaler said he didn't provide DABUS with instructions or a specific problem to solve – he simply gave it "general knowledge about the world").[37] DABUS is itself a type of Creativity Machine, or, as better described in the patent publication, "it relates to an enhanced manner of operation of

---

28 *Plotkin* (n 27).

29 Ibid.

30 Ibid.

31 Ibid.

32 Note however that some authors defend that it is possible that a specific output from an AI is so obviously relevant that it does not need further human intervention to separate the wheat from the chaff and choose the optimal solution. See Ryan Abbott, 'The Artificial Inventor Project' (*World Intellectual Property Organization (WIPO) Magazine*, December 2019) 6 <www.wipo.int/wipo_magazine/en/2019/06/article_0002.html> accessed 9 May 2021.

33 See Stephen L. Thaler, 2015, *Device and Method for the Autonomous Bootstrapping of Unified Sentience*, US patent No. 2015/0379394A1, filed January 2, 2014 and issued September 24, 2019.

34 Jurisdictions where these patents were filed include the US and the EPO; the respective analysis of these is carried out in sections 3.4.2 and 3.4.1.

35 Stephen L. Thaler, 2018, *Food Container*, European Patent Application No. 18275163.6., filed October 17, 2018.

36 Stephen L. Thaler, 2018, *Devices and Methods for Attracting Enhanced Attention*, European Patent Application No. 18275174.3, filed November 7, 2018.

37 Erika K. Carlson, 'Artificial Intelligence Can Invent but Not Patent – For Now' (2020) 6 *Engineering* 1212. See also the letter concerning the inventor submitted by the applicant in the course of European Patent Application No. 18275163.6., 1., where it is stated that "In the case of the present invention, the machine only received training in general knowledge in the field and proceeded to independently conceive of the invention and to identify it as novel and salient. If the teaching had been given to a person, that person would meet inventorship criteria as inventor." Stephen L. Thaler, 'Addendum' <https://register.epo.org/documentView?number=IB.2019057809.W&documentId=id00000053660796> accessed 9 May 2021

Creativity Machines."[38] It consists of an artificial neural network trained with general information concerning several fields (which generates novel ideas), and another artificial network (the critic) which monitors the first network and identifies new ideas (i.e., new compared to the AI's pre-existing knowledge based).[39] In addition, the critic network generates responses aimed at selectively forming or ripening ideas that it considers to have the most novelty, utility or value.[40] However, recent information available distinguishes DABUS from the Creativity Machines by claiming that it is not based upon the interplay of generator and critic nets, but instead its implementation integrates both into one system that has many disconnected neural nets, each containing interrelated memories, which are constantly combining and detaching.[41] Some cycles of learning and unlearning take place afterwards, whereby a fraction of the nets interconnect in structures that represent complex concepts, which in turn connect to other chains representing the anticipated consequences of a concept.[42] In simple terms, DABUS autonomously combines simple concepts to get more complex ones, which in turn activate a series of memories that can indicate the anticipated consequences of those ideas.[43] What follows is an ephemeral stage where these structures that represent ideas materialize and dematerialize while others take their place; if one of the represented ideas incorporates a desirable outcome, it will be selectively reinforced, while by contrast undesirable outcomes are weakened.[44] The end result is to convert the desirable ideas into long term memories, which will eventually amount to inventions.[45] According to Imagination Engines Incorporated, whose founder, President and CEO is Stephen Thaler, if it had been DABUS and not the Creativity Machine to invent a new toothbrush, "it would have combined several concepts together (e.g., hog whiskers->embedded in->bamboo stalk) with consequence chains forming as a result (e.g., scrape teeth->remove food->limit bacteria->avoid tooth decay)."[46] In this construction, it seems indeed that DABUS is more autonomous than some of its predecessors. Nevertheless, a human still needs to define the problem for DABUS to solve. In the example of the tooth brush, a human would still have to either task DABUS with searching for a solution to the problem of brushing teeth more efficiently, or to reverse engineer a

38 Thaler, *Device and Method for the Autonomous Bootstrapping of Unified Sentience* (n 33), the Summary of the Disclosure, para 18.

39 See letter concerning the inventor (id.). See also Volodymyr Mnih and Koray Kavukcuoglu, 2013, *Methods and Apparatus for Reinforcement Learning*, U.S. patent No. US 20150379394 A1, filed 5 December 2013 and issued 13 June 2017, the Summary of the Disclosure, para 18 ff.

40 Ibid.

41 'DABUS Described' (*Imagination Engines Incorporated*) < https://imagination-engines.com/dabus.html> accessed 15 May 2021.

42 Ibid.

43 Ibid.

44 Ibid.

45 Ibid.

46 Ibid.

problem from an invention generated by DABUS. Either way, the problem is defined by a human being.

3.3 Patent rationales

Justifications or rationales for patents are manifold and their conceptualization varies from one author to another.[47] One of the classic justifications for the patent system is the natural rights theory, already explored in Chapter 2 (section 2.3), according to which an individual should have natural property rights over the products of her mind.[48] As also described in Chapter 2 (section 2.3), this theory, largely based on the labour theory of the British philosopher John Locke, sees property rights as pre-existing in nature.[49] Attributing property rights over the fruits of one's labour is also somewhat connected to the idea of reward (at least for some authors[50]): the inventor has exercised her labour to shape an idea into an invention, and therefore the results of such endeavour should be hers to take. However, as devised by Locke, granting property rights over the result of one's labour should be conditioned to the fact that "there should be enough and as good left for in common for others."[51] This limitation poses specific challenges also in the context of patent law, as the idea behind granting a patent on an invention is exactly to curtail the freedom of others to make said invention – which might indicate a potential conflict between the exclusive rights that come with a patent and the need to leave "enough and as good for others."[52] The solution to this conflict might then amount to consider that a patent will leave "enough and as good for others" if those others are left with a "sufficient opportunity to invent."[53]

---

47 See Fritz Machlup and Edith Penrose, 'The Patent Controversy in the Nineteenth Century' (1950) 10 *Journal of Economic History* 1, 10.; Estelle Derclaye, 'Patent Law's Role in the Protection of the Environment – Re-assessing Patent Law and its Justifications in the 21st Century' (2009) 40 *International Review of Intellectual Property and Competition Law* 251.; Jay P. Kesan, 'Economic Rationales for the Patent System in Current Context' (2015) 22 *George Mason Law Review* 897.; Matthew Fisher, 'Classical Economics and Philosophy of the Patent System' (2005) 1 *Intellectual Property Quarterly* 1, 3.; Brigitte Andersen, 'The Rationales for Intellectual Property Rights: The Twenty-first Century Controversies' University of London (2003) <www.researchgate.net/publication/228871485_The_Rationales_for_Intellectual_Property_Rights_The_Twenty-First_Century_Controversies> accessed 15 May 2021.; William Fisher, 'Theories of Intellectual Property' (2001) <https://cyber.harvard.edu/people/tfisher/iptheory.pdf> accessed 15 May 2021.

48 *Fisher* (n 47) 6.

49 For an application of the labour theory to patents, see Ofer Tur-Sinai, 'Beyond Incentives: Expanding the Theoretical Framework for Patent Law Analysis' (2010) 45 *Akron Law Review* 1, 11 <https://papers.ssrn.com/sol3/papers.cfm?abstract_id=1697254> accessed 11 May 2021.

50 See Chapter 2 (section 2.3) and references cited therein.

51 John Locke, *Two Treatises of Government* (Peter Laslett ed., Cambridge University Press 1988) 288.

52 See e.g., Matt Fisher, *Fundamentals of Patent Law. Interpretation and Scope of Protection* (Hart Publishing 2007) 68., stating that one of the problems of using the natural rights theory to justify patents is the prohibition of both copying and independent creation inherent to patent monopoly.

53 Concept used by *Tur-Sinai* (n 49) 19.

Arguably, the theory that constitutes the main justification for the patent system is the incentive or utilitarian theory,[54] which – similarly to what happens in the copyright field – sees patents as an incentive to innovate, for the benefit of society. The theory rests on a number of assumptions, among which that inventions are necessary for industrial progress and that the level of invention will be sub-optimal without incentives.[55] In other words, absent a patent, the inventor would not be able to enjoy the same exclusivity in commercializing the invention, as she would not be able to prevent free-riders. This could in turn discourage inventors from producing new inventions, and as a result society as a whole would theoretically be worse off.[56] The incentive theory thus assumes that inventions are necessary for progress, and that patents provide the most effective way to increase the number of inventions. According to this theory, patents incentivise inventors to invent and to reveal information to the public about their inventions that furthers future innovation.[57]

A few caveats are in order, though. First, the patent system might incentivize inventors to patent, but not necessarily to invent.[58] Second, a broad view of the incentive theory considers that not only financial incentives, but also other type of incentives such as reputational benefits may be at the origin of the decision to invent.[59]

Against the background of these justification theories for the patent system, it is also necessary to consider the function of the requirements for patentability. Namely, the specific rationale for having the inventive step or non-obviousness as a patentability requirement should also be considered. In a few jurisdictions, the inventive step or non-obviousness requirement was introduced in national patent systems after the novelty condition was in place, as an additional patentability requisite.[60] It was recognised that novelty alone could not serve as a balancing

---

54 *Derclaye* (n 47) 253–255.; *Fisher* (n 47) 12–13.

55 *Fisher* (n 47) 75.

56 Chris Dent, 'An Exploration of the Principles, Precepts and Purposes that Provide Structure to the Patent System' (2008) 4 *Intellectual Property Quarterly* 456, 464–465; *Kesan* (n 47) 898–899.; Andersen (n 47) 7.; David S. Olson, 'Taking the Utilitarian Basis for Patent Law Seriously: The Case for Restricting Patentable Subject Matter' (2009) 82 *Temple Law Review* 181.

57 Jeanne C. Fromer, 'Expressive Incentives in Intellectual Property' (2012) 98 *Virginia Law Review* 1745, 1751. The author also refers to other ramifications of the utilitarian theory, though: "Utilitarian thinking comes in different flavors. One is the prospect theory, which suggests that inventors are rewarded with a patent right to centralize investment in the patented invention's commercialization and improvement, which in turn benefits society. . . . A related theory advocates for encouraging commercialization because of its valuable role in diffusion of inventions. . . . Another is the signalling theory, which proposes that patents are useful signals to financiers that the patenting firm is a worthy investment" (cit., footnotes omitted).

58 *Kesan* (n 47) 900, and references cited therein.

59 For a complete analysis of a model of "motivators," rather than the classic incentive model, see Chris Dent, 'Decisions Around Innovation and the Motivators that Contribute to Them: Patents, Copyright, Trademarks and Know-how' (2016) 6 *Queen Mary Journal of Intellectual Property* 435.

60 It is the case e.g., of the Patents Act of the United Kingdom (see Chris Dent, 'The Purpose of Patents for Invention: Regulation of Exchange Versus Incentive' (2017) 3 *Intellectual Property Quarterly* 250) and of the United States (see *Duffy* (n 4)).

tool between an incentive for research and development, and the impact that the exclusivity granted by patents has on consumer access to goods, follow-on innovators, and research and development in fields where the basic technology is patented.[61] The inventive step/non-obviousness precludes exclusive rights being granted over trivial advances, as a way to prevent the number of patents from rising to undesirable levels and potentially hindering those skilled in the art due to the ensuing patent thicket.[62] Perhaps more importantly, the inventive step/non obviousness prevents an individual from patenting obvious (but economically significant) developments that were not due to that individual's efforts.[63] The rationale or justification for the inventive step/non-obviousness requirement is thus to select the inventions that would not be created if a patent system did not exist.[64] Conversely, if the invention would be created anyways – because it is obvious and thus well within the reach of the public – granting a patent over it would be ineffective and counter-intuitive.

Underlying the grant of a patent is also the disclosure of technical information that, absent patent protection, the inventor would choose to keep secret in order to maintain a competitive advantage. This is related to another theory justifying the existence of patents – the social contract or informational theory – and which was the central justification for granting privileges to inventors in the beginnings of the patent system.[65] This theory therefore places emphasis on the value of information exchange and dissemination, and on the role that the patent system plays in achieving information disclosure. At its core, disclosure of an invention is the trade-off for the grant of patent protection. As one of the goals of the patent system is to promote innovation, disclosure makes sure that such goal is achieved.[66] In fact, apart from defining the scope of protection of the invention and distinguishing it from the state of the art, patent disclosure also provides the public with a complete survey of the state of technological development, grants information necessary for further developments, and indicates who the patent owner is for purposes of e.g., know-how licensing.[67] This is the reason why many patent laws require enablement or sufficiency of disclosure – if an invention is sufficiently disclosed and its teachings available in

---

61 Amy L. Landers, 'A Comparative Approach to the Inventive Step,' in *Takenaka* (n 4) (ed.) 454, 455.

62 Ulrich Storz, 'Patentability Requirements of Biotech Patents,' in Ulrich Storz and others (eds.), *Biopatent Law: European vs. US Patent Law* (Springer 2014) 55; Graeme Dinwoodie and others, *International and Comparative Patent Law* (LexisNexis 2002) 141. In a nutshell, the objective of the criteria relating to inventive step or non-obviousness is to exclude from patentability inventions that could be easily made by a person skilled in the art, since doing so could hamper the development of technology.

63 *Duffy* (n 4) 12.

64 Edmund W. Kitch, 'Graham v. John Deere Co.: New Standards for Patents' (1967) 49 *Journal of the Patent Office Society* 246.

65 Friedrich-Karl Beier and Josef Straus, 'The Patent System and its Informational Function – Yesterday and Today' (1977) 8 *International Review of Intellectual Property and Competition Law* 387, 389–391.

66 Alison Slade, 'Plausability: A Conditio Sine Qua Non of Patent Law?' (2020) 3 *Intellectual Property Quarterly* 180, 195.

67 *Beier and Straus* (n 65) 404–405.

a public registry, any member of the public can learn from it and use it to carry out further innovations, even if incremental. [68]

An additional, if marginal, theory to justify the grant of a patent is the personality theory, based on the writings of the philosopher Hegel and already described in Chapter 2 (section 2.3). As mentioned there, this theory views creations as an extension of the creator's personality, and property over such creations as a mechanism for self-development and personal expression.[69] Under this construction, property over creations of the mind is justified because the latter are expressions of the personality or self of its creator.[70] Hesitation to resort to the personality theory to justify the grant of patent rights is rooted on the fact that the inventor has less room to express her personality in the inventive process, due to scientific, technological and commercial constraints.[71] The outcome of the inventive process will often be dictated by the most effective way to reach a solution for a technical problem, which can be at odds with creative freedom and the expression of one's personality.

However, it has also been argued that these views are based on a narrow construction of the concept of personality, since the inventor's intellectual skills, vision or imagination also play a role in the inventive process.[72] An inventor can get recognition by others and come to be identified with her invention; empirical research reveals that in fact prestige and reputation is a prime concern among inventors.[73] Moreover, inventors also tend to link their inventions to their personality or self-concept.[74] Therefore, while the personality theory is not central to discussions on patent rationales, it can nevertheless be an ancillary basis for justifying patent rights.

3.4 Requirements for patent protection and other relevant rules

AI-generated inventions intersect with patent law in several ways, and different questions arise from that intersection. A first line of enquiry is whether AI-generated inventions are eligible subject matter for patent protection in

---

68 See also David Vaver, 'Sprucing Up Patent Law' (2010) 22 *Intellectual Property Journal* 6, 70: "[t]he purpose of disclosure is to shift the invention from being a trade secret – which only reverse engineering can reveal, and then not always, especially if it is a process – into the light of day, by laying its teaching on a public register for all to see and learn from. Anyone may experiment with the invention, try to improve it, or use the knowledge gained to move in other directions entirely," and *Drexl and others* (n 10) 20: "The sufficiency-of-disclosure requirement safeguards the fundamental objective of patent law of enhancing the stock of technological knowledge." Along the same lines, see William M. Landes and Richard A. Posner, *The Economic Structure of Intellectual Property Law* (Harvard University Press 2003) 294–295.

69 Justin Hughes, 'The Philosophy of Intellectual Property' (1988) 77 *Georgetown Law Journal* 287, 330.

70 Ibid.

71 1 *Sinai* (n 49) 27.

72 Ibid.

73 *Fromer* (n 57) 1775; see also *Sinai* (n 49).

74 *Fromer* (n 57) 1771–1772.

the jurisdictions concerned, and whether such inventions differ from human-generated inventions.

Another question is whether AI-generated inventions can meet the patentability conditions of each jurisdiction. In order to be granted a patent, an invention must comply with certain patentability requirements. Most patent laws require that inventions be new, capable of industrial application or useful, and involve an inventive step or be non-obvious in order to be granted a patent. An invention will be new if it is different from everything else that is available to the public (which is called in patent law the "state of the art"); it will be capable of industrial application or useful if it can be made or used in any kind of industry; and will involve an inventive step or be non-obvious if the invention is not obvious to someone who has general common knowledge in the technical field of the invention (which patent laws call the "person skilled in the art") – generally speaking, if the person skilled in the art would be able to devise the same invention with normal effort, then the invention does not involve an inventive step, and is therefore not patentable.

As explained in the introduction, the inventive step or non-obviousness requirement is central to an assessment of patentability, and it is also the patentability requirement that is most likely to be affected by the intervention of AI systems in the inventing process. In fact, as also discussed in section 3.1, AI systems are increasingly capable of substituting human ingenuity in the inventing process, thus generating inventions that have little human input.[75] The following sections will therefore have dedicated sub-sections where the inventive step or non-obviousness requirement will be thoroughly analysed.

The requirement of disclosure or enablement will be examined as well. This requirement implies that an invention must be described in sufficient detail to allow someone else to reproduce the invention. The present chapter is premised on the fact that the use of AI systems in the inventing process has an impact on patent law, and therefore it becomes relevant to assess whether the requirement of disclosure or enablement includes an obligation to disclose the use of an AI system for producing inventions.

Finally, a more direct question is whether an AI can be deemed an inventor (and be identified as such in a patent application).[76] For that purpose, this section will also investigate regimes of inventorship across the different jurisdictions, and discuss the extent to which said regimes might accommodate non-human inventors.

This section will analyse each of these questions in relation to each of the jurisdictions concerned – Europe,[77] United States, Australia and Japan).

---

75 *Wamsley* (n 6).

76 This question has been answered in the negative in a few jurisdictions, where patent applications named DABUS the inventor (notably, in Europe and in the US, even though appeals are currently pending).

77 Patent law is not harmonised in the EU in the same way as copyright is, in the sense that there is no EU instrument that harmonises horizontally national patent laws. There is also no EU Regulation

Where applicable, this section will also discuss neighbouring forms of protection, such as utility models, which display less strict requirements – namely, a lower level of inventive step – and which might therefore be relevant to the protection of AI-generated innovations. [78]

3.4.1 Europe

Article 52 (1) of the European Patent Convention (EPC) states that inventions must be new, involve an inventive step and be susceptible of industrial application in order to be patentable. Inventions shall also be sufficiently disclosed in the patent application (Article 83 EPC).[79] Moreover, under Articles 52(2) and (3) EPC, the subject matter of a patent application must not be excluded from patentability. The following subsections will analyse the relevant requirements in turn.

3.4.1.1 Patentable subject matter

The EPC does not give a positive definition of invention. Only a negative definition – i.e., subject matter excluded from patentability – is set forth.[80] However, positive definitional elements can be found implicitly in the EPC, namely, the fact that the invention must be concrete and have a technical character, i.e., it must involve a technical teaching that instructs a skilled person on how to use certain technical means to solve a technical problem.[81] The Synoptic Presentation

---

that creates a unitary patent title valid in all member states of the EU (note however that there will be in the near future a Unitary Patent system for participating member states of the EU – at the time of writing, the Unitary Patent system was expect to start at the beginning of 2022). The European Patent Convention – upon which analysis this book is based – is a multilateral treaty that regulates patent application and examination under a common standard, to which all member states of the EU (and beyond) are parties. Patents are granted by a single body – the European Patent Office (EPO) – and are equivalent to those granted by national patent offices. For this reason, the patent chapter will refer to "Europe" as a jurisdiction, instead of "European Union."

78 In the EU there is no utility model regime at the EU level. In 1997, the European Commission proposed a harmonisation of utility models, but no agreement was reached (the Commission formally withdrew the proposal in 2006) – see 'Internal Market, Industry, Entrepreneurship and SMEs: Utility Models' (European Commission) <https://ec.europa.eu/growth/industry/policy/intellectual-property/patents/utility-models_en> accessed 15 April 2021. Even though some countries in the EU have a national utility model regime (such as Germany or France), they will not be discussed here because this book focuses on legal regimes at the EU level. The US also doesn't have a regime of utility models. Australia has a system of protection for awarding "innovation patents" that is somehow similar to that of utility models, but it is being phased out (see infra, section 3.4.3). Japan has a system of utility models, which will be discussed in Section 3.4.4.

79 Insufficiency of disclosure can also affect the grant of a patent, as it may lead to refusal. European Patent Convention "EPC" (1973), Articles 97(2), 100(b) and 138(1)(b)).

80 EPC (1973), article 52(2) and (3) establish that the following cannot be regarded as inventions, if claimed as such: discoveries, scientific theories, and mathematical methods; aesthetic creations; schemes, rules and methods for performing mental acts, playing games or doing business, and programs for computers; presentations of information.

81 Derk Visser, *The Annotated European Patent Convention 2000* (25th ed., Kluwer Law International 2017). The author points out as another of these implicit positive elements the fact that "the invention must be such that it can be carried out by a skilled person." See also Sarah Merrifield and others,

of the EPC 1973/2000 on the Official Journal of the EPO states, in relation to Article 52(1) EPC, that one of the objectives of the use of the word "technology" therein[82] was to clarify that patent protection is available to *technical* inventions in all fields – but at the same time it recognizes that patent protection is reserved to creations in the technical field.[83]

As such, thus, there is nothing in the EPC definition of invention that would preclude AI-generated innovations from being considered as "inventions" for purposes of patentability, especially since exceptions to patentability are to be interpreted narrowly.

3.4.1.2 *Inventive step*

Article 56 of the EPC defines the inventive step requirement as follows: "An invention shall be considered as involving an inventive step if, having regard to the state of the art, it is not obvious to a person skilled in the art. If the state of the art also includes documents within the meaning of Article 54, paragraph 3 [which refers to the content of European patent applications previously filed], these documents shall not be considered in deciding whether there has been an inventive step." According to the Guidelines of the European Patent Office (EPO) the term "obvious" means something that "does not go beyond the normal progress of technology," which follows logically from prior art, and which, therefore, does not imply any ability beyond what is expected from the person skilled in the art.[84]

In assessing the inventive step, the EPO follows the so-called problem-solution approach, which stems from Rule 42(1)(c) of the Implementing Regulations to the EPC.[85] The approach consists of three steps: (1) determining the closest prior art; (2) establishing the objective technical problem to be solved; (3) considering whether the claimed invention, starting from the closest prior

---

'European Patent Convention 2000: Substantive Patent Law,' in Jochen Pagenberg and Richard Hacon (eds.), *Concise European Patent Law* (2nd ed., Kluwer Law International 2008).

82 EPC (1973), article 52(1): "European patents shall be granted for any inventions, *in all fields of technology*, provided that they are new, involve an inventive step and are susceptible of industrial application." (emphasis added)

83 1 European Patent Office, 'Revision of the European Patent Convention (EPC 2000): Synoptic Presentation of the EPC 1973/2000' (2007) Special Edition 4 European Patent Office Official Journal ISSN 0170/9291, 48 <http://archive.epo.org/epo/pubs/oj007/08_07/special_edition_4_epc_2000_synoptic.pdf> accessed 19 April 2021.

84 European Patent Office, 'Guidelines for Examination – Part G – Chapter VII-2'.

85 EPC (1973), rule 42(1)(c) establishes that the description shall "disclose the invention, as claimed, in such terms that the *technical problem*, even if not expressly stated as such, *and its solution* can be understood, and state any advantageous effects of the invention with reference to the background art."[emphasis added] Note however that the discovery or recognition that a problem exists may also consist of patentable subject matter where the identification of the problem is an inventive contribution. Catherine Seville, *EU Intellectual Property Law and Policy* (2nd ed., Edward Elgar 2016) 150.; *Merrifield* (n 81) commentary on Article 56. In these cases, the problem-solution approach might not be the best procedure, since in these "problem inventions" the question is whether the skilled person would have identified the problem, not the solution – on this point, see *Merrifield* (n 81).

art and the objective technical problem, would have been obvious to the skilled person.[86]

The selection of closest prior art (step 1) is made by comparing objectively the subject matter, objectives, and technical features of the various items of prior art.[87] The prior art reference should also relate to the same or similar technical problem, or to the same or similar technical field as the claimed invention.[88] The closest prior art will be contained in one single reference that discloses the combination of features and that constitutes the most promising starting point for an obvious development which leads to the claimed invention.[89]

The establishment of the objective technical problem to be solved (step 2) is based on technical effects of the invention not present in the closest prior art identified in step 1, which requires a comparison of the claimed invention with the closest prior art in order to identify the distinguishing features of the latter.[90]

The final step implies considering whether the claimed invention would have been obvious to the skilled person. This often entails an assessment of whether it was obvious to combine the closest prior art with other prior art to arrive at the invention.[91] AI-generated inventions become particularly relevant at this point, since what might not be obvious for a human being can be relatively 'obvious' (read simple) to an AI system that can e.g., process more data more rapidly, or make connections between fields where those connections would be unintuitive to a human inventor.

The specific question to be asked is whether a skilled person in charge of solving the objective technical problem *would* (not only *could*) have come to the claimed solution by combining the closest prior art document with another prior art document, or by adapting the closest prior art. So for example the skilled person may have had the solution in the form of the claimed invention available, but this alone is not enough to reach a finding of obviousness.[92] In other words: beyond the theoretical possibility of combining prior art documents or adapting the closest prior art, would the skilled person actually have done it in the hope of solving the technical problem, or of reaching some improvement?[93] In a concrete case, the answer to this question may again

---

86 European Patent Office, *Guidelines for Examination – Part G – Chapter VII-3*.

87 Case T-1212/01 *Pyrazolopyrimidinones for the treatment of impotence/ Pfizer Limited et al*, Boards of Appeal of the EPO, [4.4].

88 See e.g., Case T-989/93 *Scintillation Media/Fisher Scientific*, Boards of Appeal of the EPO [12].; case T-1203/97 *Recup Svenska v. Recotech Heatex & Menerga Apparatebau*, Boards of Appeal of the EPO [4.1].; case T-570/91 *A.E. PLC v. Mahle GmbH*, Boards of Appeal of the EPO [4.5].

89 Case T-254/86 *Yellow Dyes*, Boards of Appeal of the EPO.; case T-570/91 *A.E. PLC v. Mahle*, Boards of Appeal of the EPO, [4.2.]; case T-698/10 *Broadcom Corporation*, Boards of Appeal of the EPO, [3]. See also European Patent Office, *Guidelines for Examination – Part G – Chapter VII-5.1*.

90 *Visser* (n 81) commentary on Article 56.

91 Ibid.

92 *Merrifield* (n 81) commentary on Article 56.

93 *Storz* (n 62) 12.; *Seville* (n 85) 149. See also *Merrifield* (n 81) commentary on Article 56, explaining that the objective of this line of inquiry is to avoid an ex-post analysis of obviousness (so-called "hindsight").

depend if we consider the person skilled in the art to be a human being or an AI system (or a human being using an AI system to invent).

The person skilled in the art is "presumed to be a skilled practitioner in the relevant field of technology, who is possessed of average knowledge and ability and is aware of what was common general knowledge in the art at the relevant date."[94] Who the "skilled practitioner" is depends on the field in question – she may be a senior researcher, or an experienced trade professional without any formal academic qualifications, for example.[95] Common general knowledge is defined as knowledge that an experienced person in the field is expected to have, or at least be aware of so that she can look it up in a handbook if she needs it.[96] The relevant field of technology is defined by the technical problem to be solved; if the technical field of the solution differs from the technical field of the problem, the latter prevails.[97] However, the relevant technical field can encompass neighbouring fields or a broader general technical field (if the same or similar problems arose therein, and if the person skilled in the art ought to be aware of them).[98] The relevant technical field can even be a field other than a neighbouring or broader general field, if the person skilled in the art would consider looking for suggestions in that field because the materials used were related/similar, or because of widespread public debate about a technical problem common to both fields.[99] It is considered that the person skilled in the art is someone whose knowledge stands somewhere between the average member of the public at large and an advanced senior scientist.[100] Therefore, the person skilled in the art will not engage in scientific research in areas not yet explored.[101] In fact, it is considered that the skilled person is purpose-driven, and will therefore not engage in frivolous research, guided by "idle curiosity": a specific technical purpose is what guides the person skilled in the art.[102] The person skilled in the art is also presumed to have had at her disposal "the means and capacity for routine work and experimentation which are normal for the field of technology in question,"[103] but she lacks creative thinking and inventive imagination.[104] Routine work includes workshop modifications, or e.g., repeating a known measure to improve the result, provided there is a reasonable expectation of success.[105] From this it is apparent that the definition of

94 European Patent Office, *Guidelines for Examination – Part G – Chapter VII -1*.
95 Lodewijk Pesser, *The Inventiveness Requirement in Patent Law: An Exploration of its Foundations and Functioning* (Kluwer Law International 2016) 267.
96 Case T-766/91 *Decorative laminates/Boeing*, Boards of Appeal of the EPO, [8.2].
97 *Visser* (n 81) commentary on Article 56.
98 Case T-176/84 *Pencil Sharpener*, Boards of Appeal of the EPO.
99 Case T-560/89 *Filler mass/ N.I. Industries*, Boards of Appeal of the EPO, [5.2].
100 *Visser* (n 81) commentary on Article 56.
101 Case T-500/91 *Alpha-interferon II/ Biogen*, Boards of Appeal of the EPO, [2.2].
102 *Visser* (n 81) commentary on Article 56.
103 European Patent Office, *Guidelines for Examination – Part G – Chapter VII -1*.
104 *Visser* (n 81) commentary on Article 56.
105 Ibid.

the person skilled in the art is central to the topic of AI-generated inventions. An AI system, or a human being using an AI system to invent, may have a level of general knowledge and ability far superior to the average of a human being's in the same field.[106] Likewise, while a human being might not think to look into very removed technical fields for a solution to a given problem, an AI-system may be more capable of "out-of-the-box thinking" (depending of course on its underlying programming). This means that an AI system is more likely to seek suggestions from unrelated fields which would not be considered a neighbouring field or even a broader general technical field for purposes of an obviousness assessment, but which would nevertheless be within reach of said AI system.[107]

In addition to these steps, secondary indicia may be taken into account, such as the satisfaction of a long-felt need,[108] commercial success derived from the technical features of the invention,[109] the simplicity of the solution without anything in prior art that would hint at it,[110] or a surprising or unexpected effect (although it cannot make up for lack of inventiveness in an obvious solution).[111] Chiefly, in relation to this last factor, the Board of Appeals of the EPO ruled that the additional effect that is inevitably achieved by the skilled person on the basis of an obvious measure *without any effort* cannot support findings of an inventive step (even as a surprising effect)[112] which again shows the importance of a definition of the person skilled in the art, and of deciding

106 *Hartmann and others* (n 5) 110.: "AI systems probably do not have "common general knowledge," as such notion reflects what is expected of, say, a (human) technical education in the field and gained from experience." It is submitted that this definition is too narrow and does not correspond to what happens in practice. In fact, while it is true that the use of the expression "common general knowledge" has traditionally been used in relation to *human* knowledge, that does not mean that an AI system is not capable of emulating said knowledge in specific fields. On the contrary, an AI system uses troves of previous knowledge to generate output.

107 This is connected to another issue, which is the fact that prejudices in the relevant technical field can also be an indication of an inventive step if it is considered that the skilled person would not arrive to the invention due to such prejudices (see *Visser* (n 81) commentary on Article 56) – because an AI system will not have such "prejudices," it will be easier for it (or for a person using it to invent) to look beyond prejudices in the relevant field, and thus meet the requirement of inventive step with less effort.

108 Case T-699/91 *Blount*, Boards of Appeal of the EPO, [4.3], where it is explained that a finding of non-obviousness can be supported by concurrent factors, namely "an urgent need which had not been met over a long period of time."

109 Case T-1212/01 *Pyrazolopyrimidinones for the treatment of impotence/ Pfizer Limited et al*, Boards of Appeal of the EPO, [6.2.]: "To establish commercial success as an indicia of inventive step requires two evidentiary steps – first, to show that there has been commercial success and, second, to show that such success results from the claimed invention and not from one or more other causes."

110 Case T-73/95 *Enichem Synthesis v. Ciba Spezialitaetenchemie*, Boards of Appeal of the EPO. See also case T-712/92 *Cleaning lenses/Allergan*, Boards of Appeal of the EPO, [16], where the Board explains that "the simplicity of a technical solution could be indicative of inventiveness, especially if the technical field is of commercial importance and if, despite the considerable amount of activity in the field, the said solution had escaped those concerned."

111 Case T-231/97 *Emissionsarme Dispersionsfarben/Clariant*, Boards of Appeal of the EPO.

112 Case T-506/92 *AEG v. Siemens*, Boards of Appeal of the EPO.

whether such definition may include AI, or at least a human being using AI systems to invent (because it is likely that additional and surprising effects can be achieved without any efforts if the person skilled in the art is an AI system, or a human being using an AI system). It should be noted however that these indicia are indeed merely secondary, and are used to strengthen or weaken arguments of inventive step or lack thereof.[113]

3.4.1.3 Disclosure

According to Article 83 EPC, the patent application must disclose the invention in a manner sufficiently clear and complete for it to be carried out by a person skilled in the art. This means that the skilled person should be able to carry out the invention without undue burden, even though a reasonable amount of trial and error, if accompanied by adequate instructions that can lead to success, is admissible in difficult or unexplored fields.[114] When assessing the sufficiency of disclosure, the level of skill is the same as in the assessment of inventive step, with the difference that, unlike the assessment of inventive step, here it is considered that the skilled person has knowledge of the invention as disclosed (and not only of prior art).

As per rule 42(1)(e) of the Implementing Regulations to the EPC, sufficiency of disclosure implies a detailed description of at least one way of carrying out the invention.[115] It also implies that the invention is described both in terms of its structure and in terms of its function.[116] These requirements however are not akin to mandating disclosure of methods or tools (including the use of AI systems) that were used in the inventing process. Likewise, the other elements of Rule 42(1) do not convey an obligation to disclose the methods or tools used to produce the invention.[117] In fact, the disclosure of the methods and tools used

---

113 *Visser* (n 81) commentary on Article 56. See also case T-1212/01 *Pyrazolopyrimidinones for the treatment of impotence/ Pfizer Limited et al*, Boards of Appeal of the EPO, [6.1.]: "Commercial success and similar arguments can only ever be secondary *indicia* of inventiveness, which are usually only of importance in cases where an objective evaluation of the prior art has not provided a clear answer. In such cases, secondary *indicia* may show that an inventive step is involved."

114 *Seville* (n 85) 183.; European Patent Office, *Guidelines for Examination – Part F – Chapter III -1*. See also in particular the case T-226/85 *Stable bleaches*, Boards of Appeal of the EPO, [8], which explicitly states: "[e]ven though a reasonable amount of trial and error is permissible when it comes to the sufficiency of disclosure in an unexplored field or . . . where there are many technical difficulties, there must then be available adequate instructions in the specification or on the basis of common general knowledge which would lead the skilled person necessarily and directly towards success through the evaluation of initial failures or through an acceptable statistical expectation rate in case of random experiments."

115 See also European Patent Office, *Guidelines for Examination – Part F – Chapter III -1*.

116 Unless the functions of the various parts are immediately apparent. ibid.

117 EPC (1973), rule 42(1) lists the elements that should be part of the description (and that stand for a sufficiency of disclosure), which include the technical field of the invention, the relevant background art, the problem, solution and advantageous effects of the invention, and the way in which the invention is industrially applicable (when that is not obvious).

in the inventive process is often deemed irrelevant within the requirement of sufficiency of disclosure, especially since it would be difficult to enforce.[118] This would mean that, since the applicant for a patent would not be obliged to disclose the use of an AI in the inventive process, it would also not be possible to assess the impact of that use on the patentability of the invention, namely when it comes to the required inventive step. The potential disruption of AI-generated inventions to the inventive step requirement, as analysed in the previous subsection, would therefore go unnoticed (save for some possible increase in patent applications due to the greater easiness in meeting patentability requirements).[119]

3.4.1.4 Inventorship

Under Article 81 EPC, the applicant shall designate the inventor. If the applicant is not the inventor (or in case he or she is not the sole inventor), the designation "shall contain a statement indicating the origin of the right to the European patent."[120] The designation shall, among other elements, contain the family name, given names and country and place of residence of the inventor[121] a strong indication that the inventor is supposed to be a natural person.

Other provisions of the EPC reinforce a finding that AIs cannot be inventors under the law. Namely, Article 61 EPC grants the inventor the *right* to be mentioned as such before the Office. Given that machines cannot hold rights under the law, it stands to reason that AIs cannot be considered inventors under the EPC. The Boards of Appeal of the EPO have also referred to the inventor as a natural person.[122]

The question of inventorship in relation to AIs was analysed in the patent applications filed by Thaler, which designated as inventor the AI DABUS.[123] The EPO found that the right to an invention (Article 60 EPC) and the moral

---

118 *Drexl and others* (n 10) 5.
119 The Motion for a European Parliament Resolution on intellectual property rights for the development of artificial intelligence technologies, from October 2020, might start a debate on recasting disclosure requirements (or at least how disclosure is assessed by IP Offices) in the framework of AI inventions, inventions that have AI applications, or inventions that are AI-generated and AI-aided, since it mentions that "the challenge of assessing AI applications creates a need for some transparency requirements and the development of new methods as, for instance, adaptive learning systems may recalibrate following each input, making certain ex ante disclosures ineffective" – see European Parliament (Committee on Legal Affairs), 'Report on Intellectual Property Rights for the Development of Artificial Intelligence Technologies' (2020/2015(INI)) 7 <www.europarl.europa.eu/doceo/document/A-9-2020-0176_EN.pdf> accessed 2 May 2021.
120 EPC (1973), article 81.
121 Implementing Regulations to the Convention on the Grant of European Patents (1973), rule 19(1).
122 Case J-7/99 *Heavy-duty Power*, Boards of Appeal of the EPO, [6]: "the right to be designated as the inventor in accordance with Article 81 EPC is an important moral right of the inventor as the natural person who has performed the creative act of invention (as opposed to the company or legal person which is usually the applicant."
123 Stephen L. Thaler, *Devices and Methods for Attracting Enhanced Attention*, European Patent Application No. EP3563896, filed on November 7, 2018 and issued on November 6, 2019 and Stephen L. Thaler, *Food Container*, European Patent Application No. EP3564144, filed on October 17, 2018 and issued on November 6, 2019.

right to be designated as the inventor (Article 62 EPC) could only belong to a natural person, given that only natural persons can hold moral and property rights.[124] In the same proceedings, the Office held that the preparatory works of the EPC demonstrate that the inventor must be a human being.[125] At the time of writing, these decisions are under appeal.[126] It should be noted though that, should the final decision be that DABUS cannot be the inventor because only human beings can claim inventorship, the substantial impact on the patentability of AI-generated innovations will likely be minimal. In fact, a negative decision might incentivize applicants to indicate a human being as the inventor, with the assurance that the EPO does not verify the accuracy of the designation of the inventor.[127] This suggests that in Europe naming the inventor is a mere formality, and that no other consequences – namely, a requirement that an inventor must have substantially contributed to the invention to be named as such – should be derived from the EPO's findings in the DABUS case or from Article 81 EPC (without prejudice to national laws that may have such requirement).[128] To put it differently, under the EPC, the human being that partially contributes to an invention will probably qualify as an inventor; the extent of the human contribution needed (if any) to meet a threshold of inventorship is a matter for national law.[129]

3.4.2 United States

3.4.2.1 Patentable subject matter

US law does not have a detailed definition of "invention" as such. 35 US Code, Section 100, states that the term 'invention' means invention or discovery, while Section 101 further clarifies that inventions patentable are (new and

---

124 Summons to Attend Oral Proceedings for Application 18275163.6 from European Patent Office to Williams Powell (September 13, 2019), Annex, 2 <https://register.epo.org/application?docum entId=E3SDI9ZN5969498&number=EP18275163&lng=en&npl=false> accessed 9 April 2021.

125 Ibid., 2–3: "The drafters of the EPC were in agreement as to the fact that the inventor must be a natural person, a human being. The preparatory works demonstrate this by documenting discussions on 'development of invention by [a] person', 'inventions made jointly by several persons' . . . 'the inventor being an employed person' . . . the possibility for the inventor to renounce 'his' right to be mentioned."

126 The decisions have been the object of appeal to the Legal Board of Appeal as cases J-8/20, Board of Appeal of the EPO and J-9/20 Board of Appeal of the EPO.

127 As clearly stated in the Implementing Regulations to the Convention on the Grant of European Patents (1973), rule 19(2).

128 In the same sense, see *Hartmann and others* (n 5) 100 ("Naming the inventor is, in other words, a formal requirement that a human person be named as inventor, nothing more."). Contra, see *Kim* (n 1) 448, who, while stating that "the EPC does not explicitly stipulate any qualitative or quantitative criteria with regard to the inventing activity that should give rise to the inventor entitlement; such criteria can be found under national patent law statutes and courts' jurisprudence," still affirms that "the underlying principle that there should be a substantial contribution to the development of an invention, as a qualifying factor for the inventor entitlement, can still be valid in situations where a technical solution might be found by applying AI."

129 *Hartmann and others* (n 5) 102.

useful) processes, machines, manufactures, or composition of matter, or any new and useful improvement thereof. Only subject matter that falls under one of these categories can amount to patentable subject matter.[130] Moreover, such subject matter should exist in a physical or tangible form.[131]

The Supreme Court has in addition ruled that "laws of nature, physical phenomena and abstract ideas" are not patentable in the context of Section 101,[132] as finding otherwise could hinder, rather than promote, innovation.[133] Further case law[134] has clarified that, should the patent claim a law of nature, natural phenomena or abstract idea, such subject matter might still be eligible for patent protection if the claim contains an "inventive concept" sufficient to transform the law of nature, natural phenomena or abstract idea into patentable subject matter.[135] The decisions thus exclude from patentability conventional (as opposed to "inventive") applications of laws of nature, natural phenomena or abstract ideas.[136] The Supreme Court did not establish a rule to decide what constitutes an abstract idea; to decide whether a claim embodies an abstract idea or a patent-eligible subject matter, courts carry out a comparison between the case before them and claims found to be directed to an abstract idea in previous cases[137] – i.e., the assessment will necessarily be done on a case-by-case basis.

While these decisions are important to delimit patentable subject matter independently of whether said subject matter is generated by an AIs or a human, they highlight that current AIs are akin to a tool in the inventive process, as in

---

130 *In re Petrus A.C.M. Nuijten*, 500 F.3d 1346, 1354, 84 USPQ2d 1495, 1500 (Fed. Cir. 2007): "[the] four categories together describe the exclusive reach of patentable subject matter."

131 *Digitech Image Techs. v. Electronics for Imaging*, 758 F.3d 1344, 1348, 111 USPQ2d 1717, 1719 (Fed. Cir. 2014).

132 *Diamond v. Chakrabarty*, 447 U.S. 303, 309 (1980).

133 See *Mayo Collaborative Services v. Prometheus Laboratories*, 566 U.S. 66 (2012), 71, 101. See also *Mayo v. Prometheus*, Syllabus: "Rewarding with patents those who discover laws of nature might encourage their discovery. But because those laws and principles are 'the basic tools of scientific and technological work' . . . there is a danger that granting patents that tie up their use will inhibit future innovation, a danger that becomes acute when a patented process is no more than a general instruction to 'apply the natural law,' or otherwise forecloses more future invention than the underlying discovery could reasonably justify" (footnotes omitted).

134 *Mayo Collaborative Services v. Prometheus Laboratories (ibid.)* and *Alice Corp. v. CLS Bank International*, 134 S. Ct. 2347 (2014).

135 "To transform an unpatentable law of nature into a patent-eligible application of such a law, a patent must do more than simply state the law of nature while adding the words 'apply it'. . . . It must limit its reach to a particular, inventive application of the law" (*Mayo Collaborative Services v. Prometheus Laboratories*, references omitted). See also Jeffrey A. Lefstin and others, 'Final Report of the Berkeley Center for Law & Technology Section 101 Workshop: Addressing Patent Eligibility Challenge' (2016) University of California Hastings College of the Law Legal Studies Research Paper Series, 9 <https://papers.ssrn.com/sol3/papers.cfm?abstract_id=3050093> accessed 26 April 2021, explaining that "[i]n *Alice Corp.*, the Court extended the Mayo framework to computer-implemented inventions, confirming that Mayo's requirement for an 'inventive concept' in the claim represents the new test for patent-eligible subject matter under §101" (footnotes omitted).

136 *Lefstin* (n 135) 20–21.

137 *Enfish, LLC v. Microsoft Corp.*, 822 F.3d 1327, 1334 (Fed. Cir. 2016).

most cases there is a need for a human inventor to further (inventively) apply the abstract ideas generated by an AI. Other than that, the definition of patentable subject matter is quite broad and can in principle accommodate AI- and human-generated inventions alike.

3.4.2.2 Non-obviousness

The requirement that an invention displays an inventive step, which in the US translates into the non-obvious condition for patentability, amounts to an invention not having been obvious to someone with ordinary skill in the art to which the invention's subject matter pertains. Until the Patent Act of 1952, US statutory law did not have a non-obviousness requirement.[138] The case *Hotchkiss v. Greenwood* set the ground for a requirement of non-obviousness by demanding a sufficient degree of ingenuity and skill higher than the ordinary person "acquainted with the business" in order for a patent to be valid.[139] This standard gave rise to different interpretations by different courts – some more stringent than others[140] – which ultimately caused the US Congress to enact Section 103 of the 1952 Patent Act.[141]

The current version of the provision (35 U.S.C. Section 103) states that a patent cannot be obtained

> if the differences between the claimed invention and the prior art are such that the claimed invention as a whole would have been obvious before the effective filing date of the claimed invention to a person having ordinary skill in the art to which the claimed invention pertains. Patentability shall not be negated by the manner in which the invention was made.

The provision thus requires the examiner or judge to define the field under which the invention falls ("the art"), the level of skill of the person skilled therein, and whether the invention is obvious to that person.[142]

---

138 see John H. Barton, 'Non-obviousness' (2003) 43 *IDEA* 475, 476, and generally Donald S. Chisum, *Chisum on Patents – A Treatise on the Law of Patentability, Validity and Infringement* (vol. 2, LexisNexis 2017) sec. 5.02 for the background of the Patent Act and the insertion therein of the non-obviousness requirement.

139 *Hotchkiss v. Greenwood*, 52 U.S. 248 (1850).

140 Among the decisions that followed *Hotchkiss v. Greenwood* where strict interpretations were put forth, *Cuno Engineering Corp. v. Automatic Devices Corp.* 314 U.S. 84 (1941) (with Mr. Justice Douglas, delivering the opinion of the US Supreme Court) established that to obtain a patent a given device had to involve "more ingenuity . . . than the work of a mechanic skilled in the art. . . . [T]he new device, however useful it may be, must reveal the flash of creative genius" id. [90–91].

141 World Intellectual Property Organization (WIPO) Secretariat of the Standing Committee on the Law of Patents, 'Study on Inventive Step' (SCP/22/3, Geneva, 6 July 2015) 3 <www.wipo.int/edocs/mdocs/scp/en/scp_22/scp_22_3.pdf> accessed 15 January 2018.; *Chisum* (n 138) sec. 5.02 para 4; *Duffy* (n 4) 39–43.

142 Joseph P. Meara, 'Just Who is the Person Having Ordinary Skill in the Art – Patent Law's Mysterious Personage' (2007) 77 *Washington Law Review* 273.

In a trilogy of cases on Section 103 – *Graham v. John Deere Co.*,[143] *Calmar v. Cook Chemical Co*,[144] *United States v. Adams*[145] – the US Supreme Court further considered the scope of that provision and the test for obviousness. The *Graham v. John Deere* decision lays down the approach that should be adopted by the patent office and the lower courts.[146] The approach consists of a step-by-step inquiry determining: the scope and content of the prior art; differences between the prior art and the claimed invention; the level of ordinary skill in the pertinent art; and secondary considerations that can provide objective evidence of non-obviousness, such as "commercial success, long felt but unsolved needs, [and] failure of others," that "may have relevancy" as "indicia of obviousness or non-obviousness."[147]

In relation to the first factor – the scope and content of the prior art – it is necessary to determine both to which art the claimed invention pertains, and what the "prior art" is.[148] The pertinent art should be defined as the art dealing with the problem to be solved (and not the art relating to the industry in which the invention is used).[149] "The art to which the claimed invention pertains" comprises analogous arts, i.e., arts from the same field independently of the problem addressed, and arts from a different field but that solve the same problem or have the same purpose.[150] That is, analogous arts include those areas where a person having ordinary skill in the art (hereinafter, "PHOSITA") looking to solve the same problem as the inventor would be inclined to research for a solution.[151] Non-analogous art, on the other hand, cannot be used when judging whether the invention is obvious or non-obvious.[152] Several Supreme Court decisions reveal a trend to expand the notion of analogous art that must

---

143 *Graham v. John Deere Co*, 379 U.S. 956 (1965).

144 *Calmar v. Cook Chemical Co.*, 380 U.S. 949 (1965).

145 *United States v. Adams*, 380 U.S. 949 (1965).

146 *Chisum* (n 138) sec. 5.02 para 5 and references cited therein.

147 *Graham v. Deere* (n 143) [17–18].

148 *Chisum* (n 138) sec. 5.03.

149 Ibid. para 1b, and references cited therein. See also United States Patent and Trademark Office (USPTO), 'Manual of Patent Examining Procedure' (2019) Chapter 2141.01(a): "In determining whether a reference is reasonably pertinent, an examiner should consider the problem faced by the inventor, as reflected – either explicitly or implicitly – in the specification. . . . The question of whether a reference is reasonably pertinent often turns on how the problem to be solved is perceived."

150 Jacob S. Sherkow, 'Negativing Invention' (2011) 4 *Brigham Young University Law Review* 1091, 1109–1110. The author gives as an example of arts from the same field but that solve different problems toothbrushes and hairbrushes; and provides the case of cone-shaped caps for oil decanters and cone-shaped caps for bags of popcorn as an example of arts that exist in different fields of endeavour but solve the same problem or have the same purpose. See also MPEP, 2141.01(a).

151 Jeffrey T. Burgess, 'The Analogous Art Test' (2009) 7 *Buffalo Intellectual Property Law Journal* 63, 67. See also *Scientific Plastic Products, Inc. v. Biotage AB*, 766 F.3d 1355, 1360 (Fed. Cir. 2014): "the analogous art inquiry does not exclude references 'not within the field of endeavour' if a person of ordinary skill would reasonably look to that reference in order to solve the problem confronting the inventor."

152 Ibid.

be considered prior art.[153] Moreover, the Federal Circuit has ruled that the Patent Office Classification system (which can be used for prior art searches) has limited value in deciding the analogous/non-analogous question, since the criterion for such system differs from considerations "relating to a person of ordinary skill seeking solution for a particular problem."[154] As for the sources where the prior art can be found, Section 102 of the Patent Act lists patents, published patent applications, publications, public use, sale or otherwise availability to the public before the effective filing date of the claimed invention.[155]

Like what was mentioned in relation to Europe and the concept of neighbouring fields, the concept of analogous arts in the obviousness analysis is of particular importance for AI-generated inventions. Depending of course on its underlying programming, an AI system is more likely than a human to seek solutions in far removed fields, which would not be traditionally considered analogous art for purposes of an obviousness assessment. In other words, the concept of analogous arts may conceptually be stretched in the case of AI-generated or AI-aided inventions, as what is non-analogous for a human being might be analogous for an AI system.

The second factor refers to the differences between prior art and the claimed invention, which implies first construing the patent claims of the claimed invention, and then comparing the subject matter as a whole with the prior art.[156]

The third factor – the level of ordinary skill in the pertinent art – is defined taking into account several criteria: (1) the educational level of the inventor; (2) type of problems encountered in the art; (3) prior art solutions to those problems; (4) rapidity with which innovations are made; (5) sophistication of the technology; (6) educational level of active workers in the field.[157] However, not all criteria are necessarily present in every case, and one or more factors may predominate in a particular case.[158] Some court decisions seem to draw a difference between high level skilled-fields (where there are specialized subfields, people with advanced degrees, or the use of substantial resources in problem-solving), and low level skilled-fields (where typically people have limited education and/ or experience); in principle, a low level of skill will favour a determination of

---

153 See e.g., *Cuno Engineering Corp. v. Automatic Devices Corp.*, 314 U.S. 84 (1941), where the patent on an automobile cigarette lighter with a thermostatic control was invalidated because similar thermostats had been used in analogous arts (such as toasters or irons), or *Jungersen v. Ostby & Barton Co.*, 335 U.S. 560 (1949), which considered jewellery casting to be analogous to dental casting for purposes of prior art references – these and other cases referred in *Chisum* (n 138) sec. 5.03 para 1.

154 *Chisum* (n 138) sec. 5.03 para 1a, citing *In re Mlot-Fijalkowski*, 676 F.2d 666, 669 (C.C.P.A. 1982).

155 See *Burgess* (n 151) 66. Even though Section 102 does not deal with obviousness, the comments to the 1952 Patent Act reveal that the "prior art" of Section 102 is the "antecedent [basis]" for its use in Section 103. The author adds that "in general, a reference that does not fall into any statutory category under Section 102 can be excluded from an obviousness analysis."

156 *Chisum* (n 138) sec. 5.03 para 5, and references cited therein.

157 1 *Custom Accessories, Inc. v. Jeffrey-Allan Indus., Inc.*, 807 F.2d 955, 962 (Fed. Cir. 1986); *In re GPAC Inc.*, 57 F.3d 1573, 1579 (Fed. Cir. 1995); *Environmental Designs, Ltd. v. Union Oil Co*, 713 F.2d 693 (Fed. Circ. 1983).

158 1 *Environmental Designs, Ltd. v. Union Oil Co.* (n 157).

non-obviousness, while a high level of skill favours the reverse.[159] This, together with the criterion relating to the sophistication of technology, could contribute to findings of obviousness in fields where the use of AI systems to invent is more prevalent, as AI systems might be considered substantial resources/sophisticated technology used in problem-solving (the prevalent use of AI in a given field would probably have to be common knowledge that an examiner would likely have, since the applicant would not necessarily have to disclose the use of AI in the inventive process – see infra section 3.4.2.3).

Regarding the secondary considerations, the US Supreme Court would point out in *Calmar v. Cook Chemical*, they focus on "economic and motivational rather than technical issues," lending a "helping hand" to the judiciary and helping to avoid hindsight.[160] On the other hand, as explained by M.J. Adelman et al., these seem no longer secondary as per the Federal Circuit's ensuing case law (even though the patentee must show a link between the invention and these considerations).[161] Specifically, authors defend that, if there is a long-felt need and failure of others to address those needs, these are strong indicia of non-obviousness.[162] The view vis-à-vis secondary considerations that is adopted in this book – and one that is also followed by a few authors and courts – is that secondary considerations are always relevant when assessing non-obviousness, even though their level of probative force might vary on a case-by-case basis.[163]

After performing an analysis of these factors, the examiner or judge is to reach a conclusion regarding obviousness or non-obviousness of the invention as a whole.[164] This includes an assessment of the discovery of the problem, since an obvious solution to a non-obvious problem might comply with the non-obviousness requirement.[165] The assessment of obviousness is made from the perspective of the PHOSITA, who is, as per the Supreme Court's case *KSR*

---

159 *Chisum* (n 138) sec. 5.03 para 4e, and references cited therein. The author notes however that "if the inventor's solution in fact has gone unnoticed for a substantial period of time despite the high level of skill, that fact tends to support a conclusion of non-obviousness."

160 *Calmar v. Cook Chemical Co*. (n 144) [35–36].

161 Martin J. Adelman and others., *Cases and Materials on Patent Law* (4th ed., West Academic Publishing 2015) 342–343.

162 1 *Meara* (n 142) 295–296., advocates that long-felt need and failure of others should be taken as objective evidence of actual skill in the art, stating that "when a problem is old in the art and has been the subject of more than de minimis research, it suggests that no one of any skill level was able to solve it. When combined with actual evidence that others failed to solve the problem, one can infer that the solution has eluded those of ordinary skill."

163 This is also the stance of *Chisum* (n 138) sec. 5.05 (and references cited therein). The author notes that in relation to secondary considerations there are three schools of thought: one that views secondary considerations as truly secondary, i.e., to be used only when in doubt or to "tip the scales"; another that takes secondary considerations as not secondary at all, making them the basis for a decision on obviousness; and the third one, which the author calls "the balanced and preferred view," which is also adopted here.

164 *Chisum* (n 138) sec. 5.04, and references cited therein.

165 See *In re Kaslow*, 707 F.2d 1336 (Fed. Cir. 1983) and *In re Sponnoble*, 405 F.2d 578 (C.C.P.A. 1969) both cited in David J. Abraham, 'Shinpo Sei: Japanese Inventive Step Meets U.S. Non-obviousness' (1995) 77 *Journal of the Patent and Trademark Office Society* 528, 533.

v. Teleflex,[166] someone who has "ordinary creativity."[167] Moreover, if a problem only has a finite number of identified, predictable solutions, it may be obvious to try them all, and if so the invention might fail the non-obviousness test.[168] This is particularly relevant for AI-generated inventions, as an AI system will have the computing power to try a considerable higher number of solutions – which might be identified and predictable for said AI-system, but not necessarily so for a human being.

In *KSR v. Teleflex*, the Court also referred to the teaching-suggestion-motivation (TSM) test used by the Federal Circuit, which dictates that a claimed invention will be obvious where there is a teaching, suggestion or motivation to combine prior art teachings.[169] The Supreme Court softened the focus put by the Federal Circuit on this test and ruled that the TSM test is not the only way to support a finding of obviousness – instead, the assessment of obviousness should also include "common sense" and take into account modern technology.[170]

The US Patent Office reflected these jurisprudential developments in its Manual of Patent Examining Procedure (MPEP), and expanded the list of factors that support an obviousness finding from the TSM test to a (non-exhaustive) list of rationales which besides the TSM test include e.g., '"obvious to try" (following KSR v. Teleflex, this amounts to choosing from a finite number of identified, predictable solutions, with a reasonable expectation of success).[171]

The last sentence of Section 103 states that the patent cannot be negated due to the way the invention was made. According to the historical and revision notes on this section, this means "it is immaterial whether it resulted from long toil and experimentation or from a flash of genius."[172] In other words, it is the outcome of

---

166 550 U.S. 398 (2007).

167 Ibid. 421 (2007): "A person of ordinary skill is also a person of ordinary creativity, not an automaton." See also Harold C. Wegner, 'Making Sense of KSR and Other Recent Patent Cases' (2007) 106 *Michigan Law Review First Impressions* 39, 41.

168 Ibid.: "In *KSR v. Teleflex*, the Supreme Court held that a patent claim may be proved obvious by "showing that the combination of elements was obvious to try. When there is a design need or market pressure to solve the problem and there are a finite number of identified, predictable solutions, a person of ordinary skill has good reason to pursue the know options within his or her technical grasp. If this leads to anticipated success, it is likely the product not of innovation but of ordinary skill and common sense. In that instance the fact that a combination was obvious to try might show that it was obvious under §103."

169 For the origins of the TSM test, see chiefly *ACS Hospital Systems, Inc. v. Montefiore Hospital*, 732 F.2d 1572, 1577 (Fed. Cir. 1984): "Obviousness cannot be established by combining the teachings of the prior art to produce the claimed invention, absent some teaching or suggestion supporting the combination. Under section 103, teachings of references can be combined only if there is some suggestion or incentive to do so. The prior art of record fails to provide any such suggestion or incentive."

170 See *KSR v. Teleflex* (n 166). See also *Sherkow* (n 150) 1118–1119.

171 USPTO, 'Manual of Patent Examining Procedure' (2019), Chapter 2143.

172 '35 U.S. Code § 103 – Conditions for patentability; Non-obvious Subject Matter' (Legal Information Institute) <www.law.cornell.edu/uscode/text/35/103> accessed 16 January 2021. See also *Pacific Contact Labs, Inc. v. Solex Labs, Inc.*, 209 F.2d 529, 532–533 (9th Circ. 1953): "[A]s we

the inventive process that is evaluated in the framework of the non-obviousness analysis. US Courts have extensively confirmed this.[173] Subjective tests – such as considering the inventor's efforts, methods or talent to come up with the invention – are thus expressly barred.[174] US patent law awards patent rights to "accidental or lucky inventors" as well.[175] The argument could then be made that inventions developed by an AI by chance (or as a result of a semi-automated process where multiple trial-and-error experiments are conducted, for example) cannot be negated by the manner in which they were made. This conclusion is reinforced by the fact that the inventor does not have to "know why the new and beneficial result was obtained"[176] – an understanding of the invention, and of how it works to solve the problem as such, is not required, which speaks in favour of the patentability of inventions that are generated by an AI system.[177]

However, some court decisions have lent some flexibility to the prohibition to negate the patent due to the way in which the invention was made. In *Brunswick Corporation v. Champion Spark Plug Company*, the Court, while recognizing that the obviousness assessment is based on objective rather than subjective factors, also states that it believes there are no "iron laws," and that therefore there are instances where the level of knowledge and awareness of the inventor should be taken into account.[178] What is important to note here is that the Court bases these findings on patent rationales, stating that "as a policy matter . . . it may be inconsistent with the goals of the patent monopoly to allow plaintiff's "teaching away" theory to defeat a claim of obviousness," adding that the "ignorance and naivete" of the inventor are "presumably not qualities which the patent monopoly is specifically designed to reward."[179] In *Pfizer, Inc. v. Apotex, Inc*, the Federal Circuit considered that the routine testing carried out by the patent owner was akin to verification of prior art results, rather than to trial and error testing aimed at discovering a new compound.[180]

---

understand it, the Congress by enacting Sec. 103 showed its fear that the meaning of the phrase 'flash of creative genius' . . . would result in excluding from patentability most if not all mechanical advances derived from study and experimentation."

173 See case law cited in *Chisum* (n 138) sec. 5.04A para 2. See in particular *Radiator Speciality Co. v. Buhot*, 39 F.2d 373, 376 (3rd Cir. 1930): "Invention is not always the offspring of genius; more frequently it is the product of plain hard work; not infrequently it arises from accident or carelessness; occasionally it is a happy thought of an ordinary mind; and there have been instances where it is the result of sheer stupidity. It is with the inventive concept, the thing achieved, not the manner of its achievement or the quality of the mind which gave it birth, that the patent law concerns itself."

174 *Duffy* (n 4) 18 and 43.

175 *Adelman and others* (n 161) 314.

176 *General Tire & Rubber Co. v. Jefferson Chem. Co.*, 497 F.2d 1283, 1291 (2nd Cir. 1974).

177 Even though, if the inventor does not have a complete understanding of the invention, challenges might arise in relation to enablement – see section 3.4.2.3.

178 *Brunswick Corp. v. Champion Spark Plug Co.*, 689 F.2d 740, 750 (7th Cir. 1982).

179 Ibid.

180 480 F.3d 1348 (2007). See also comment on this case in *Chisum* (n 138) sec. 5.04 para 2., noting that three judges in the case wrote dissenting opinions stating that the panel's decision was at odds with the last sentence of Section 103.

In *Mayo Collaborative Services v. Prometheus Laboratories, Inc.*,[181] the US Supreme Court gave as one of the reasons to invalidate a patent the fact that the claimed invention involved "well-understood, routine, conventional activity, previously engaged in by researchers in the field" – i.e., the Court focused on *how* the invention had been implemented, despite the prohibition of Section 103.[182] It is also possible to argue that the last sentence of Section 103 was intended by the US legislator to level the different inventive processes that can be undertaken by humans – not machines.[183]

3.4.2.3 *Enablement*

Section 112 of the Patent Act states that "[t]he specification shall contain a written description of the invention, and of the manner and process of making and using it, in such full, clear, concise and exact terms as to enable any person skilled in the art to which it pertains, or with which it is most nearly connected, to make and use the same, and shall set forth the best mode contemplated by the inventor or joint inventor of carrying out the invention." In a 1923 case, the Court of Appeals stated that sufficiency of disclosure should be judged against the difficulty or novelty of the art concerned, the development of that art, the kind and degree of skill which must be present to apply it, and the particular invention at stake.[184] The enablement requirement includes the "best mode requirement" mentioned in the enablement provision (the specification shall set forth the best mode contemplated by the inventor of carrying out the invention). It should be noted however that the best mode requirement refers to the best mode of making and using ("carrying out") the invention, not the inventing process behind it. The enablement requirement concerns only the invention itself, not the method of inventing it,[185] which means that in theory the applicant is not obliged to disclose that an invention was AI-generated, or that an AI has played a prominent role in the inventive process. However, in some cases it might be difficult to separate the disclosure of the invention from the disclosure of the method of inventing it. In fact, examples of factors that help assess whether an enablement is sufficient include the quantity of experimentation necessary, the amount of guidance presented in the specification, the presence or absence of working examples of the invention, the nature of the invention, the state of the prior art, the relative skill of those in the art,

181 566 U.S. 66 (2012), Docket nr. 10–1150.
182 Jacob S. Sherkow, 'And How: *Mayo v. Prometheus* and the Method of Invention' (2013) 122 *Yale Law Journal Forum* 351, 351–352.
183 Ben Hattenbach and Joshua Glucoft, 'Patents in an Era of Infinite Monkeys and Artificial Intelligence' (2015) 19 *Stanford Technology Law Review* 32, 44.
184 *A.B. Dick Co. v. Barnett*, 288 Fed. 799 (2nd Cir. 1923), as analysed in William H. Francis and others, *Cases and Materials on Patent Law, Including Trade Secrets* (7th ed., West Academic Publishing 2017) 576. See also USPTO, 'Manual of Patent Examining Procedure' (2019) section 2164.01(a).
185 *Wamsley* (n 6) 31.

or the breadth of the claims.[186] Some of these factors might indirectly require mentioning the use of an AI system – e.g., in some cases, it would be difficult to describe the quantity of experimentation necessary without disclosing the use of an AI system in the inventive process, as such use might determine how much experimentation is necessary

(that would be the case, for instance, if the invention requires a particular strain of microorganism which is only available after extensive screening performed with the help of an AI). According to the MPEP, Section 2164.01(b), following *In Re Ghiron*,[187] if the practice of a method requires a particular apparatus, the latter must be sufficiently disclosed if it is not readily available.

3.4.2.4 Inventorship

35 US Code, Section 100(f) defines the inventor as "the individual, or, if a joint invention, the individuals collectively who invented or discovered the subject matter of the invention." A few cases have been decided on this issue, and courts have clarified that states or corporations cannot be named as inventors, as the inventors are the individuals who conceive of the invention and who can perform the needed mental act.[188] Conception is indeed "the touchstone of inventorship, the completion of the mental part of the invention."[189] It implies "the formation in the mind of the inventor of a definite and permanent idea of the complete and operative invention, as it is hereafter to be applied in practice."[190] The idea will be definite and permanent when it is specific, in the sense that it presents a particular solution to the problem at hand, rather than a general goal or research plan (even though the inventor does not need to know at the conception stage that the invention will work, as that is part of its reduction to practice).[191]

What does not seem to be a valid basis for inventorship is the stage before conception, i.e., "[providing] the inventor with well-known principles or [explaining] the state of the art without ever having a firm and definite idea of the claimed combination as a whole".[192] The fact that this prior stage cannot in principle lead to inventorship is particularly relevant in the context of AI-generated inventions: it indicates that feeding the AIs information in the context of machine learning should not give rise to an inventorship claim.[193]

---

186 *In re Wands*, 858 F.2d 731, 737 (Fed. Cir. 1988).

187 442 F.2d 985, 991 (C.C.P.A. 1971).

188 *University of Utah v. Max-Planck-Gesellschaft*, 734 F.3d 1315 (Fed. Cir. 2013); *Beech Aircraft v. EDO*, 990 F.2d 1237 (Fed. Cir. 1993).

189 *Burroughs Wellcome Co. v. Barr Labs., Inc.*, 40 F.3d 1223, 1229 (Fed. Cir. 1994). See also *Fiers v. Revel*, 984 F.2d 1164, 1168 (Fed. Circ. 1993)

190 Ibid., citing *Hybritech Inc. v. Monoclonal Antibodies, Inc.*, 802 F.2d 1367, 1376, 231 USPQ 81, 87 (Fed. Cir. 1986). The Court added that "the test for conception is whether the inventor had an idea that was definite and permanent enough that one skilled in the art could understand the invention."

191 Ibid.

192 Ibid.

193 In the same sense see W. Michael Schuster, 'Artificial Intelligence and Patent Ownership' (2018) 75 *Washington and Lee Law Review* 1945, 1962: "To initiate AI invention, a person may input seed information, including existing technologies, e.g., for neural networks, or relevant parameters to

The requirement of "conception" of the invention as a threshold of inventorship is also explicitly stated in the Manual of Patenting Examining Procedure (MPEP), where Section 2137.01-II clarifies that "[t]he threshold question in determining inventorship is who conceived the invention." Further, Section 2138.04 defines conception as "the complete performance of the mental part of the inventive act," amounting to "the formation in the mind of the inventor of a definite and permanent idea."[194] The same Section states that "conception requires contemporaneous recognition and appreciation of the invention," which includes an understanding of the invention as having the features that comprise the inventive subject matter at issue.[195] This would hint that, as machines cannot as such perform a "mental act," nor can they recognize or appreciate an invention, AIs cannot be considered as inventors. Moreover, 35 US Code, Section 115 requires the inventor to submit an oath whereby he or she believes himself or herself to be the original inventor of the claimed invention. It is difficult to fathom a scenario where an AIs could actually perform this in the way that the law intended, as again AIs do not have content states such as beliefs.[196]

The exclusion of AIs from claims of inventorship was confirmed by the USPTO, which issued a petition decision explaining that only a natural person could be named as an inventor in a patent application. The decision follows an application that named DABUS, a creativity machine that produced the invention, as the inventor. The legal representative of DABUS, as well as the assignee of the right, was Stephen Thaler, who was also the inventor of DABUS.[197] According to him, the machine was not created to solve any particular problem, and it was not trained on any relevant data.[198] It had been DABUS that recognized the novelty and salience of the invention.[199] According to the USPTO, the patent statutes consistently refer to the inventors as natural persons. It is the case, e.g., of Section 101, that states that "*Whoever* invents or discovers any new and useful process, machine, manufacture or composition of matter . . . may obtain a patent therefore"(emphasis added), which suggests a natural person; or of Section 115(h)(1), which specifically refers to "any *person* making a statement."[200] The USPTO concludes that interpreting such

---

be optimized, e.g., for genetic algorithms. Such acts merely provide the AI with access to existing knowledge in the field, which Nartron held is not invention" [footnotes omitted]).

194 Referring to *Townsend v. Smith*, 36 F.2d 292, 295, 4 USPQ 269, 271 (C.C.P.A 1929).

195 See inter alia *Silvestri v. Grant*, 496 F.2d 593, 596, 181 USPQ 706, 708 (C.C.P.A 1974) and *Langer v. Kaufman*, 465 F.2d 915, 918, 175 USPQ 172, 174 (C.C.P.A 1972).

196 See *supra* section 2.2.

197 See *supra* section 3.2.

198 Commissioner for Patents of the United States Patent and Trademark Office (USPTO), 'The Decision on the Petition: Application No. 16/524,360 for Devices and Methods for Attracting Enhanced Attention' (filed January 20, 2020 under 37 CFR 1.181) <www.uspto.gov/about-us/news-updates/petition-decision-inventorship-limited-natural-persons> accessed 19 April 2021. See also supra Section 3.2.

199 Ibid.

200 Other sections referred by the USPTO are e.g., Section 115(b)(2) ("An oath or declaration under subsection (a) shall contain statements that . . . such individual believes himself or herself to be the original inventor or an original joint inventor of a claimed invention in the application"),

provisions broadly so as to cover machines would contradict the literal or plain meaning of the statutes, and go against the case law mentioned above.

One of the arguments of the applicant was that an interpretation of the statutes as denying AI inventorship would compel applicants to "name a natural person even where the person does not meet the inventorship criteria."[201] The USPTO contended that naming a natural person that did not invent or discover the subject matter of the invention would be in conflict with the patent statutes, and that therefore it was not suggested that an applicant is compelled to name a natural person that does not meet the inventorship criteria. The discussion stopped short of an in-depth look into what would happen where no natural person could be an inventor under the statutes (because no natural person would have conceived the invention).

Another issue is the possibility of the natural person having only a minor role in producing the invention. For instance, in the case of an invention that was "conceived" by an AIs (not in the anthropomorphic sense of formation of ideas in the mind of the inventor, but rather as a production derived from the operation of neural networks), but "understood" by a natural person (i.e., it is the natural person who understands the invention as having the features that comprise inventive subject matter), would it be legitimate to indicate the natural person as an inventor? Following US case law on joint inventorship,[202] the answer would probably be affirmative, provided that the contribution of that person is significant.[203,204]

Section 102(a) ("A person shall be entitled to a patent unless"), Section 116(c) ("Whenever through error a person is named in an application for patent as the inventor," or Section 185 ("Notwithstanding any other provisions of law any person, and his successors, assigns, or legal representatives, shall not receive a United States patent for an invention if that person, or his"). Note that after this book went into production, the US District Court for the Eastern District of Virginia issued a ruling upholding the USPTO's views that an AI cannot be an inventor under current patent law.

201 *The Decision on the Petition* (n 198) 6.

202 One court noted that "to claim inventorship is to claim at least some role in the final conception of that which is sought to be patented. Perhaps one need not be able to point to a specific component as one's sole idea, but one must be able to say that without his contribution to the final conception, it would have been less-less efficient, less simple, less economical, less something of benefit." (*Mueller Brass Co. v. Reading Indus.*, 352 F.Supp. 1357, 1372 (E.D.Pa.1972), aff'd, 487 F.2d 1395 (3d Cir.1973). It follows that each contributor does not have to make the same type or amount of contribution (as per *Burroughs Wellcome Co. v. Barr Labs., Inc.*, 40 F.3d 1223 (Fed. Cir. 1994) See also 35 U.S. Code 116(a)). See also *Nartron Corp. v. Schukra USA Inc.*, 558 F.3d 1352, 1353 (Fed. Cir. 2009), quoting *Pannu v. Iolab Corp.*, 155 F.3d 1344, 1351 (Fed. Cir. 1998): "a joint inventor must "contribute in some significant manner to the conception or reduction to practice of the invention [and] make a contribution to the claimed invention that is not insignificant in quality, when that contribution is measured against the dimension of the full invention."

203 It is submitted that the cases on joint inventorship could be applied here by analogy, regardless of the fact that one of the "inventors' – the AI – should not be considered as such under US patent law. In fact, the cases on joint inventorship mentioned in the previous footnote all focused on the analysis of whether *one* of the inventors (who would be the natural person in the case of an invention produced by an AI and a natural person) could have a valid claim of inventorship. This should be considered independently of the status of the other inventor (in our case, the AI system).

204 See also Noam Shemtov, 'A Study on Inventorship in Inventions Involving AI Activity' (*European Patent Office*, February 2019) 13 <http://documents.epo.org/projects/babylon/eponet.nsf/0/39

3.4.3 Australia

The Australian Patent Act (APA)[205] regulates the grant of two types of patents: standard patents and innovation patents. The standard patent is closer to the patent regime of other jurisdictions examined in this book (such as Europe), while the innovation patent has laxer patentability requirements (notably, it requires the less stringent requirement of "innovative step," instead of "inventive step"), and has a shorter period of protection (eight years). The innovation patent is also not subject to a substantive examination (although such examination will be necessary for the innovation patent to become legally enforceable).[206] As the requirements for protection, procedures and scope of each of these patents vary, that could in turn influence findings regarding the patentability of AI inventions. For example, the innovation patent is supposedly ideal for fast-innovation industries (such as the tech industry), where products are quickly superseded by newer ones on the market.[207] This in theory could bode well with the fast – and over time potentially cheaper – rate of production of AI generated inventions. It would not be far-fetched to imagine that AI-generated inventions could find a rapid and cheaper form of protection in the regime of innovation patents. However, the innovation patent is being phased out: the last day an applicant may file an innovation patent is 25 August 2021.[208] Discussions around the innovation patent become therefore rather theoretical, and will only be carried out where relevant.

The Intellectual Property Amendment Bill 2019 that mandated the phasing out of innovation patents also inserted a new Section 2A in the APA – the

---

18F57B010A3540C125841900280653/$File/Concept_of_Inventorship_in_Inventions_involving_AI_Activity_en.pdf> accessed 15 April 2021: "both at present as well as in the foreseeable future invention processes are likely to require "intellectual domination" by human actors, even if the "inventive" and "non-obvious" part was produced by an AI system." (the author bases this conclusion inter alia on case *Morse v. Porter*, 155 USPQ 280, 283 (Bd. Pat. Inter. 1965), where it is stated that a person will be the inventor "so long as he maintains intellectual domination of the work of making the invention down to the successful testing, selecting or rejecting as he goes").

205 Patents Act (1990).

206 Section 120(1A) APA.

207 As explained on 'Types of Patents' (*Australian Government Intellectual Property Office*) <www.ipaustralia.gov.au/patents/understanding-patents/types-patents#standard> accessed 6 September 2020.

208 As per the Intellectual Property Amendment (Productivity Commission Response Part 2 and Other Measures) Bill 2019, which abolishes the innovation patent. The Productivity Commission is the Australian Government's independent research and advisory body. The Government decided to abolish the innovation patent following the Productivity Commission's Report "Intellectual Property Arrangements," which recommended its abolishment on the grounds that "the innovation patent system is unlikely to provide net benefits to the Australian community or to the small and medium sized enterprises (SMEs) who are the intended beneficiaries of the system," and that "the system imposes significant costs on third parties and the broader Australian community." 'Australian Government Response to the Productivity Commission Inquiry into Intellectual Property Arrangements' (*The Department of Industry, Innovation and Science of the Australian Government*, August 2017) <www.industry.gov.au/sites/default/files/government_response_to_pc_inquiry_into_ip_august_2017.pdf?acsf_files_redirect> accessed 6 September 2020.

so-called "objects clause," which clarifies that the objective of the APA is to provide a patent system that promotes economic well-being through techno-logical innovation and dissemination of technology. The second part of the provision further adds: "In doing so, the patent system balances over time the interests of producers, owners and users of technology and the public." Accord-ing to the IP Office of Australia, this clause provides the guiding principles that can guarantee that the patent system remains flexible and fit-for-purpose over time, and it is an interpretation tool that courts can use where legislation is uncertain or ambiguous.[209] As such, this clause can also provide guidance with regard to the question of patentability of AI-generated inventions (even though it cannot alter the meaning of legislation, or reverse established precedents[210])

In order to be granted a standard patent, an invention must amount to eligible subject matter,[211] and be novel, useful, and involve an inventive step; in addition, the invention may not have been secretly used in the patent area by the patentee or by someone on his behalf or with his authority before the priority date.[212]

3.4.3.1 Patentable subject matter

Section 18(1)(a) APA establishes that an invention will be patentable if it is "a manner of manufacture within the meaning of Section 6 of the Statute of Monopolies." Section 6 of the Statute of Monopolies – an act passed by the English Parliament in 1623 and enacted in 1624 – excludes from the ban on monopolies any "manner of new manufactures" that are not "contrary to the law nor mischievous to the state by raising prices of commodities at home, or hurt of trade, or generally inconvenient." The rationale behind Section 6 was to incentivize inventions in new industry fields, and to encourage more exploita-tion of existing resources.[213]

While there is no statutory definition of "manner of new manufacture," courts have interpreted the concept rather broadly. A "manner of new manufacture" may include e.g., processes.[214] The key legal principle to decide on the ques-tion of patentable subject matter was established in the landmark case *NRDC v. Commissioner of Patents*: "Is this a proper subject of letters patent according to the principles which have been developed for the application of section 6 of the

209 'Intellectual Property Laws Amendment (Productivity Commission Response Part 2 and Other Measures) Act 2020' (*Australian Government Intellectual Property Office*) <www.ipaustralia.gov. au/about-us/public-consultations/archived-public-consultations/intellectual-property-laws-amendment-productivity-commission-response> accessed 20 September 2020.

210 Ibid. as per the Australian Government Intellectual Property Office explanation.

211 The definition of eligible subject matter can be found in Patents Act (1990), section 18 and sched-ule I, and in The Statute of Monopolies 1624, section 6 as will be explored further below.

212 Patents Act (1990), section 18.

213 Justin Pila, 'The Common Law Invention in its Original Form' (2001) 3 *Intellectual Property Quar-terly* 209, 224.

214 The possibility of "a manner of new manufacture" including processes was first established in *Crane v. Price* (1842) 1 WPC 393.

Statute of Monopolies?"[215] This gives the concept of "manner of manufacture" a rather broad and flexible scope. Courts have indeed considered that the concept develops on a case-by-case basis, and have relied on it to broach several significant phrases that further convey the meaning of the concept of "manner of manufacture," including e.g., "an artificially created state of affairs of economic significance" or "an artificially created state of affairs providing economic utility".[216] Ultimately, though, as eloquently put by the Federal Court, "[t]he approach to be taken to deciding whether a claimed method or product is properly the subject of letters patent must be flexible and must allow for new technologies presently unknown."[217] The APA however restricts this flexibility to a (very) limited extent – for standard patents, Section 18(2) prescribes that human beings and biological processes for their generation are not patentable inventions.

The requirement to not be contrary to the law is now expressed in the APA as well, in Section 50(1)(a).[218] Patent examiners are however supposed to only refuse to accept a patent under Section 50(1)(a) "in the clearest of circumstances."[219] Case law has interpreted "contrary to the law" to mean that either the primary use of the invention would amount to a criminal act, or that its use would be an offence because of its prohibition under current laws and regulations.[220] The Australian Patent Office Manual has further added that objections under Section 50(1)(a) "should only be taken where an unlawful use, but no lawful use, of an invention has been disclosed."

It is also not clear when an invention will be "generally inconvenient" so as to not be considered patentable subject matter. Possibly, it refers to a broad public benefit test, whereby an invention that was not in the public interest would be contrary to the act (and would therefore not be patentable subject matter).[221] This might impose a test that requires patents to be in line with the policy objectives of the patent system.[222]

In Australia, the exception of "generally inconvenient" has mainly been discussed in relation to methods of medical treatment for humans and isolated genes, with courts normally being reluctant to deny patentability on grounds of general inconvenience.[223] Some case law on general inconvenience as a bar

---

215 *NRDC v. Commissioner of Patents* (1959) 102 CLR 252, 269.

216 Mark J. Davison and others, *Australian Intellectual Property Law* (4th ed., Cambridge University Press 2020) sections 10.4.2–10.4.3., and references cited therein.

217 *Research Affiliates LLC v. Commissioner of Patents* [2014] FCAFC 150, para 116.

218 Note that Patents Act (1990), section 50 lists other grounds on which the office may refuse to accept a patent application namely if the specification claims as an invention a substance that is capable of being used as food or medicine, and is a mere mixture of known ingredients, or a process producing such a substance by mere admixture (Section 50 (1)(b)).

219 Australian Patent Office, *Patent Manual of Practice and Procedure*, Section 2.9.3.1.

220 *Official Rulings* (1923) RPC 40, appendix iv.

221 Chris Dent, '"Generally Inconvenient": The 1624 *Statute of Monopolies* as Political Compromise' (2009) 33 *Melbourne University Law Review* 415, 446.

222 Ibid., 453.

223 *Davison and others* (n 216) section 10.5, and references cited therein.

to patentability seemed to equate it to a need to consider the interests of other members of the public.[224] However, in *Rescare* – a case concerning a method for treating sleep apnoea decided by the Full Bench of the Federal Court of Australia – Wilcox J pointed out that courts have no particular expertise on issues of ethics and social policy, and if the legislator chose not to include such exceptions in patent law, it should not be the courts' role to apply them.[225] A similar observation on the role of courts vis-à-vis that of the legislator was made in the *Bristol-Myers* case, where it is stated: "[i]n my opinion, medical treatment and surgical process are patentable under the legislation and, if public policy requires a different result, it is for the Parliament to amend the 1990 Act."[226] In a nutshell, even though courts have the power to consider whether an invention is generally inconvenient, they seem unwilling to exercise that power where matters of complex policy are involved if they can resort to other grounds for rejecting a patent.[227]

To date, no patent has been invalidated by having these grounds has a primary basis for invalidity.[228] Because it is unclear what "generally inconvenient" really amounts to, the Australian Patent Office Manual even urges examiners to "refrain from taking this objection."[229]

The requirements that the invention be a new manner of manufacture and not contrary to the law do not bring any added difficulty for AI-generated inventions to be considered as patentable subject matter. The same can be said of the requirement not to be generally inconvenient, with the added argument that there seems to be little political and/or institutional will to operationalise the latter. Eventually, if e.g., an invention complies with all patentability requirements but was easily and autonomously produced by an AI system, one could argue that granting a patent would be contrary to the goals of the patent system, as there is no incentive needed for producing more inventions – the machine does not respond to incentives, and the humans using it already have a machine that can invent (almost) effortlessly, which makes the benefit/cost analysis for producing new products an easy equation to solve. However, judging from past examples mentioned above, it does not look like this argument would be looked into by the Australian Patent Office or by courts.

3.4.3.2 *Inventive step*

The Productivity Commission – Australian Government's independent research and advisory body – found in its 2016 Inquiry Report that Australia provides stronger patent rights than other advanced economies, and that many

---

224 See e.g., *Rolls-Royce Ltd's. Application* [1963] RPC 251, a case from the United Kingdom Patent Appeals Court concerning a method of operating an aircraft to reduce noise, where the court considered that granting the patent would be adding to the pilot's burden.

225 *Anaesthetic Supplies Pty. Ltd. v. Rescare Ltd* [1994] FCA 304.

226 *Bristol-Myers Squibb Co. v. FH Faulding & Co. Ltd* (2000) 97 FCR 524 [142].

227 *Davison and others* (n 216) section 10.5, and references cited therein.

228 Australian Patent Office, *Patent Manual of Practice and Procedure*, section 2.9.3.3.

229 Ibid.

low-value patents were burdensome for innovators – both factors being costly for Australia.[230] According to the Commission, one of the reasons for this scenario is a more lenient inventive step threshold when compared with e.g., the EU. The Commission was especially concerned with the fact that, in Australia, the standard required for an invention to advance the prior art was a mere "scintilla of inventiveness."[231] Therefore, the recommendation of the Commission was that the inventive step be raised.[232] These findings were despite the fact that, just a few years before, the APA had already been amended,[233] and the inventive step threshold had already increased through the reform of a couple of definitions, as shall be seen below.

Assessing whether an invention involves an inventive step requires determination of whether the invention would have been obvious to a person skilled in the relevant art in light of the common general knowledge as it existed before the priority date.[234] Australian courts have defined the term "obvious" as something which is "perfectly evident to the person thinking on the subject" or "very plain."[235]

Like other IP offices, the IP Office of Australia uses a problem–solution approach to assess whether an invention complies with the inventive step requirement. The approach is comprised of a series of elaborate steps:

1   Determine the problem that the claimed invention solves
2   Identify the person skilled in the art in the field of the problem
3   Determine, where applicable, whether in the context of the problem, any pieces of prior art information under consideration are such that the person skilled in the art could be reasonably expected to have combined them
4   Determine the relevant common general knowledge
5   Determine whether, in the context of the problem, the claimed invention is: a technical equivalent; a workshop improvement; an obvious selection

---

230 See Productivity Commission 2016, 'Intellectual Property Arrangements' *(Inquiry Report nr. 78,* September 2016) 13ff. <www.pc.gov.au/inquiries/completed/intellectual-property/report/intellectual-property-overview.pdf> accessed 20 September 2020.

231 See e.g., *Samuel Parkes & Co. Ld. v. Cocker Brothers Ld.* (1929) 46 RPC 241; *Meyers Taylor Pty. Ltd. v. Vicarr Industries Ltd.* (1977) 137 CLR 228

232 *Productivity Commission 2016.* Interestingly, the Commission also noted that "[m]easures of patent quality suggest that thresholds in the US and EU fall short of the ideal, and so are not sufficiently high benchmarks." However, the Commission cautioned against raising the inventive step threshold above that of other countries: "Going further and significantly raising the threshold above the level applied in other countries would, however, entail risks. Such endeavour is best pursued in collaboration with like-minded countries."

233 This was the so-called *Raising the Bar Act 2012*, which went into full effect on 15 April 2013.

234 Patents Act 1990, section 7(2) and Australian Patent Office, *Patent Manual of Practice and Procedure*, section 2.5.1.3. Compare with the (much) less stringent requirement of innovative step for innovation patents, in Section 7(4) APA: an invention will not involve an innovative step if it only varies from the information in the prior art base in ways that make *no substantial contribution to the working of that invention.*

235 *Olin Mathieson v. Biorex* [1970] RPC 157, 188.; *General Tire & Rubber Company v. Firestone Tyre and Rubber Company Ltd* [1972] RPC 457, 497.

or special inducement; or an obvious combination of features of common general knowledge

6   Consider whether: the prior art information teaches away from the solution; the invention overcomes practical difficulties in seeking the solution; the invention resides in identifying the "real nature" of the problem

7   If relevant, consider whether there has been a prior perceived need using the tests of: long felt need; failure of others; copying of invention in preference to prior art; commercial success[236]

In practice, an invention will not pass the inventive step threshold if steps 3 and 5 are met, while steps 6 and 7 speak in favour of a compliance with the inventive step.[237] Further, the Australian Patent Office Manual clarifies that it is not necessary to carry out a detailed analysis of every issue in each procedural step, but only of the relevant ones to the particular invention being examined.[238] The lines that follow will examine the steps of the problem-solution approach deemed more relevant to the question of patentability of AI-generated inventions.

In relation to step 2, the person skilled in the art in the field of the problem is identified in light of the problem to be solved, not in light of the solution. This hypothetical person is not an inventive person, but one with ordinary skills in the relevant field, with common general knowledge that is typically available to all such persons in that field.[239] The person skilled in the art (or persons, given that the "person skilled in the art" can be a team) has a practical interest in the subject matter of the invention.[240] The art includes any related field of technology where the skilled person would be expected to look for a solution to the problem, so it does not include remote fields, as the person skilled in the art is not inventive.[241] In a case concerning an artificial sweetener composition, the Federal Court of Australia considered that the person skilled in the art was a team that together had a rudimentary knowledge of chemistry, some skills of a food technologist, an understanding of the sensory evaluation of foods, and some appreciation of the commercial use and application of artificial sweeteners.[242] It is therefore possible that the "person skilled in the art" is a team that comprises specialists in more than one art. Usually, the person skilled in the art will be a team where it is normal in the field in question to have a team working together.[243] The person skilled in the art is also supposed to have the best available equipment.[244]

---

236 Australian Patent Office, *Patent Manual of Practice and Procedure*, section 2.5.1.6A.

237 Ibid.

238 Ibid.

239 Ibid, section 2.5.2.4.A. See also *H Lundbeck A/S v. Alphapharm Pty. Ltd.* (2009) 177 FCR 151.

240 *NutraSweet Australia Pty. Ltd. v. Ajinomoto Co. Inc* (2005) 224 ALR 200 [28].

241 Australian Patent Office, *Patent Manual of Practice and Procedure*, section 2.5.2.4.

242 Ibid.

243 *Davison and others* (n 216) section 10.8.2., referring to *General Tire & Rubber Co v. Firestone Tyre & Rubber Co. Ltd* (1972) RPC 457, 485; *ICI Chemicals & Polymers Ltd. v. Lubrizol Corp Inc* (2000) 106 FCR 214 [61].

244 *Davison and others* (n 216) section 10.8.2., referring to *Genentech Inc v. Wellcome Foundation Ltd* [1989] RPC 147, 278 (Mustill LJ), 241 (Dillon J).

Step 3 – determining whether the person skilled in the art would be reasonably expected to combine pieces of prior art information – is, by its nature, entirely dependent on the notion of "person skilled in the art" as defined above, and in that sense poses interesting questions to AI-generated inventions. This step involves ascertaining whether the nature and content of the documents combined make it likely or unlikely for the person skilled in the art to combine them; the closeness or distance of the fields where the documents originate from; or whether the art would have taught away from the combination (because, e.g., the documents seemed inherently incompatible).[245] However, the default position of the office is, if there is a combination of documents, lack of inventive step will arise only where there is a suggestion or motivation (either in the documents themselves or in the knowledge available to the person skilled in the art) to combine the disclosures of the documents; if that motivation is not immediately apparent, it is up to the examiner to provide a reasoned argument as to why the disclosures may be combined.[246] The problem is that an AI could, more easily than a human, combine disclosures from seemingly incompatible or distant fields. In such a case, it could be easier to obtain a patent should the use of an AI for that purpose not be disclosed in the patent application, and/or should the examiner not have access to the same technology. The "default position" in those situations would be a(n) (easy) compliance with at least this step in the process. This scenario would be reinforced by other circumstances that the examiner may consider,[247] such as the number of documents to be combined (an AI is able to combine a higher number of documents than a human, thus increasing the impression that the person skilled in the art would not be able to combine them); or the fact that the combination would involve a change to the principle of operation of any of the elements of the combination (an AI is, by its nature, less prone to be constrained by previous, sometimes biased, knowledge frameworks).

The definition of common general knowledge (step 4) has been put forth by Aickin J. in *Minnesota Mining & Manufacturing Co. v. Beiersdorf (Australia) Limited*: "The notion of common general knowledge itself involves the use of that which is known or used by those in the relevant trade. It forms the background knowledge and experience which is available to all in the trade in considering the making of new products, or the making of improvements in old, and it must be treated as being used by an individual as a general body of knowledge."[248] The scope of "common general knowledge" has been expanding over time – namely, since the *Raising the Bar Act*, it is no longer limited to knowledge existing in Australia. In a recent case, the court found that common general knowledge "must be generally accepted and assimilated by the person skilled in the art and known and accepted without question by the bulk of those

---

245 Australian Patent Office, *Patent Manual of Practice and Procedure*, section 2.5.2.5.5A.
246 Ibid., section 2.5.2.5.6.
247 Ibid.
248 *Minnesota Mining & Manufacturing Co v.* Beiersdorf (Australia) Limited (1980) 144 CLR 253, 292.

who are engaged in the particular art."[249] Those "engaged in the particular art" of the invention set the tone of what "common general knowledge" amounts to: as explained in another case, "if the field is occupied by practical tradesmen, rather than scientists, claims to an invention should be considered against the background of that field, not of some unreal field peopled by a technological elite. What must be taken into account is the common general knowledge and the skill of the relevant calling".[250] It is therefore important to assess the context of the field, which could be updated to read that it is important to consider the use (or lack thereof) of AI in generating inventions in that field.

In step 5, the examiner is supposed to determine whether, in the context of the problem, the claimed invention is: a technical equivalent; a workshop improvement; an obvious selection or special inducement; or an obvious combination of features of common general knowledge. As mentioned, any of these factors will support a finding of obviousness/lack of inventive step. The last two factors deserve a mention. There will be an obvious selection or special inducement where a problem has several possible solutions and the person skilled in the art would inevitably have chosen that solution or that particular selection over others.[251] Special inducements occur when the prior art or the common general knowledge teach towards the solution, or when the other solutions are impractical.[252] Likewise, where the invention has a particular combination of features, it will lack inventive step if the combination is obvious to the person skilled in the art having regard to the common general knowledge.[253] In all these cases, a selection or a combination might not be obvious to a person skilled in the art considering that the latter is a human without access to an AI that can automate or facilitate the inventive process, or generate the solution itself. Conversely, if the person skilled in the art is considered to use an AI (or if it is considered that the person skilled in the art is the AI itself), the selection or combination might be deemed obvious due to the heightened capabilities of an AI and its impact on the inventive process.

Steps 6 and 7 of the Australian problem-solution approach aggregate factors that support a finding of inventive step. Of these, some are relevant to the issue of AI-generated inventions. For instance, the fact that the identification of the real nature of the problem will speak in favour of a finding of inventive step. This occurs when a problem is known, but its cause unknown. An invention that identifies the cause of the problem (the "real nature" of the problem) has, under this factor, more probability of meeting the inventive step requirement.[254] In situations where an AI with a high processing power is used, it is possible that finding

---

249 *Idenix Pharmaceuticals LLC v. Gilead Sciences Pty. Ltd.* [2017] FCAFC 196 [192].

250 *Davison and others* (n 216) section 10.8.3., referring to *Leonardis v. Sartas No. 1 Pty. Ltd.* (1996) 67 FCR 126, 146.

251 Australian Patent Office, *Patent Manual of Practice and Procedure*, section 2.5.3.4.

252 Ibid.

253 Ibid., section 2.5.3.5.

254 Ibid., section 2.5.3.6.

the cause of a problem will be made trivial or at least much easier, simply because of the sheer number of experiments that such a machine can run in comparison to a human being. That is, this is one factor where an AI, or a human being using an AI, might have a clear advantage in the inventive step assessment.

3.4.3.3 *Disclosure*

Provisional and complete patent specifications must "disclose the invention in a manner which is clear enough and complete enough for the invention to be performed by a person skilled in the relevant art."[255] Complete patent specifications must moreover "disclose the best method known to the applicant of performing the invention."[256] Failure to comply with these criteria is grounds for opposition or revocation of the patent.[257]

The requirement to the disclose the invention clearly and completely enough for it to be performed by the person skilled in the art is similar to what is found in other jurisdictions, namely in Europe. This is not surprising, given that the express intention of the *Raising the Bar Act*, which introduced the current wording of Section 40(2)(a), was indeed to give the provision the same effect as the corresponding provisions of the European Patent Convention and UK legislation, to the extent possible.[258]

Sufficient disclosure of the invention entails that sufficient information is provided to enable the whole width of the claimed invention to be performed by the skilled person without undue burden, or the need for further invention.[259] There isn't much guidance in Australian case law on what is "undue burden," and therefore the Australian Patent Office relies on decisions in the UK and Europe to formulate principles in that regard.[260]

As for disclosing the best method of performing the invention, such assessment is a matter of fact that must be done "in a practical and common sense manner."[261] The extent of the best method obligation therefore varies depending on the concrete circumstances of a given case, such as the qualifications, knowledge and capabilities attributed to the notional skilled addressee, the importance of the information in question, the practicality of disclosing it, and the extent of the burden imposed on the skilled addressee.[262] So, for instance,

255 Patents Act 1990, sections 40(1) and 40(2)(a).
256 Ibid., section 40(2)(aa).
257 Ibid., sections 59(c) & 138(3)(f), respectively.
258 'Explanatory Memorandum: Intellectual Property Laws Amendment (*Raising the Bar*) Act 2011 (Cth)' (The Parliament of the Commonwealth of Australia 2011), schedule 1, item 8: "The intention is that paragraph 40(2)(a) be given, as close as is practicable, the same effect as the corresponding provisions of UK legislation and the European Patent Convention."
259 Ibid.
260 Australian Patent Office, *Patent Manual of Practice and Procedure*, section 2.11.3.4.3A.
261 *GlaxoSmithKline Consumer Healthcare Investments (Ireland) (No 2) Limited v. Generic Partners Pty. Limited* [2018] FCAFC 71 [187].
262 Ibid. [190], [192].

in a case concerning an extension drilling system on a semi-automatic drilling rig, the court determined that a key aspect of the best method of performing the invention was an adequate water seal, even though the seal was not part of the invention described in the specification.[263] This could lead to an interpretation of disclosure that would entail an obligation to disclose the use of an AI in the making of an invention – with potential consequences to the assessment of inventive step derived therefrom. However, disclosing the method of manufacture of a product invention seems to only be necessary when the method is material to the advantages arguably brought by the invention; when the additional details concern the applicant's own manufacturing methods and are irrelevant for the purposes of describing the best method known of performing the invention, disclosure of those manufacturing methods does not seem to be mandatory under the best method obligation.[264] As a consequence, if an AI is involved in the manufacture of an invention for reasons of making the process easier, faster, or cheaper, the disclosure of its use is likely not mandatory in light of the best method obligation. Conversely, the applicant might have to disclose the use of an AI in the inventive process should that use have an impact on advantages that the applicant claims the invention to have.

3.4.3.4 Inventorship

Section 15 APA defines who may be granted a patent: the inventor; a third person who is either entitled to have the patent assigned to him/her, or that derives title to the invention from the inventor or from such assignee; or the legal representative of any of the former. The act does not define "inventor," even though the wording of Section 15 points to a human being.[265] A "person," in Australian law, means any legal person, including a body politic (e.g., Commonwealth of Australia) and a body corporate (i.e., a company, as well as an individual.[266] Each patent applicant must be a "person" for purposes of Section 15 APA and, unless a person is mentioned in that provision, that person has no entitlement to the patent.[267] Because AI systems cannot be considered a "person," bar a change in the current law AI systems should not be able to be named as inventors.[268]

Courts support this interpretation: under current case law in Australia, an invention necessarily involves *human* intervention.[269] Case law has also clarified

---

263 See *Davison and others* (n 216) section 10.13.7.2, referring to case *Sandvik Intellectual Property AB v. Quarry Mining & Construction Equipment Pty. Ltd* (2017) 126 IPR 427, paras. 125–126.

264 Ibid., section 10.13.7.2 and case law cited therein.

265 Patents Act (1990), section 15 and its references to "person," "he or she," or "Australian citizen."

266 Acts Interpretation Act (1901) (Cth), section 2C(1). See also Australian Patent Office, *Patent Manual of Practice and Procedure*, section 2.6.1.1.

267 *Polwood Pty. Ltd. v. Foxworth Pty. Ltd.* [2008] FCAFC 9 [54].

268 Note however that, under Patents Act 1990, section 22A, a patent is not invalid merely because it was granted to a person who is not entitled, or not granted to a person who is entitled.

269 *Research Affiliates LLC v. Commissioner of Patents* [2014] FCAFC 150 [116], where the court refers to the need of understanding "what has been the work of, the output of, and the result of, human

that the inventor will be the one who makes a material contribution to the invention.[270] In a case concerning the question of joint inventorship, the Federal Court of Australia decided that the contribution should be to the conception of the invention, which is the *"formation in the mind of the inventor, of a definite and permanent idea of the complete and operative invention, as it is hereafter to be applied in practice."*[271] As argued in relation to other jurisdictions that have similar rules,[272] because machines do not "conceive" an invention in this sense, AI systems cannot be considered as inventors.[273]

3.4.4 Japan

The requirements for patentability in Japan are similar to the previous jurisdictions, i.e., in order to be patentable an invention must be new, industrially applicable, and non-obvious (which in Japanese law is formulated as not being able to easily make the invention).[274]

Next to the regular patent regime, Japan grants protection to certain small innovations of devices through the utility model regime, regulated in the Utility Model Act.[275] The utility model protects devices related to the shape or structure of an article or combination of articles, has a lower threshold of inventive step or non-obviousness, and lasts for a shorter period of time (10 years) when compared to patents. The process of examination is also different from that of a patent, as it does not comprise substantive examination. As argued in relation to the Australian innovation patent, since the requirements for protection, procedures and scope of the utility model are less strict than those of the patent regime, utility models might be relevant to the issue of protection of AI-generated innovations. Therefore, in addition to an analysis of patentable subject matter (section 3.4.4.1), inventive step/non-obviousness (section 3.4.4.2), disclosure/enablement (section 3.4.4.3), and inventorship (section 3.4.4.4),

---

ingenuity" when assessing whether an invention constitutes patentable subject matter; *D'Arcy v. Myriad Genetics Inc* [2014] FCAFC 115 [11]: "human intervention that creates an artificial state of affairs that has some discernible effect is essential."

270 *University of Western Australia v Gray* (2009) 179 FCR 346 [248].

271 *Polwood v. Foxworth* (n 267) [48], and earlier case law cited therein.

272 See Chapter 3 section 3.4.2.4.

273 Note however that some academic commentators support a positive change in current law to accommodate AI as inventors – see Nick Li and Tzeyi Koay, 'Artificial Intelligence and Inventorship: An Australian Perspective' (2020) 15 *Journal of Intellectual Property Law and Practice* 399. Also, after this book went into production, the Federal Court of Australia ruled (on 30 July 2021) that an AI system (DABUS, in the specific case) could be named as inventor in the patent application. However, as pointed out by commentators, this decision "was mostly based on unverified assumptions regarding the technical capabilities of AI systems in general and DABUS in particular", among other shortcomings – see Daria Kim et al., 'Artificial Intelligence Systems as Inventors? A Position Statement of 7 September 2021 in View of the Evolving Case-Law Worldwide' (2021).<https://papers.ssrn.com/sol3/papers.cfm?abstract_id=3919588> accessed 29 September 2021.

274 Patent Act No. 121 (1959) (hereinafter, "JPA"), Article 29.

275 Act 123 (1959).

section 3.4.4.5 will focus on the regime of utility models in Japan as a potential route of protection of AI-generated innovations.

3.4.4.1 Patentable subject matter

The JPA defines invention as "the highly skilled advanced creation of technical ideas utilizing the laws of nature" (Article 2 (1)). An "invention" will be completed through several steps: (1) establishing the technical problem to be solved; (2) employing technical means to solve the problem; (3) confirming that the technical configuration produces an effect that contributes to achieving the goal.[276]

The reference to laws of nature means that an invention must embody the principle of cause and effect that is usually inherent to a natural phenomenon (i.e., the invention must be repeatable). Courts have in the past narrowly interpreted "laws of nature" to mean "the production of objects," but have meantime abandoned it.[277] Moreover, several revisions of the guidelines of the Japanese Patent Office have lent increasing flexibility to the interpretation of the term "invention,"[278] and academics have also warned that the requirement "laws of nature" should be interpreted flexibly in order to not leave out of the concept of invention new developments in technology.[279]

A few court decisions have also ruled that it is not necessary for the patentee to understand the causal or theoretical relation between the cause and effect for an invention to be considered as such.[280]

The broad interpretation of "laws of nature," combined with the fact that the patentee does not need to fully understand the theoretical underpinnings of the invention (which might be the case in some AI-generated innovations), seem to indicate that there is no *prima facie* reason for AI-generated innovations not to be considered as inventions under the JPA.

3.4.4.2 Inventive step/non-obviousness

The Japanese standard for non-obviousness has its roots in the US patent system,[281] even though the concrete formulation of the standard in the law bears

---

276 Mizuki Hashiguchi, 'The Global Artificial Intelligence Revolution Challenges Patent Eligibility' (2017) 13 *J Bus & Tech* 11, 24 and references cited therein.

277 Ibid. 34 and references cited therein.

278 Ibid.

279 As explained by Nobuhiro Nakayama, *Patent Law* (2nd ed., Koubundou Publishers 2012) 98–107.

280 See in particular Tokyo District Court judgment *Mutai Saishu* (October 29, 1987), as referenced by *Nakayama* (n 279) 101.

281 Tomotaka Homma, 'Comparing Japanese and US standards of Obviousness: Providing Meaningful Guidance after KSR' (2008) 48 *IDEA* 449, 452: "[J]apanese patent law copied US patent law's obviousness requirement in a 1959 amendment because the US was the only jurisdiction that included obviousness as one of the requirements for patentability in its examination procedure." Note however that the Japanese standard for obviousness/inventive step was considered to be

differences to its American counterpart. Should there be an invention according to Article 2(1) JPA, Article 29(2) JPA prescribes that a patent shall not be granted where, prior to the filing of the patent application, a person ordinarily skilled in the art would have been able to easily make the invention. This implies following a step-by-step methodology. The examiner must (1) identify the claimed invention; (2) identify one or more prior art relevant to the claimed invention; (3) select the closest prior art (also called "primary prior art"), compare that prior art and the claimed invention, and find similarities and differences; (4) evaluate the differences: determine the reasons for denying inventive step, based on the content of the selected prior art or other relevant prior art (also called "secondary prior art"), and the common general knowledge.[282]

The identification of the claimed invention (step 1) is made based on the claims, even though the examiner can take the description, drawings and common general knowledge into account for purposes of interpreting the claims.[283]

The relevant prior art to be compared with the claimed invention (steps 2 and 3) is selected from the valid prior art as defined by Article 29(1) JPA: inventions publicly known or publicly worked before the filing date, and inventions that were described in a distributed publication, or made publicly available before that date. The relevant art of a given invention is to be decided on a case-by-case basis taking into account the elements of the invention (e.g., its constitution, purpose or effects).[284] In principle, the relevant art will include the so-called "adjacent art," as the Examination Guidelines of the JPO states that all technical matters in the field relevant to the problem should be considered.[285] Just as pointed out in relation to other jurisdictions, an AI would probably be more capable of using prior art elements from distant technical fields, with the result that something that could be considered adjacent or relevant following an AI intervention would not be necessarily so for a human being not using an AI system to invent.

The reasoning that follows (step 4) evaluates the differences between the invention and the prior art and it is based on several factors – some which support the inexistence of inventive step, and others that, by contrast, indicate such existence.[286] One relevant factor that supports the inexistence of inventive step is the motivation or suggestion derived from prior art to combine or modify certain elements therein. This particular factor comprises a few points that the

stricter than the non-obviousness requirement in the US – see Shoichi Okuyama, 'Patent Prosecution and Patentability Requirements: Recent Intellectual Property High Court Decisions in Japan on Inventive Step', in Schüßler-Langeheine and Hansen (eds.), *Patent Practice in Japan and Europe: Liber Amicorum for Guntram Rahn* (Kluwer Law International 2011) 157, 158.

282 *WIPO Secretariat of the Standing Committee on the Law of Patents* (n 141) 14.; Japan Patent Office, *Examination Guidelines for Patent and Utility Model in Japan*, Part III, Chapter 2, sections 2.3 and 3.

283 Ibid., section 3.2.

284 *Nakayama* (n 279) 135.

285 *WIPO Secretariat of the Standing Committee on the Law of Patents* (n 141) 7.

286 Japan Patent Office, *Examination Guidelines for Patent and Utility Model in Japan*, Part III, Chapter 2, section 2.3. See also *Abraham* (n 165) 531.

examiner must consider to reach a decision, among which the similarity or relation of technical fields, the similarity of problems to be solved, the similarity of operations or functions, and the suggestions shown in the content of the prior art[287] – all indications that a person ordinarily skilled in the art would be led ("motivated") to apply or combine elements from the prior art to make the invention. Also here, the use of an AI system in the inventive process becomes relevant, as such use might approximate technical fields, problems and operations or functions, with the consequence that the prior art might then contain suggestions that would motivate a combination of elements (and lead to a finding of obviousness should that AI use be disclosed).

If the examiner finds that it would not be possible for a person skilled in the art to arrive at the claimed invention from the available prior art, the invention will be deemed to have inventive step. If on the other hand the examiner determines that it is possible to reason that a person skilled in the art would easily arrive at the claimed invention, then further enquiries are necessary and the examiner must comprehensively assess several factors that might support the existence of an inventive step, among which advantageous effects of the claimed invention as compared to the prior art, or the existence of obstructive factors that could stand in the way of an application of secondary prior art to primary prior art (i.e., factors that would make an otherwise obvious combination of prior art non-obvious).[288] The advantageous effects factor might be of particular relevance to AI-generated inventions. The effects are considered advantageous when the invention has an unexpected effect of a different nature from, or significantly superior to, that of the prior art.[289] Because AI systems are capable of processing more data, and with the increased research capabilities that come with it, it is possible that the effects of a given invention generated by an AI system go beyond what a person skilled in the art would have expected given the state of the art.

After this enquiry, the examiner is to make her final assessment of whether or not the skilled person would easily make the invention, i.e., whether or not the claimed invention involves an inventive step. Apart from the described methodology, other considerations can also be taken into account when assessing the inventive step requirement. Indicators of the existence of inventive step include situations where the problem to be solved by the claimed invention is novel and inconceivable by a person skilled in the art, and cases of commercial success and long-felt need (even though the latter may only be considered if

---

287 See at length Japan Patent Office, *Examination Guidelines for Patent and Utility Model in Japan*, Part III, Chapter 2, section 2.3.
288 Ibid.; *Abraham* (n 165) 532.
289 Ibid., which also contains the following example: "The claimed invention relates to motilin which has a specific amino acid sequence, shows six to nine times more active than the motilin of the prior art, and has advantageous effects in increasing intestinal motility. Where such effects exceed what is predictable based on the state of the art at the time of filing, these effects are factors in support of the existence of an inventive step."

such facts are due to the technical features of the invention and not to other factors such as advertising and marketing techniques).[290]

Like other jurisdictions, the assessment is made from the perspective of "a person ordinarily skilled in the art," who is defined as a person who: has common general knowledge of inventions in the technical field of the claimed invention; is able to use ordinary technical means for research and development; is able to exercise ordinary creativity in selecting materials and changing designs; and is able to understand all the matter in the state of the art in the technical field of the claimed invention, as well as all technical matters in the field relevant to the problems to be solved by the invention.[291]

The Intellectual Property High Court has clarified that, in order to reach a finding that the person skilled in the art could have made the invention, it is necessary that there is a suggestion that she must have attempted to do it with the intention of "reaching the characteristics of the invention."[292] It has been pointed out that this bears some resemblance to the EPO's could-would approach and to the US TSM test.[293] It is telling however that the person skilled in the art should have the *intention* of reaching the characteristics of the invention, as it seems that not only the definition of invention, but also this patentability requirement, are at odds with arbitrariness in the inventive process. Moreover, the same Court has pointed out that "easily making the invention" may refer additionally to "easily setting the problem to be solved" (since, according to the court, if it was easy to adopt a solution to a problem, but "uniqueness can be found in the setting or viewpoint of the problem to be solved," the invention might have an inventive step) – which incidentally obliges the examiner to accurately identify the specific problem to be solved.[294] Under this decision, more inventions – including AI-generated inventions – could be able to pass the patentability hurdle, provided that the problem to be solved is not easily defined by the person skilled in the art. However, this apparently laxer standard set by the Intellectual Property High Court might be offset by a few decisions that place emphasis on the *effort* put in by the inventor in coming up with the invention: the court has specifically linked "significant effort"[295] in conceiving the invention with a finding that such invention could not have been easily made by the person skilled in the art. This might indicate

290 Ibid. and *Nakayama* (n 279) 137.

291 Japan Patent Office, *Examination Guidelines for Patent and Utility Model in Japan*, Part III, Chapter 2, section 2.3.

292 "Circuit-connecting Member" case (Intellectual Property High Court, No. 10096 (*Gyo-Ke*), January 28, 2009).

293 Takanori Abe and Keishi Yoshkawa, 'Japan: Hindsight Excluded in Inventive Step' (*ManagingIP*, 2013) <www.managingip.com/Article/3284653/Japan-Hindsight-excluded-in-inventive-step.html> accessed 13 May 2021.

294 "Exhaust Fan Filter" case (Intellectual Property High Court, No. 10075 (*Gyo-Ke), January 31, 2011).

295 See e.g., Intellectual Property High Court judgment *Gyo-Ke* 10186, (March 21, 2017) ("Friction heat-based thermochromic writing implement" case) and Intellectual Property High Court judgment *Gyo-Ke* 10111 (January 28, 2013).

that a special or high level of effort is a factor to be taken into account when assessing the inventive step requirement in Japan, which is relevant in case the inventing effort needed to satisfy the inventive step requirement mainly originates from an AI and not from the patent applicant.

3.4.4.3 Disclosure

Japan also prescribes an obligation that the description of the invention contains in its detailed explanation a statement "clear and sufficient as to enable any person ordinarily skilled in the art to which the invention pertains to work the invention."[296] This enablement requirement means that disclosure should be sufficient for the invention to be carried out, i.e., produced and used.[297] The previous version of this provision stated that the detailed explanation of the invention must state the purpose, composition and effects of the invention in a manner sufficient for the invention to be easily carried out by a person having ordinary skill in the art to which the invention pertains. The law was changed to align Japanese law with other countries and to make it more technology-neutral, but it is argued that the amendment did not change the original function of the provision – to enable the disclosure of the invention.[298] The Examination Guidelines of the JPO also clarify that the description must state "specific features" of the product such as its structure, and may also describe its function, characteristics, etc.

The JPO has issued a reference document entitled "Case examples pertinent to AI technology" which complements the Examination Guidelines and which include further instructions for examination procedures of AI related technology.[299] These instructions relate however to the patentability of AI technology itself, or to inventions where AI is applied, and not to outcomes created by or through AI technologies.[300]

3.4.4.4 Inventorship

The JPA does not contain a provision that defines inventorship. From a few court decisions, however, it is possible to derive the scope of the concept. Only a person involved in the part of the invention that distinguishes it from the prior art can be considered an inventor under Japanese law.[301] That is, only the person

---

296 The JPA, Article 36(4)(i).

297 1 *Nakayama* (n 279) 190.; Japan Patent Office, *Examination Guidelines for Patent and Utility Model in Japan*, Part II, Chapter 1, sections 1.2–1.3.

298 Japan Patent Office, *Kōgyō Shoyūken Hō Chikujō Kaisetsu* [Dai 16 Han] (Industrial Property Laws Section-by-Section Summary [16th ed.]) (Japan Institute of Invention and Innovation, 2001), translation by the Institute of Intellectual Property, commentary on Section 36.

299 'Case Examples Pertinent to AI-related Technology' (Japanese Patent Office) <www.jpo.go.jp/e/system/laws/rule/guideline/patent/document/ai_jirei_e/jirei_e.pdf> accessed 13 May 2021.

300 This was confirmed to the author by patent attorneys Gai Matsushita and Seigo Suzuki in relation to the previous version of the reference document and continues to be the case.

301 *Fine Granule Medicine v. Pfeizer* (Tokyo District Court, No. 7196 (Wa) 2001, August 27, 2002).

involved in the inventive process that will lead to the completion of creation of technical ideas should be deemed the inventor.[302] The basis for a claim of inventorship is thus the creative nature of the acts that result in the invention.[303]

It follows that it is necessary to assess who is involved in the relevant stage of making the invention. Japanese courts have used two different tests to perform this assessment. The first one amounts to excluding from inventorship claims people who played only an ancillary role, such as administrators, assistants or sponsors.[304] The second one entails dividing the inventive process into two steps: conception of the problem (or direction for the solution), and reduction to practice. The person involved in step one will be the inventor if the conception is somewhat concrete; the person who reduced the conception to practice should be the inventor unless that reduction is obvious for the person skilled in the art.[305] When two or more people are involved at the different relevant stages, they might be considered co-inventors. [306]

In the case of inventions produced with the contribution of an AI, it would be likely that the human inventor involved in the creative process – be it at the conception stage or at the point of reduction to practice – would be identified as the inventor.[307]

3.4.4.5 *Utility models*

Utility models protect devices related to the shape or structure of an article or combination of articles, but methods of using a device, pharmaceuticals, chemical substances and similar innovations cannot be protected by a utility model.[308] To be protected, a device must be new and not be "exceedingly easy" for a person skilled in the art to make, based on publicly known art.[309] The difference to the inventive step test, which in Japan is whether a person skilled in the art could easily make the invention, is thus a matter of degree: the utility

302 See Kengo Sengai, 'Part III: Inventors and Inventors' Rights – Case No. 13: Rights Over the Invention – Inventorship', in Christopher Heath and Atsuhiro Furuta (eds.), *Japanese Patent Law: Cases and Materials* (Kluwer Law International 2019) 145–154, section 3b and case law cited therein.

303 *Shemtov* (n 204) 15.

304 Ibid. The author gives the example of someone who "only introduced an ordinary subject without any concrete conception or a person who gave general advice or instructions during the inventive process."

305 Ibid., and case law cited therein. The author also points out that the two steps approach is different in the chemistry field, since there the consequences of reducing to practice are difficult to foresee at the time of conception (therefore, in that field, experiments play a more relevant role in the inventive process).

306 Ibid.

307 Ibid.

308 *Jitsuyō shin'an-hō* (Utility Model Act), art. 1 (Law No. 123, 1959).

309 *Jitsuyō shin'an-hō* (Utility Model Act), art. 3 (Law No. 123, 1959). See also Masashi Kurose, 'Utility Model Law: The Present and Future of Japan's Utility Model System,' in Dirk Schüßler-Langeheine and Bernd Hansen (eds.), *Patent Practice in Japan and Europe: Liber Amicorum for Guntram Rahn* (Kluwer Law International 2011) 802.

model cannot be *exceedingly* easy to make. The "inventive step" in the utility model regime is a lower threshold as compared to patents.

The examination of the application for a utility model is mostly conducted on formalities; the utility model will be registered without substantive examination (although, in order to enforce the rights granted by the utility models, the owner will need to request a Utility Model Technical Opinion from the Patent Office and present the report to the infringer as a warning).[310] Due to the lack of substantive examination, obtaining utility model rights is relatively fast,[311] but the protection period is shorter than that of patents (ten years).[312]

It has been pointed out by scholars that the utility model regime has two important drawbacks: the substantive validity of a given utility model is unclear (which makes them of limited use in cases of technology transfer); and claims for injunctive relief are not likely to succeed within the protection period of ten years.[313] These might explain the modest figure of 7000 applications for utility models per year.[314]

Nevertheless, it is conceivable that the less stringent inventive step requirement for utility models may play a role in decisions to apply for a utility model instead of a patent, especially if the fact that an invention was generated by an AI will be seen as an obstacle to the fulfilment of the (more demanding) inventive step requirement for patents (and provided of course that such fact is known to the examiner). In other words, if the fact that an invention was generated by an AI is known or taken into account, it might be more difficult for that invention to meet the inventive step requirement, given that an AI (or a person using an AI system in the inventive process) might be able to more easily make the invention – which might in turn lead to an increase in the number of applications for a utility model.

3.5 Conclusions and recommendations

3.5.1 Conclusions

The questions that the increasing use of AI raises for patent law are of a slightly different nature than the ones dealt with in the realm of copyright law. This is because the structure of copyright and patent differ from one another. In patent law, a human being is needed to (at least) formulate the problem, which is a relevant stage of the inventing process. Another relevant stage of the inventing process where a human is needed is machine learning. Indeed, the stage of machine learning is important to patent law. This is because the process of

---

310 1 *Jitsuyō shin'an-hō* (Utility Model Act), articles 14–2, 29–2 (Law No. 123, 1959).; Kurose (n 308) 802–805.

311 Kurose (n 309) 805.

312 *Jitsuyō shin'an-hō* (Utility Model Act), art. 15 (Law No. 123, 1959).

313 S Okuyama, 'Part III: Specific issues, 3. Utility models, Case No. 66: Technical Assessment Report', in *Heath and Furuta* (n 301) 691–700, section 1.

314 Ibid., and references cited therein.

getting a patent implies a prior art search. An inventor who applies for a patent will need to know – and explain – how the invention differs from, or adds to, the state of the art. Feeding the AI system with available information from the state of the art becomes a pertinent action in that regard – which is not to say that knowledge of the state of the art is relevant per se for an inventorship claim,[315] or that such knowledge is an autonomous requirement for patentability; rather, the state of the art is something which will be considered when a patent is applied for, and it is in that sense that it should be regarded as an important element of the process.

Because of the different structure of patent law and how it conceives of the inventing process in terms of patentability assessment, an AI system cannot be considered as autonomous in patent law as it is in copyright law (even though the degree of human intervention needed will vary from one field of technology to the other). An AI is a tool – albeit a sophisticated one – in the inventing process.

Nevertheless, the use of AI systems to invent brings about its own challenges to patent law and policy. This chapter aimed at analysing the main areas where the development and increasing use of AI in the inventing process may impact patent law, and at suggesting recommendations to mitigate negative consequences derived from that impact. It was submitted that the main areas to look into were patentable subject matter, inventive step or non-obviousness, disclosure, and inventorship. Where applicable, the regime of utility models was also either mentioned (Australia) or analysed (Japan).

The first conclusion to be drawn from a comparative analysis of the four jurisdictions is that there is a relatively high level of international harmonisation of current patent laws. This high level of legal harmonization is perhaps not surprising, given the tendency of likeminded countries to seek harmonization of their national laws through e.g., plurilateral and bilateral free trade agreements.[316] Moreover, in some instances, legislators have unilaterally revealed the intention to harmonize their laws with those of other countries (namely their trading partners) – it is the case e.g., of Australia, where the Raising the Bar Act expressly referred to the intention to have the provision on disclosure as close as possible to UK legislation and to the European Patent Convention.[317] By contrast, at the level of patent offices and courts, some elements might differ (in terms of procedure and interpretations of the legal provisions). Nevertheless, some initiatives exist at the level of patent offices that try to streamline different national practices. An example is the forum "Five IP Offices," whose vision includes, inter alia, patent harmonisation of practices and procedures.[318]

---

315 In some jurisdictions, such as the US, this question is expressly settled in the sense that the prior stage of explaining the state of the art or providing the inventor with well-known principles cannot give rise to inventorship claims – see section 3.4.2.3.

316 *Miyamoto* (n 9) 46.

317 *Explanatory Memorandum: Intellectual Property Laws Amendment (Raising the Bar) Act 2011 (Cth)* (n 258) and section 3.4.3.3 of this book.

318 'About IP 5 Co-operation' (Five IP offices) <www.fiveipoffices.org/about> accessed 17 May 2021. The "Five IP Offices" forum comprises the Patent Offices of some of the jurisdictions in this book (the EPO, the USPTO and the JPO), in addition to the Korean Intellectual Property Office and

A first point of similarity at the level of patent laws is that none of the laws in the jurisdictions examined contain any provisions that would exclude patentability of subject matter because of how the invention was generated, or who generated it. Therefore, AI-generated innovations can in principle be patentable subject matter in all four jurisdictions, meaning that there is no difference between AI-generated inventions and traditional inventions in what concerns eligibility of subject matter for patent protection.

Another commonality concerns the inventive step or non-obviousness as a patentability requirement: all jurisdictions analysed grant patents to inventions that display an inventive step or that are non-obvious, and said requirement might be put at strain with the increased use of AI systems in the inventive process. The reasoning or justification behind the inventive step/non-obviousness requirement is common to the four jurisdictions: to not grant patents to inventions that could be easily made by someone skilled in the art, so as to not hinder the development of technology.[319] In that vein, it can be argued that the laws in the four jurisdictions are similar. The notion of "easily conceived" is inherent to the Japanese test, but not to the tests of other jurisdictions, even though it is considered that the Japanese test is akin to obviousness as understood in the US.[320] The difference between "inventive step" and "non-obviousness" is not necessarily negligible (as the former relates to the relation between the invention and prior art, while the latter refers to the mental process of the person skilled in the art),[321] but again the underlying goal of the provision approximates the laws in spirit if not in drafting.

The approach taken by the four Offices is similar in the sense that they all compare the invention with prior art and assess the differences between them. Moreover, the Offices limit the scope of prior art by relating it to the specific field of the claimed invention, but all four include adjacent, related, analogous or neighbouring fields in the scope of prior art. Common to the procedures is also the fact that it is possible to use secondary considerations – such as commercial success – in the assessment of inventive step/non-obviousness (although this must be linked to the technical features of the invention and not to exogenous factors such as marketing or advertising).

The assessment of inventive step/non-obviousness is made from the perspective of the person skilled in the art in all four jurisdictions. Also in all of them the person skilled in the art is presumed to have had access to all publicly available state of the art information and is able to comprehend all technical

---

the National Intellectual Property Administration of the People's Republic of China. Together, the Offices handle around 80% of the patent applications worldwide.

319   See also *Dinwoodie* (n 62) 141.

320   Kotaro Kageyama, 'Determining Inventive Step or Non-obviousness for a Patent Requirement in View of the Formation Process of an Invention' (2016) 7 *Beijing Law Review* 238, 241–242.

321   Ove Granstrand, 'Are We on Our Way in the New Economy with Optimal Inventive Steps?,' in Ove Granstrand (ed.), *Economics, Law and Intellectual Property. Seeking Strategies for Research and Teaching in a Developing Field* (Springer 2003) 223, 237.

matters in the relevant art.[322] However, in Japan and the US the threshold for patentability might be higher because it is considered that the person skilled in the art has an ordinary level of creativity. Conversely, in Europe, the person skilled in the art will not engage in scientific research in areas not yet explored, which could be read as meaning that the person skilled in the art will not use AI in a field where AI is not widely used; and in Australia, the person skilled in the art is considered to be "non-inventive," although such person may also have access to the best available equipment (which, it is submitted, could be an AI system if the AI system is widely or moderately used to invent in the field).

Even though the laws are similar and the approach taken by the four offices is similar in some aspects, the remaining differences in guidelines and procedures for examination might lead to divergent solutions when an invention generated by an AI system is at stake, not least because the inventive step/non-obviousness test is highly subjective. As observed by J. Duffy in relation to the US, the step-by-step procedure for examination allows for an understanding of the differences between a claimed invention and the prior art, but does not clarify how examiners and judges ought to determine whether those differences are obvious.[323] The same line of reasoning can be applicable, *mutatis mutandis*, to the examination procedures in the other jurisdictions: the formalistic nature of the obviousness/ inventive step enquiry does not necessarily lead to a clear determination of compliance (or lack thereof) with this patentability requirement, which might mean that a specific solution should be sought for the examination of AI-generated inventions in relation to their compliance with the inventive step or non-obviousness requirement.

With regard to inventorship, the state of the art in the field of AI and the fact that an AI is not completely autonomous in the inventing process also means that the question of inventorship – i.e., whether an AI can be considered an inventor in its own right – is less relevant. It is in the AI capabilities to expedite and optimize the inventing process that the main impact of AI on patent law lies. Nevertheless, there are strong indications in all the jurisdictions concerned that the inventor must be a human being for purposes of inventorship claims. Provisions in patent laws and/or office guidelines often imply that the inventor is a human being – see e.g., the need for the formation, in the *mind* of an inventor, of the complete and operative invention (US, Australia) or the necessary *creative* nature of the acts that result in the invention (Japan).[324] These are among the concepts that, although not expressly, seem to require a human being. Recent decisions from the EPO and the USPTO in relation to the DABUS applications – which refused to grant inventorship status to the AI DABUS – confirm this.

Calls have been made to recognize the status of inventor to AI systems, citing reasons of legal certainty (since, if the AI cannot be named the inventor, there

322 See WIPO (n 141) point 25.
323 *Duffy* (n 4) 62.
324 Specifically for the differences between human creativity and AI creativity, see Chapter 2 section 2.2 of this book.

might be uncertainty as to who should be designated instead), and consistency with the patent system (because attributing inventorship to a human being who did not deploy intellectual effort in conceiving the invention is damaging to the integrity of the patent system).[325] As pointed out above, granting inventorship status to AI systems is not necessary (or correct) at present, since there is always a human involved at some point in the inventing system. The problem lies in detecting the human contribution and evaluating whether there is a sufficient claim for inventorship – and if so who is entitled to such claim. The question of contribution to the invention and the rise of inventorship claims derived therefrom is a relevant issue in the jurisdictions analysed in this book, bar Europe (where the question might nevertheless be dealt with in the national laws of the EPC countries).[326] For instance, in the US, it is necessary that the inventor, to be considered as such, conceives of the invention, i.e., that he or she carries out a "complete performance of the mental part of the inventive act," while contemporaneously recognizing and appreciating the invention.[327] Other jurisdictions will also have their own rules for assessing inventorship under their respective laws. Ultimately, finding the inventor of an AI-generated invention will depend on the particular circumstances of the situation and will have to be assessed on a case-by-case basis.

If, for a given invention, no human being fits the definition of "inventor" – either because the human contribution was not deemed enough for a claim of inventorship under national law, or because AI technology evolves to a point where human beings are not needed along the inventing process – then this might mean that the invention is not patentable. Indeed, the logic underlying the patent system is connected to *human* ingenuity. In general, examples of technical developments that may be excluded from patent protection include discoveries and substances already existing in nature.[328] It could be argued that, if no human being is involved in the inventing process, the resulting output is akin to a discovery, i.e., to a pre-existing product (in the sense that the product exists prior and independently to human intervention). For example, in the US, the Supreme Court, citing Committee Reports accompanying the 1952

---

325 *Li and Koay* (n 273) 402–403. See also Abbott, *The Reasonable Robot* (n 2) 86–87, who defends that AI should be considered as inventors under a "dynamic interpretation of the current law." For earlier thoughts from the same author, Ryan Abbott, 'I think, Therefore I Invent: Creative Computers and the Future of Patent Law' (2016) 57 *Boston College Law Review* 1079.

326 Still, in a report submitted by the President of the European Patent Office, it is stated that there will be multiple options for inventorship in the case of AI-related patents – see the report submitted by the President of the European Patent Office, "Update of legal aspects of artificial intelligence and patents," cit., p. 5: "Depending on where the invention lies, the inventor may e.g., be the software developer who set up an AI system, the person who trained the machine with data, the person who interpreted the output of an ML algorithm, the person who improved an AI algorithm to obtain a certain technical effect or who identified the technical application of the output of an AI system (or a combination thereof)."

327 See section 3.4.2.3 of this book.

328 World Intellectual Property Organization, *Introduction to Intellectual Property: Theory and Practice* (2nd ed., Kluwer Law International 2017) 158–159.

Act, recalled that "Congress intended statutory subject matter to include anything under the sun that is made by man."[329] The case was not about artificial intelligence, but it provides a strong indication that it's man-made innovations that should be the subject matter of patents.[330] Ergo, in the absence of "man," the product should not be deemed patentable subject matter. In Australia, the High Court has ruled that "[f]or a claimed invention to qualify as a manner of manufacture [i.e., patentable subject-manner] it must be something more than a mere discovery."[331] This case was also not about artificial intelligence, but likewise it highlighted something fundamental: the difference between a "discovery" (as pre-existing material), and an "invention."

While not all jurisdictions have an express exclusion for discoveries or substances found in nature (and even though artificially produced output that are AI-generated are not exactly the same as substances found in nature), patent laws generally tend to presume the intervention of human beings at some point in the inventing process, and it seems that the absence of a human would not only twist the logic of the patent system, but make it misaligned with its own rationales and justifications, as shall be seen below. Another argument standing for the necessity of a human inventor relates to the requirement that an inventor be named. This requirement is connected to the need of recognizing the true inventor, akin to a moral right of attribution.[332] Moreover, identifying an inventor traces the invention to a certain space and time, allowing for a follow-up of the invention's substance and existence.[333] This function of naming an inventor and its connection to humanness – as recognition speaks to humans, not machines, and only a human could further defend an invention's substance and existence properly – indicates that, in the absence of a human inventor, patentability stands on shaky grounds. In any case, it is unclear how relevant this exercise is, since patent offices do not generally object to the reported (human) inventor[334] – which could mean that a human proxy would be able to pass as an inventor, undisputed.

As argued in this chapter, AI systems that generate inventions might not be completely autonomous, but it is undeniable that they augment the inventing capabilities of human beings. They allow human beings to move more easily into more remote fields of technology. They might aid in producing new inventions that would be considered non-obvious or displaying an inventive step, when in reality the automated process of idea production, speed of

---

329 *Diamond v. Chakrabarty*, 447 U.S. 303 (1980).
330 Even though, ironically, the statement in *Diamond v. Chakrabarty* was intended as a support for a broad construction of patentability subject matter.
331 *D'Arcy v. Myriad Genetics Inc.* [2015] HCA 35 [126].
332 Graham Dutfield, 'Collective Invention and Patent Law Individualism, 1877–2012 – or, the Curious Persistence of the Inventor's Moral Right,' in Stathis Arapostathis and Graham Dutfield (eds.) *Knowledge Management and Intellectual Property – Concepts, Actors and Practices from the Past to the Present* (Edward Elgar 2013) 109, 122–123.
333 Ibid.
334 *Abbott*, 'The Artificial Inventor Project' (n 32).

inventing process, easiness of testing or other factors combined are obvious to someone using an AI system to invent. Failing to consider the role of AI systems in the inventing process might thus lead to lowering the bar for patentability in practice, and have the market flooded with obvious "inventions." This increases the risk of patent thickets, which namely the inventive step/non-obviousness requirement tries to combat.

The main theory used to justify patents – the utilitarian theory – rests, among others, on the premise that the level of invention will be sub-optimal without incentives; but is that necessarily so if AI systems are able to process large amounts of data and to invent at little cost? It could be argued that incentives would be needed to use the AI system in the first place, due to the costs such systems involve. However, that incentive is linked to the AI system per se, not to eventual output that it may produce. On the other hand, it should also be considered that, beyond economic incentives, other type of motivations such as reputational benefits may be at the origin of the decision to invent. Is it possible to rely on reputational incentives to justify patents when a great part of the inventing process is carried out by a machine? Just as economic incentives, there will be reputational incentives connected to the AI system itself, but the AI system and the inventions generated by using it are not one and the same thing – even though, admittedly, the reputational incentives to invent might still be present in some cases where a human being has a more prominent role during the inventing process (since, as argued before, the level of intervention of human beings in the inventing process differs according to the field of technology, but also depending on the particular AI system at stake).

As for other theories, such as the Lockean labour theory, the monopoly afforded by a patent generally conflicts with the need to leave "enough and as good for others," which is a premise of said theory. This makes the labour theory less relevant in the patent field. In the case of AI-generated inventions, the labour theory seems to be even more ill-fitting. First, because, if the bar for patentability is lowered due to an AI intervention in the inventing process, with the consequent flooding of the market with patents, there will be less left for others, as the minefield of monopolies will curtail their freedom to operate. Second, and depending on the AI-system at stake, the labour that deserves a reward might often originate from the AI-system, not the human being using it – which means that the necessary link between (human) labour and the output produced by it becomes elusive. The same can be said, *mutatis mutandis*, of the personality rights theory: the original criticisms of using it to justify the patent system, based on the fact that the inventor has less room to express her personality in the inventive process, is potentiated in the case of AI-generated inventions, where traces of human intervention become less visible.

All in all, it is possible to conclude that the use of AI in the inventing process puts a strain on the original justifications to grant a patent. It is thus necessary to examine which measures could be taken to realign the patent system with its rationales where AI-generated inventions are concerned. This will be done in the next section.

3.5.2 Recommendations

Inventions where an AI is used in the inventing process mean that the justifications for granting patents might be diminished or strained – although not totally extinguished, since a human being is still, to a greater or lesser extent, involved. This in turn calls for revisiting current patent law and policy.

Recommendations should focus on an international, rather than national or regional, level; even though international harmonization of patent law has never been a goal of the patent system per se, it is a way to address challenges that require international solutions, such as, *inter alia*, the need for accessibility, cost-effectiveness, legal certainty, and patent quality. [335] Because AI-generated inventions are a source of uncertainty and have an impact on the patent system – namely, in terms of patent quality if as a result of the intervention of AI systems in the inventing process more patents are granted – recommendations concerning this area are a natural candidate to a more internationally-looking perspective.

Any type of recommendation suggested should also take into account patent rationales, in the sense of it being needed to bring the patent system more aligned with its original justifications. The question to be asked should thus be: how can it be considered that patents are leaving others with a sufficient opportunity to invent (Lockean theory), while at the same time guaranteeing that inventors have enough incentive to innovate, thus keeping inventions in society at an optimal level (utilitarian theory)?

Inventions differ in their level of complexity, and therefore in the time, effort and resources employed in its generation. It has been noted that the more costly the inventing process, the more defensible the patent grant, as the monopoly will allow for the inventor to recover the inventing costs.[336] This speaks directly to patent rationales, and specifically to the idea of reward underlying natural rights theories – the labour in creating the invention should be connected to the reward the inventor gets for that creation. The incentive theory also relates to this, since it can be argued that inventors need (more) incentives to engage in (more) costly inventing processes. However, creating a "multi-speed" patent system, where the scope of a patent is connected to the complexity of the invention (i.e., the more complex the invention, the broader the patent protection), is not feasible. The transaction costs, subjectivity and lack of legal certainty, to name but a few hurdles inherent to such utopic system, would be too high to overcome.

Some quick-fix solutions could be pondered, such as setting up higher fees for registering or maintaining a patent. Yet, that would not prevent inventors and firms from applying for patents for inventions generated by AI systems, if the resulting invention is deemed commercially valuable. Indeed, it has been argued that, where an invention is obvious but also commercially valuable,

---

335 *Miyamoto* (n 9) 53.
336 Sherkow, 'Negativing invention' (n 150) 1134.

there is really no good substitute for the inventive step/non-obviousness requirement.[337] Another solution would be to deem AI-generated inventions non-patentable. However, that is not aligned with the patent system justifications either – as demonstrated throughout this chapter, AI-generated inventions need a human at some stages of the inventing process. Failing to acknowledge human intervention – and to assess that intervention in the context of patentability claims – could chill technological development and/or lead the owners of AI machines to resort to trade secrets rather than patents.

It is submitted that the most sensible solution for the misalignment between the patent system and its rationales lies in the patentability requirements. Setting the optimal threshold for patentability is of course quite a difficult (if not impossible) task; if the patentability requirements are set too low that can lead to patent flooding, but if they are set too high innovation and inventive activities might be prejudiced. To add to this difficult balance, drawbacks inherent to patenting new technologies should also be considered: it has been widely discussed in literature that patents on early-on technology or subject matter can prevent other innovators from working on the same issue, thus hindering second generation products.[338] Nevertheless, it seems that the easiness to invent brought by AI, on the one hand, and the need to not hinder subsequent innovation, on the other hand, point to increasing the patentability bar as a preferred solution.

The crux of the matter in terms of patentability is the inventive step or non-obviousness requirement, which, while being the most difficult to assess, is also central to defining an invention. Ideally, then, the inventive step or non-obviousness requirement should be rethought in light of technological development. The main problem with this approach is that, regardless of the jurisdiction, the tendency seems to be to assess the achievement of the invention (i.e., whether it is non-obvious) and to disregard the (necessarily subjective) achievement of the inventor and the history behind the invention/the inventing process.[339] Moreover, while the laws are similar in the four jurisdictions analysed, some differences show at the procedural level, i.e., regarding Office guidelines and examination processes. This indicates that amending laws would not be a viable solution. In addition, amending laws to take into account AI developments would not be technology-neutral. They would run the risk of becoming outdated in the future. Changing laws is also burdensome due to the political processes involved, and does not therefore amount to a realistic path. A better course of action is to develop common guidelines on this subject between the Patent Offices. In that regard, several measures can be adopted.

Clear common guidelines on the notion of analogous, neighbouring, related or adjacent art should be adopted. Independently of the question of AI-generated inventions, such guidelines seem in any case to be needed, as distinguishing

337 *Duffy* (n 4) 12–13.
338 see e.g., Suzanne Scotchmer, 'Standing on the Shoulders of Giants: Cumulative Research and the Patent Law' (1991) 5 *Journal of Economic Perspectives* 29.; Kesan (n 47) 900.
339 Putting forth a similar observation regarding the European system, *Seville* (n 85) 147.

analogous from non-analogous art can be subjective and arbitrary.[340] The use of AI in the inventing process can cause the field of analogous arts to be broadened in practice, given the real possibility that AI systems will look for solutions to problems in non-analogous fields. The case of the Benevolent Platform, mentioned in section 3.2, provides a good illustration of this. As explained, the system establishes links between an entire spectrum of drug discovery and makes it possible to produce knowledge graphs that connect e.g., a disease, the genes associated with it, and the substances that affect it – which might or might not emanate from related or analogous fields.

Since non-analogous art cannot be used when judging whether the invention is obvious or non-obvious, the scope of "analogous/neighbouring/related/adjacent art" should be broadened in Examination Guidelines, as a way to counteract the effects of a potential "race to patent" derived from the easiness to invent in the context of AI (as the broader the pertinent art, the more likely it is to find prior art that makes the invention obvious/lacking inventive step). An analysis of what the relevant art is should thus specifically consider the technological advances and the amount to which interdisciplinary collaboration is common in a given field of technology.[341] In some areas, researchers are more prone to combine teachings from different and distant fields, while in others (such as nuclear engineering) not much interdisciplinarity is visible.[342] These differences between fields ought to be taken into account.

However, what should also be considered in an assessment of whether the field is remote or analogous is that AI systems need to be programmed. Ultimately, it is the programming and the setting of an AI system that leads it to "look" into removed fields. In some cases, there will be a clear link between that programming and the capabilities of the AI to look into other fields; but in other cases the out-of-the-box thinking might surprise even the programmer who input data on the AI that ultimately led the latter to "invent." In other words, the determination to look into remote fields might be a direct consequence of programming the AI to look into specific, yet removed fields (in which case there is a direct link between the search for a solution in said fields and the initiative of a human being), but it might also be a consequence of the design of the AI system itself, which can e.g., ingest data from several different

340 Sherkow, 'Negativing Invention' (n 150) 1110ff.

341 This proposal seems to be in line with what some courts have advocated. See especially in the US, *KSR v. Teleflex* (n 166) [418]-[419]: "The diversity of inventive pursuits and of modern technology counsels against confining the obviousness analysis by a formalistic conception of the words teaching, suggestion, and motivation, or by overemphasizing the importance of published articles and the explicit content of issued patents. In many fields there may be little discussion of obvious techniques or combinations, and market demand, rather than scientific literature, may often drive design trends. Granting patent protection to advances that would occur in the ordinary course without real innovation retards progress and may, for patents combining previously known elements, deprive prior inventions of their value or utility."

342 Brenda M. Simon, 'The Implications of Technological Advancement for Obviousness' (2013) 19 *Michigan Telecommunications and Technology Law Review* 2013, 331, p. 358.

fields that are not analogous or related, and come up with an unexpected solution that combines teachings from remote fields (in which case the link between programming the AI system and the solution that it finds is feebler). The different types of AI systems and respective programming they require is a factor that should be taken into account when assessing whether a field is remote or analogous, for purposes of analysing the inventive step requirement.

Technological development in general and the use of AI specifically should also be taken into account when assessing who the person skilled in the art is. In a world where AI systems are capable of ingesting and processing more information than a human could ever dream of, would the standard of an unimaginative, average person skilled in the art still stand?

AI might indeed affect the level of skill of the person skilled in the art and her level of creativity.[343] In that regard, it would be advisable that the European and Australian practices become aligned with the Japanese and US ones, in the sense of considering that the person skilled in the art has ordinary creativity.

Moreover, it should specifically be considered what means the skilled person has at her disposal. Both the EPO and JPO Guidelines mention that the skilled person has ordinary or normal technical means for experimentation/research and development. In Australia, there are references to the person skilled in the art having the best available equipment – admittedly, a higher standard than the "normal means" in Europe and Japan. However, in Australia, the context of the field needs to be taken into account, which is to say that the extent to which technology is used in general in the particular field needs to be assessed. This might bring references to the "best available equipment" down to the "normal" levels of Europe and Japan, or at least it might call for a reformulation of the "best available equipment" as being the "best available equipment" amongst those generally used in the field. The USPTO Guidelines do not contain a reference to means of experimentation in the same way as the other jurisdictions, but mention the sophistication of technology and the rapidity with which inventions are made as a factor when determining the level of ordinary skill in the pertinent art. Moreover, the US Supreme Court specifically stated that an assessment of obviousness should take into account modern technology.[344] It would thus be possible to build on these existing practices and consider the use of AI in the inventing process in the following fashion: if the use of AI is not a normal means of experimentation in the relevant art, a patent can be granted if the invention is not obvious for a person skilled in the art without the use of AI (even if AI was used by the inventor in question). Conversely, if the use of AI is a normal means of experimentation in the relevant art, the skills of the person skilled in the art improve and AI use is taken into account – which means that a patent can be granted if the invention is not obvious for a person skilled in the art who uses the AI (even if AI was not used by the inventor in question).

343 Ibid., 347.
344 See *KSR v. Teleflex* (n 166).

The question – and problem – then becomes how the examiner or judge can determine if the use of the AI amounts to a normal means of experimentation. The AI field is constantly evolving, and new AI applications and systems are regularly being developed, making it hard to keep up with trends in any given art. Moreover, the use of AI is not necessarily disclosed in the patent application. Even though there is an enablement or disclosure requirement, neither laws nor Examination Guidelines seem to mandate that the applicant indicate the means through which she created the invention. The enablement or disclosure obligation concerns only the invention itself, not the method of inventing it. Therefore, disclosure of the inventing process is not per se mandatory in any of the jurisdictions analysed. In the US, this is further reinforced by the last sentence of Section 103 of the Patent Act (stating that patentability shall not be negated by the manner in which the invention was made), although it can be claimed, in line with the analysis carried out in section 3.4.2, that the provision has more flexibility than it appears. In any case, from a technical perspective, the "black box" nature of AI might make it challenging to clearly disclose all the elements of the entire process by which an AI system generated an invention. Moreover, an AI system may not be able to explain why the invention works in a certain way, or how it makes a contribution.[345] One tentative solution that has been put forth is the creation of a deposit system for AI algorithms, assuming that it is possible to sufficiently describe an algorithm for that purpose, both from a technical and legal perspectives (as the mandatory disclosure of the algorithm might conflict with trade secret laws, for example).[346]

A more straightforward solution might then be to harmonize the Guidelines of the four Offices, making the disclosure of the inventing process mandatory therein. This could be politically feasible, considering the momentum for more transparency in AI. For example, following the Report "Towards the Promotion of International Discussion on AI Networking" from the Japanese Ministry of Internal Affairs and Communications, a few principles were issued, among which the principle of transparency. This principle specifically calls on developers to pay attention to the "verifiability of inputs/outputs and the explainability of their judgments."[347] Similar calls for transparency have been made, to a greater or lesser extent, in other jurisdictions.[348]

---

345 *Hartmann and others* (n 5) 112.

346 Ibid. "The idea of requiring disclosure/deposit of algorithms, and possibly also of a description of the way in which the AI that assisted in the inventive process was trained, including a reference to the training data and its main characteristics, training technique and method used, may be required in appropriate cases."

347 Fumio Shimpo, 'The Principal Japanese AI and Robot Strategy Toward Establishing Basic Principles,' in H. Barfield and U. Pagallo (eds.), *Research Handbook on the Law of Artificial Intelligence* (Edward Elgar 2018) 114, 122–123.

348 See e.g., in Europe, 'Report on Intellectual Property Rights for the Development of Artificial Intelligence Technologies'; (n 119); in the US, The White House Office of Science and Technology Policy, 'American Artificial Intelligence Initiative: Year One Annual Report' (February 2020) <www.nitrd.gov/nitrdgroups/images/c/c1/American-AI-Initiative-One-Year-Annual-Report.

In the US, the need for transparency might be further supported by the fact that the assessment of enablement (i.e., the determination of whether the enablement of the invention is sufficient) is based on a number of factors, namely the quantity of experimentation necessary, the amount of guidance presented in the specification, the presence or absence of working examples of the invention, the nature of the invention, the state of the prior art, the relative skill of those in the art, or the breadth of the claims – some of which might require, even if indirectly, disclosing the use of an AI system in the inventing process. The use of these or similar factors in other Offices could help operationalize the assessment of enablement or sufficiency of disclosure so that it becomes more difficult not to reveal the use of an AI system in the inventing process.

Furthermore, all the four jurisdictions take secondary indicia into consideration. Many of those secondary indicia – such as commercial success – are the same, and are part of the Examination Guidelines of their respective Patent Offices. It would therefore be advisable to consider adding a "made by AI' factor as an indication of obviousness. Secondary considerations are relevant to the assessment of inventive step, even though their probative force might differ per jurisdiction and even on a case-by-case basis. The fact that these indicia are not central to the examination, and that they must be balanced with other factors, means that an invention being AI-generated is not a deal-breaker in terms of inventive step/non-obviousness compliance (therefore not chilling AI use and technological development). This measure would face the same difficulties as the previous one – the applicant does not necessarily disclose the use of AI – but reference could be made to the general trend in the field of the pertinent art.

The solutions proposed – to broaden the scope of analogous arts; to take into account the use of AI and technological development when defining the person skilled in the art; to consider the AI intervention in the context of secondary indicia – imply increasing the threshold for a finding of inventive step/non-obviousness, i.e., increasing the patentability threshold, at the level of Patent Offices. Said solutions also make the grant of a patent justifiable in light of patent rationales. The financial and reputational incentives given to inventors – or better said, to participants in the inventing process – are still in place, but for inventions which would not be created absent the patent system. The trade-off inherent to the patent system is also in place – in case a patent is granted in a given AI-generated innovation, information is exchanged in the form of disclosure/enablement. The intellectual labour of the human being participating in the inventing process (e.g., in setting the problem to be solved, or in applying the technical teachings) is rewarded, while some is left for others to invent due to the higher patentability threshold. In passing, and even though

pdf> accessed 22 May 2021.; in Australia, Australian Government (Department of Industry, Science, Energy and Resources), 'An AI Action Plan for All Australians: A Call for Views – Discussion Paper' (Australian Government Department of Industry, Science, Energy and Resources, 2020) <https://consult.industry.gov.au/digital-economy/ai-action-plan/supporting_documents/AIDiscussionPaper.pdf> accessed 22 May 2021.

the personality theory is less relevant in the patent field, the intervention of the human being who participates in the inventing process is also still protected, thus being aligned with that theory.

An alternative way to address the challenges brought by the intervention of AI systems in the inventing process would be to consider a legislative solution such as a regime of utility models for AI generated innovations. Utility models (or similar regimes such as the innovation patents in Australia) usually have lower thresholds for patentability, namely in what concerns the inventive step or non-obviousness requirement. With the lower threshold of patentability comes also a reduced scope of protection (chiefly, in terms of duration of protection). Intuitively, given the easiness to invent brought by AI and the fears of innovation lock-ins lasting for 20 years, utility models or similar forms of lighter protection seem attractive. Creating a utility model regime to protect AI-generated innovations would not be a foreign move to legislatures that introduce special, sui generis rights (such as database laws) to protect new subject matter that is left unprotected due to the impossibility to stretch existing intellectual property regimes.[349] In the case of the utility model, it is generally accepted that it serves the purpose of protecting incremental (as opposed to breakthrough) innovation.[350]

However, creating a utility model regime for this purpose is not without drawbacks. The fact that the regime has a lower inventive step threshold might lead to an incentive to apply for utility models, which in turn could lead to more litigation and to more barriers for third parties.[351] From the jurisdictions analysed in this book, only Japan has a stable utility model regime. Australia is in the process of phasing out its innovation patent system (akin to a utility model regime), following the recommendation of the Productivity Commission, which is the Australian Government's independent research and advisory body. The recommendation of the Productivity Commission was to abolish innovation patents given their unlikelihood to provide net benefits, against the significant costs on third parties they generated.[352] In the EU, as mentioned, no agreement was reached regarding the harmonisation of utility model regimes.[353] Moreover, in a 2015 Study that analysed nine European countries that had a system of utility model, the authors of the Study found that utility models were less of a route to protect minor inventions and more of a tool used

---

349 see Uma Suthersanen, 'Utility Models: Do They Really Serve National Innovation Strategies?,' in Josef Drexl and Anselm Kamperman Sanders (eds.), *The Innovation Society and Intellectual Property* (Edward Elgar 2019) 8. "Sui generis rights (such as utility model, design, semiconductor chip, geographical indications or database laws) emanate from the inability of legislators and jurists to stretch the existing three bulwarks of the intellectual property regime to accommodate new things to protect."
350 Ibid., 11–12.
351 Alfred Radauer and others, 'Study on the Economic Impact of the Utility Model Legislation in Selected Member States' (*European Commission*, April 2015) 168–171. <https://op.europa.eu/en/publication-detail/-/publication/830fedd7-a1cf-46bd-a460-ba4a9eb01e63> accessed 22 May 2021.
352 See supra Section 3.4.3.
353 See supra n. 78.

by savvy IP professionals to overcome the shortcomings of the patent system.[354] This is in line with another Study that analysed the Australian Innovation Patent, and which found that the reasons to choose an innovation patent instead of a standard patent were faster turnaround times and lower fees (while the lower inventive step was the least cited motive to go for an innovation patent).[355] Likewise, the Japanese utility model system was originally used to ensure technology transfer from western economies, as protection would then be granted to Japanese innovators who would carry out small improvements of foreign technology.[356] The fact that a utility model system might be used to distort, or to work around of, the patent system is a real possibility.

On balance, the utility model system can be part of a strategy to push incremental innovation forward and, under certain circumstances and provided other policy measures are taken, improve the economy.[357] However, AI is not concerned only with incremental innovation or small improvements; the reason why AI-generated inventions might be deemed more obvious than other types of inventions has to do with the easiness of the inventing process brought about by AI, not with the fact that the inventions themselves are incremental. In that sense, it is doubtful that protecting AI-generated innovations via a utility model regime is in line with the latter's rationale. It would have to be assessed whether protection of AI-generated innovations via utility models would indeed lead to more incremental innovation that would be beneficial to society – which would also depend on the particular economy at stake (e.g., utility models are said to be more important in less mature economies, as, among other reasons, these produce a higher number of incremental innovations). Further economic studies would thus be needed to weigh the benefits and disadvantages of a utility model system for AI-generated innovations, knowing however that a harmonised, international regime of utility models would not be an adequate solution due to the fact that the success of a utility model system depends very much on the economic context of a given country.

References

Primary sources

35 U.S. Code
A.B. Dick Co. v. Barnett, 288 Fed. 799 (2nd Cir. 1923)
ACS Hospital Systems, Inc. v. Montefiore Hospital, 732 F.2d 1572, 1577 (Fed. Cir. 1984)
Acts Interpretation Act (1901)

---

354 *Radauer and others* (n 351) 182.
355 John Zeitsch, 'The Economic Value of the Australian Innovation Patent' (*IP Australia*, March 2013) 40–41. <www.ipaustralia.gov.au/sites/default/files/economic_value_of_the_innovation_patent_-_final_report_-_verve_economics_-_24_mar_2013.pdf> accessed 22 May 2021.
356 *Radauer and others* (n 351) 20–21 and references cited therein.
357 Ibid. According to the authors, an example of other policy measures to be taken include "a fine-tuning of utility model provisions with those of other (particularly patent) laws."

Alice Corp. v. CLS Bank International, 134 S. Ct. 2347 (2014)

Anaesthetic Supplies Pty Ltd v Rescare Ltd [1994] FCA 304

Australian Patent Office, Patent Manual of Practice and Procedure

Beech Aircraft v. EDO, 990 F.2d 1237 (Fed. Cir. 1993)

Bristol-Myers Squibb Co v FH Faulding & Co Ltd (2000) 97 FCR 524

Brunswick Corp. v. Champion Spark Plug Co., 689 F.2d 740, 750 (7th Cir. 1982).

Burroughs Wellcome Co. v. Barr Labs., Inc., 40 F.3d 1223 (Fed. Cir. 1994)

Calmar v. Cook Chemical Co., 380 U.S. 949 (1965)

Case J-7/99 Heavy-duty Power, Boards of Appeal of the EPO

Case T-1203/97 Recup Svenska vs. Recotech Heatex & Menerga Apparatebau, Boards of Appeal of the EPO

Case T-1212/01 Pyrazolopyrimidinones for the treatment of impotence/ Pfizer Limited et al, Boards of Appeal of the EPO

Case T-1212/01 Pyrazolopyrimidinones for the treatment of impotence/ Pfizer Limited et al, Boards of Appeal of the EPO

Case T-176/84 Pencil Sharpener, Boards of Appeal of the EPO

Case T-226/85 Stable bleaches, Boards of Appeal of the EPO

Case T-231/97 Emissionsarme Dispersionsfarben/Clariant, Boards of Appeal of the EPO

Case T-500/91 Alpha-interferon II/ Biogen, Boards of Appeal of the EPO

Case T-506/92 AEG vs. Siemens, Boards of Appeal of the EPO

Case T-560/89 Filler mass/ N.I. Industries, Boards of Appeal of the EPO

Case T-570/91 A.E. PLC vs. Mahle GmbH, Boards of Appeal of the EPO

Case T-699/91 Blount, Boards of Appeal of the EPO

Case T-712/92 Cleaning lenses/Allergan, Boards of Appeal of the EPO

Case T-73/95 Enichem Synthesis v. Ciba Spezialitaetenchemie, Boards of Appeal of the EPO

Case T-766/91 Decorative laminates/Boeing, Boards of Appeal of the EPO

Case T-989/93 Scintillation Media/Fisher Scientific, Boards of Appeal of the EPO

"Circuit-connecting Member" case (Intellectual Property High Court, No. 10096 (Gyo-Ke), 28 January 2009)

Crane v Price (1842) 1 WPC 393

Cuno Engineering Corp. v. Automatic Devices Corp. 314 U.S. 84 (1941)

Custom Accessories, Inc. v. Jeffrey-Allan Indus., Inc., 807 F.2d 955, 962 (Fed. Cir. 1986)

D'Arcy v Myriad Genetics Inc [2014] FCAFC 115

D'Arcy v. Myriad Genetics Inc. [2015] HCA 35

Diamond v. Chakrabarty, 447 U.S. 303 (1980)

Digitech Image Techs. v. Electronics for Imaging, 758 F.3d 1344, 1348, 111 USPQ2d 1717, 1719 (Fed. Cir. 2014)

Enfish, LLC v. Microsoft Corp., 822 F.3d 1327, 1334 (Fed. Cir. 2016)

Environmental Designs, Ltd. v. Union Oil Co, 713 F.3d 693 (Fed. Circ. 1983)

European Patent Convention (1973)

European Patent Office, Guidelines for Examination

'Exhaust Fan Filter' case (Intellectual Property High Court, No. 10075 (Gyo-Ke), 31 January 2011)

'Explanatory Memorandum: Intellectual Property Laws Amendment (Raising the Bar) Act 2011 (Cth)' (The Parliament of the Commonwealth of Australia 2011)

Fiers v. Revel, 984 F.2d 1164, 1168 (Fed. Circ. 1993)

Fine Granule Medicine v. Pfeizer (Tokyo District Court, No. 7196 (Wa) 2001, August 27, 2002)

General Tire & Rubber Co. v. Jefferson Chem. Co., 497 F.2d 1283, 1291 (2nd Cir. 1974)

General Tire & Rubber Company v Firestone Tyre and Rubber Company Ltd [1972] RPC 457

GlaxoSmithKline Consumer Healthcare Investments (Ireland) (No 2) Limited v Generic Partners Pty Limited [2018] FCAFC 71

Graham v. John Deere Co, 379 U.S. 956 (1965)

H Lundbeck A/S v Alphapharm Pty Ltd (2009) 177 FCR 151

Hotchkiss v. Greenwood, 52 U.S. 248 (1850)

Idenix Pharmaceuticals LLC v Gilead Sciences Pty Ltd [2017] FCAFC 196

Implementing Regulations to the Convention on the Grant of European Patents (1973)

In Re Ghiron 442 F.2d 985, 991 (C.C.P.A. 1971)

In re GPAC Inc., 57 F.3d 1573, 1579 (Fed. Cir. 1995)

In re Kaslow, 707 F.2d 1336 (Fed. Cir. 1983)

In re Mlot-Fijalkowski, 676 F.2d 666, 669 (C.C.P.A. 1982)

In re Petrus A.C.M. Nuijten, 500 F.3d 1346, 1354, 84 USPQ2d 1495, 1500 (Fed. Cir. 2007)

In re Sponnoble, 405 F.2d 578 (C.C.P.A. 1969)

In re Wands, 858 F.2d 731, 737 (Fed. Cir. 1988)

Japan Patent Office, Examination Guidelines for Patent and Utility Model in Japan

Jitsuyō shin'an-hō (Utility Model Act) (Law No. 123, 1959)

Jungersen v. Ostby & Barton Co., 335 U.S. 560 (1949)

Langer v. Kaufman, 465 F.2d 915, 918, 175 USPQ 172, 174 (C.C.P.A 1972)

Mayo Collaborative Services v. Prometheus Laboratories, 566 U.S. 66 (2012)

Mueller Brass Co. v. Reading Indus., 352 F.Supp. 1357, 1372 (E.D.Pa.1972), aff'd, 487 F.2d 1395 (3d Cir.1973)

Meyers Taylor Pty Ltd v Vicarr Industries Ltd (1977) 137 CLR 228

Minnesota Mining & Manufacturing Co v Beiersdorf (Australia) Limited (1980) 144 CLR 253

Mnih V and Kavukcuoglu K, 2013, Methods and Apparatus for Reinforcement Learning, U.S. patent No. US 20150379394 A1, filed December 5, 2013 and issued June 13, 2017

Nartron Corp. v. Schukra USA Inc., 558 F.3d 1352, 1353 (Fed. Cir. 2009)

NRDC v Commissioner of Patents (1959) 102 CLR 252

NutraSweet Australia Pty Ltd v Ajinomoto Co Inc (2005) 224 ALR 200

Official Rulings (1923) RPC 40

Olin Mathieson v Biorex [1970] RPC 157

Pacific Contact Labs, Inc. v. Solex Labs, Inc., 209 F.2d 529, 532–533 (9th Circ. 1953)

Pannu v. Iolab Corp., 155 F.3d 1344, 1351 (Fed. Cir. 1998)

Patents Act (1990)

Pfizer, Inc. v. Apotex, Inc 480 F.3d 1348 (2007)

Polwood Pty Ltd v Foxworth Pty Ltd [2008] FCAFC 9

Radiator Speciality Co. v. Buhot, 39 F.2d 373, 376 (3rd Cir. 1930)

Research Affiliates LLC v Commissioner of Patents [2014] FCAFC 150

Rolls-Royce Ltd's. Application [1963] RPC 251

Samuel Parkes & Co. Ld. v. Cocker Brothers Ld. (1929) 46 RPC 241

Scientific Plastic Products, Inc. v. Biotage AB, 766 F.3d 1355, 1360 (Fed. Cir. 2014)

Silvestri v. Grant, 496 F.2d 593, 596, 181 USPQ 706, 708 (C.C.P.A 1974)

Thaler SL, 1997, Device for the Autonomous Generation of Useful Information, U.S. Patent No. 5,659,666, filed October 13, 1994 and issued August 19, 1997 <www.google.com/patents/US5659666> accessed 13 May 2021

——— Device and Method for the Autonomous Bootstrapping of Unified Sentience, US Patent No. 2015/0379394A1, filed January 2, 2014 and issued September 24, 2019

———— Devices and Methods for Attracting Enhanced Attention, European Patent Application No. EP3563896, filed on November 7, 2018 and issued on November 6, 2019

———— Device for the Autonomous Bootstrapping of Useful Information, U.S. Patent No. 7,454,388B2, filed May 8, 2006 and issued November 18, 2008 <https://patents.google.com/patent/US7454388B2/en> accessed?

———— Food container, European Patent Application No. EP3564144, filed on October 17, 2018 and issued on November 6, 2019

Tokkyohō (Patent Act) (Law No. 121, 1959)

Tokyo District Court judgment Mutai Saishu (October 29, 1987)

Townsend v. Smith, 36 F.2d 292, 295, 4 USPQ 269, 271 (C.C.P.A 1929)

United States Patent and Trademark Office (USPTO), 'Manual of Patent Examining Procedure' (2019)

United States v. Adams, 380 U.S. 949 (1965)

University of Utah v. Max-Planck-Gesellschaft, 734 F.3d 1315 (Fed. Cir. 2013)

University of Western Australia v Gray (2009) 179 FCR 346

Secondary sources

'35 U.S. Code § 103 – Conditions for Patentability; Non-obvious Subject Matter' (Legal Information Institute) <www.law.cornell.edu/uscode/text/35/103> accessed 16 January 2021

'35th Trilateral Conference – European Patent Office, Japan Patent Office and United States and Trademark Office' (Seville, March 2017) <www.trilateral.net/conferences/35conference.pdf> accessed 22 May 2021

'5737-B19 IBM Watson for Drug Discovery' (2009) IBM United States Sales Manual <https://www-01.ibm.com/common/ssi/ShowDoc.wss?docURL=/common/ssi/rep_sm/9/897/ENUS5737-B19/index.html&lang=en&request_locale=en> accessed 14 May 2021

Abbott R, 'I think, Therefore I Invent: Creative Computers and the Future of Patent Law' (2016) 57 *Boston College Law Review* 1079

———— 'The Artificial Inventor Project' (World Intellectual Property Organization Magazine, December 2019) 6 <www.wipo.int/wipo_magazine/en/2019/06/article_0002.html> accessed 9 May 2020

———— *The Reasonable Robot – Artificial intelligence and the Law* (Cambridge University Press 2020)

Abe T and Yoshkawa K, 'Japan: Hindsight Excluded in Inventive Step' (ManagingIP, 2013) <www.managingip.com/Article/3284653/Japan-Hindsight-excluded-in-inventive-step.html> accessed 13 May 2021

'About IP 5 Co-operation' (FiveIPoffices) <www.fiveipoffices.org/about> accessed 17 May 2021

Abraham DJ, 'Shinpo Sei: Japanese Inventive Step Meets U.S. Non-obviousness' (1995) 77 *Journal of the Patent and Trademark Office Society* 528

Adelman MJ and others, *Cases and Materials on Patent Law* (4th ed., West Academic Publishing 2015)

Andersen B, 'The Rationales for Intellectual Property Rights: The Twenty-first Century Controversies', University of London (2003) <www.researchgate.net/publication/228871485_The_Rationales_for_Intellectual_Property_Rights_The_Twenty-First_Century_Controversies> accessed 15 May 2021

Ann C, 'Patent Trolls – Menace or Myth?', in Wolrad P zu Waldeck und Pyrmont et al. (eds.), *Patents and Technological Progress in a Globalized World* (Springer Science and Business Media 2009)

Australian Government (Department of Industry, Science, Energy and Resources), 'An AI Action Plan for All Australians: A Call for Views – Discussion Paper' (Australian Government Department of Industry, Science, Energy and Resources, 2020) <https://consult.industry.gov.au/digital-economy/ai-action-plan/supporting_documents/AIDiscussion-Paper.pdf> accessed 22 May 2021

'Australian Government Response to the Productivity Commission Inquiry into Intellectual Property Arrangements' (The Department of Industry, Innovation and Science of the Australian Government, August 2017) <www.industry.gov.au/sites/default/files/government_response_to_pc_inquiry_into_ip_august_2017.pdf?acsf_files_redirect> accessed 6 September 2020

Barton JH, 'Non-obviousness' (2003) 43 *IDEA* 475

Beier FK and Straus J, 'The Patent System and its Informational Function – Yesterday and Today' (1977) 8 *International Review of Intellectual Property and Competition Law* 387

Blok PH, 'The Inventor's New Tool: Artificial Intelligence – How Does it Fit the European Patent System?' (2017) 39 *European Intellectual Property Review* 69

Brown N, 'Introduction', in Nathan Brown (ed.), *Artificial Intelligence in Drug Discovery* (Royal Society of Chemistry 2021)

Burgess JT, 'The Analogous Art Test' (2009) 7 *Buffalo Intellectual Property Law Journal* 63

Carlson EK, 'Artificial Intelligence Can Invent but Not Patent – For Now' (2020) 6 *Engineering* 1212

'Case Examples Pertinent to AI-related Technology' (Japanese Patent Office) <www.jpo.go.jp/e/system/laws/rule/guideline/patent/document/ai_jirei_e/jirei_e.pdf> accessed 13 May 2021

Chan HCS and others, 'Advancing Drug Discovery via Artificial Intelligence' (2017) 40 *Trends in Pharmaceutical Sciences* 592

Chisum DS, *Chisum on Patents – A Treatise on the Law of Patentability, Validity and Infringement* (vol. 2, LexisNexis 2017)

Commissioner for Patents of the United States Patent and Trademark Office (USPTO), 'The Decision on the Petition: Application No. 16/524,360 for Devices and Methods for Attracting Enhanced Attention' (filed January 20, 2020 under 37 CFR 1.181) <www.uspto.gov/about-us/news-updates/petition-decision-inventorship-limited-natural-persons> accessed 19 April 2021\

'DABUS Described' (Imagination Engines Incorporated)<https://imagination-engines.com/dabus.html> accessed 15 May 2021

Davison, Mark J and others, *Australian Intellectual Property Law* (4th ed., Cambridge University Press 2020)

Dent C, 'An Exploration of the Principles, Precepts and Purposes that Provide Structure to the Patent System' (2008) 4 *Intellectual Property Quarterly* 456

———— 'Decisions Around Innovation and the Motivators that Contribute to Them: Patents, Copyright, Trademarks and Know-how' (2016) 6 *Queen Mary Journal of Intellectual Property* 435

———— '"Generally Inconvenient": The 1624 Statute of Monopolies as Political Compromise' (2009) 33 *Melbourne University Law Review* 415

———— 'The Purpose of Patents for Invention: Regulation of Exchange Versus Incentive' (2017) 3 *Intellectual Property Quarterly* 250

Derclaye E, 'Patent Law's Role in the Protection of the Environment – Re-assessing Patent Law and its Justifications in the 21st Century' (2009) 40 *International Review of Intellectual Property and Competition Law* 249

Dinwoodie G and others, *International and Comparative Patent Law* (LexisNexis 2002)

Drexl J and others, 'Artificial Intelligence and Intellectual Property Law: Position Statement of the Max Planck Institute for Innovation and Competition of 9 April 2021 on the current debate' (2021) Max Planck Institute for Innovation and Competition Research Paper No. 21–10, 23 <www.ip.mpg.de/fileadmin/ipmpg/content/stellungnahmen/MPI_PositionPaper__SSRN_21-10.pdf> accessed 2 May 2021

Duffy JF, 'Inventing invention: A case study of legal innovation' (2007) 86 *Texas Law Review* 1

Dutfield G, 'Collective Invention and Patent Law Individualism, 1877–2012 – or, the Curious Persistence of the Inventor's Moral Right', in Stathis Arapostathis and Graham Dutfield (eds.), *Knowledge Management and Intellectual Property – Concepts, Actors and Practices from the Past to the Present* (Edward Elgar 2013) 109

European Parliament (Committee on Legal Affairs), 'Report on Intellectual Property Rights for the Development of Artificial Intelligence Technologies' (2020/2015(INI)) <www.europarl.europa.eu/doceo/document/A-9-2020-0176_EN.pdf> accessed 2 May 2021

European Patent Office, 'Revision of the European Patent Convention (EPC 2000): Synoptic Presentation of the EPC 1973/2000' (2007) *Special Edition 4 European Patent Office Official Journal* ISSN 0170/9291, 48 <http://archive.epo.org/epo/pubs/oj007/08_07/special_edition_4_epc_2000_synoptic.pdf> accessed 19 April 2021

Fisher M, 'Classical Economics and Philosophy of the Patent System' (2005) 1 *Intellectual Property Quarterly* 1

———— *Fundamentals of Patent Law. Interpretation and Scope of Protection* (Hart Publishing 2007)

Fisher W, 'Theories of Intellectual Property' (2001) <https://cyber.harvard.edu/people/tfisher/iptheory.pdf> accessed 15 May 2021.

Fleming N, 'How Artificial Intelligence is Changing Drug Discovery' (Nature, May 30, 2018) <www.nature.com/articles/d41586-018-05267-x> accessed 15 May 2021.

Fraser E, 'Computers as Inventors – Legal and Policy Implications of Artificial Intelligence on Patent Law' (2016) 13 *SCRIPTed* 305.

Fromer JC, 'Expressive Incentives in Intellectual Property' (2012) 98 *Virginia Law Review* 1745

Granstrand O, 'Are We on Our Way in the New Economy with Optimal Inventive Steps?', in Ove Granstrand (ed.), *Economics, Law and Intellectual Property. Seeking Strategies for Research and Teaching in a Developing Field* (Springer 2003)

Hale C, 'IBM to Wind Down Watson's Work in AI-based Drug Discovery: Report' (Fierce Biotech, April 19, 2019) <www.fiercebiotech.com/medtech/ibm-to-wind-down-watson-s-work-ai-based-drug-discovery-report> accessed 14 May 2021

Hartmann C and others, 'Trends and Developments in Artificial Intelligence. Challenges to the Intellectual Property Rights Framework' (2020) 106 <www.ivir.nl/publicaties/download/Trends_and_Developments_in_Artificial_Intelligence-1.pdf> accessed 22 May 2021

Hashiguchi M, 'The Global Artificial Intelligence Revolution Challenges Patent Eligibility' (2017) 13 *J Bus & Tech* 11

Hattenbach B and Glucoft J, 'Patents in an Era of Infinite Monkeys and Artificial Intelligence' (2015) 19 *Stanford Technology Law Review* 32

Homma T, 'Comparing Japanese and US Standards of Obviousness: Providing Meaningful Guidance After KSR' (2008) 48 *IDEA* 449

Hughes J, 'The Philosophy of Intellectual Property' (1988) 77 *Georgetown Law Journal* 287

'IEI's Patented Creativity Machine Paradigm' (Imagination Engines Incorporated) <http://imagination-engines.com/iei_cm.php> accessed 25 March 2021

'Intellectual Property Laws Amendment (Productivity Commission Response Part 2 and Other Measures) Act 2020' (Australian Government Intellectual Property Office) <www.ipaustralia.gov.au/about-us/public-consultations/archived-public-consultations/intellectual-property-laws-amendment-productivity-commission-response> accessed 20 September 2020

'Internal Market, Industry, Entrepreneurship and SMEs: Utility Models' (European Commission) <https://ec.europa.eu/growth/industry/policy/intellectual-property/patents/utility-models_en> accessed 15 April 2021

Iribarren M, 'IBM's Watson for Drug Discovery Program No Longer Taking New Clients' (Voicebot, April 22, 2019) <https://voicebot.ai/2019/04/22/ibms-watson-for-drug-discovery-program-no-longer-taking-new-clients/> accessed 14 May 2021

Kageyama K, 'Determining Inventive Step or Non-obviousness for a Patent Requirement in View of the Formation Process of an Invention' (2016) 7 *Beijing Law Review* 238, 241–242

Kesan JP, 'Economic Rationales for the Patent System in Current Context' (2015) 22 *George Mason Law Review* 897

Kim D, '"AI-generated Inventions": Time to get the Record Straight?' (2020) 69 (5) *GRUR International* 443

Kim D et al., 'Artificial Intelligence Systems as Inventors? A Position Statement of 7 September 2021 in View of the Evolving Case-Law Worldwide' (2021).< https://papers.ssrn.com/sol3/papers.cfm?abstract_id=3919588> accessed 29 September 2021

Kitch EW, 'Graham v. John Deere Co.: New Standards for Patents' (1967) 49 *Journal of the Patent Office Society* 246

Kurose M, 'Utility Model Law: The Present and Future of Japan's Utility Model System', in Dirk Schüßler-Langeheine and Bernd Hansen (eds.), *Patent Practice in Japan and Europe: Liber Amicorum for Guntram Rahn* (Kluwer Law International 2011)

Landers AL, 'A Comparative Approach to the Inventive Step', in Toshiko Takenaka (ed.), *Research Handbook on Patent Law and Theory* (2nd ed., Edward Elgar 2019) 454

Landes WM and Posner RA, *The Economic Structure of Intellectual Property Law* (Harvard University Press 2003)

Lefstin JA and others, 'Final Report of the Berkeley Center for Law & Technology Section 101 Workshop: Addressing Patent Eligibility Challenge' (2016) University of California Hastings College of the Law Legal Studies Research Paper Series <https://papers.ssrn.com/sol3/papers.cfm?abstract_id=3050093> accessed 26 April 2021

Li N and Koay T, 'Artificial Intelligence and Inventorship: An Australian Perspective' (2020) 15 *Journal of Intellectual Property Law and Practice* 399

Locke J, *Two Treatises of Government* (Peter Laslett ed., Cambridge University Press 1988) 288

Machlup F and Penrose E, 'The Patent Controversy in the Nineteenth Century' (1950) 10 *Journal of Economic History* 1.

Meara JP, 'Just Who is the Person Having Ordinary Skill in the Art – Patent Law's Mysterious Personage' (2007) 77 *Washington Law Review* 273

Merrifield S and others, 'European Patent Convention 2000: Substantive Patent Law', in Jochen Pagenberg and Richard Hacon (eds.), *Concise European Patent Law* (2nd ed., Kluwer Law International 2008)

Miyamoto T, 'International Treaties and Patent Law Harmonization: Today and Beyond', in Toshiko Takenaka (ed.), *Research Handbook on Patent Law and Theory* (2nd ed., Edward Elgar 2019)

Nakayama N, *Patent Law* (2nd ed., Koubundou Publishers 2012)

Okuyama S, 'Part III: Specific issues, 3. Utility models, Case No. 66: Technical Assessment Report', in Christopher Heath and Atsuhiro Furuta (eds.), *Japanese Patent Law: Cases and Materials* (Kluwer Law International 2019)

———'Patent Prosecution and Patentability Requirements: Recent Intellectual Property High Court Decisions in Japan on Inventive Step', in Schüßler-Langeheine and Hansen (eds.), *Patent Practice in Japan and Europe: Liber Amicorum for Guntram Rahn* (Kluwer Law International 2011) 157

Olson DS, 'Taking the Utilitarian Basis for Patent Law Seriously: The Case for Restricting Patentable Subject Matter' (2009) 82 *Temple Law Review* 181

Pesser L, *The Inventiveness Requirement in Patent Law: An Exploration of its Foundations and Functioning* (Kluwer Law International 2016)

Pila J, 'The Common Law Invention in its Original Form' (2001) 3 *Intellectual Property Quarterly* 209

Plotkin R, *The Genie in the Machine- How Computer-Automated Inventing is Revolutionizing Law and Business* (Stanford University Press 2009)

Productivity Commission 2016, 'Intellectual Property Arrangements' (Inquiry Report nr. 78, September 2016) 13ff. <www.pc.gov.au/inquiries/completed/intellectual-property/report/intellectual-property-overview.pdf> accessed 20 September 2020)

Radauer A and others, 'Study on the Economic Impact of the Utility Model Legislation in Selected Member States' (European Commission, April 2015) <https://op.europa.eu/en/publication-detail/-/publication/830fedd7-a1cf-46bd-a460-ba4a9eb01e63> accessed 22 May 2021

Schuster WM, 'Artificial Intelligence and Patent Ownership' (2018) 75 *Washington and Lee Law Review* 1945

Scotchmer S, 'Standing on the Shoulders of Giants: Cumulative Research and the Patent Law' (1991) 5 *Journal of Economic Perspectives* 29

Sengai K, 'Part III: Inventors and Inventors' Rights – Case No. 13: Rights Over the Invention – Inventorship', in Christopher Heath and Atsuhiro Furuta (eds.), *Japanese Patent Law: Cases and Materials* (Kluwer Law International 2019)

Seville C, *EU Intellectual Property Law and Policy* (2nd ed., Edward Elgar 2016)

Shemtov N, 'A study on Inventorship in Inventions Involving AI Activity' (European Patent Office, February 2019) <http://documents.epo.org/projects/babylon/eponet.nsf/0/3918F57B010A3540C125841900280653/$File/Concept_of_Inventorship_in_Inventions_involving_AI_Activity_en.pdf> accessed 15 April 2021

Sherkow JS, 'And How: Mayo v. Prometheus and the Method of Invention' (2013) 122 *Yale Law Journal Forum* 351

———'Negativing Invention' (2011) 4 *Brigham Young University Law Review* 1091

Simon B, 'The Implications of Technological Advancement for Obviousness' (2013) 19 *Michigan Telecommunications and Technology Law Review* 331

Shimpo F, 'The Principal Japanese AI and Robot Strategy Toward Establishing Basic Principles', in H Barfield and U Pagallo (eds.), *Research Handbook on the Law of Artificial Intelligence* (Edward Elgar 2018)

Sinai OT, 'Beyond Incentives: Expanding the Theoretical Framework for Patent Law Analysis' (2010) 45 *Akron Law Review* 1

Slade A, 'Plausability: A Conditio Sine Qua Non of Patent Law?' (2020) 3 *Intellectual Property Quarterly* 180

Story U, 'Patentability Requirements of Biotech Patents', in Ulrich Storz and others (eds.), *Biopatent Law: European vs. US Patent Law* (Springer 2014)

Straus J and Klunker NS, 'Harmonization of International Patent Law' (2017) 38 *International Review of Intellectual Property and Competition Law* 907

Summons to Attend Oral Proceedings for Application 18275163.6 from European Patent Office to Williams Powell (September 13, 2019), Annex, 2 <https://register.epo.org/application?documentId=E3SDI9ZN5969498&number=EP18275163&lng=en&npl=false> accessed 9 April 2021

Suthersanen M, 'Utility Models: Do They Really Serve National Innovation Strategies?', in Josef Drexl and Anselm Kamperman Sanders (eds.), *The Innovation Society and Intellectual Property* (Edward Elgar 2019)

Thaler S, 'Addendum' <https://register.epo.org/documentView?number=IB.2019057809.W&documentId=id00000053660796> accessed 9 May 2021

The White House Office of Science and Technology Policy, 'American Artificial Intelligence Initiative: Year One Annual Report' (February 2020), <www.nitrd.gov/nitrdgroups/images/c/c1/American-AI-Initiative-One-Year-Annual-Report.pdf> accessed 22 May 2021

'Types of Patents' (Australian Government Intellectual Property Office) <www.ipaustralia.gov.au/patents/understanding-patents/types-patents#standard> accessed 6 September 2020

University of Cambridge, "Artificially Intelligent Robot Scientist "Eve" Could Boost Search for New Drugs' (Phys Org, February 3, 2015) <https://phys.org/news/2015-02-artificially-intelligent-robot-scientist-eve.html> accessed 15 May 2021

Vaver D, 'Sprucing Up Patent Law' (2010) 22 *Intellectual Property Journal* 6

Visser D, *The Annotated European Patent Convention 2000* (25th ed., Kluwer Law International 2017)

Wamsley CSD, 'Flashes of Genius, Toiled Experimentation, and Now Artificial Creation: A Case for Inventive Process Disclosures' (Master of Laws, The George Washington University Law School, 2011) <https://scholarspace.library.gwu.edu/concern/gw_etds/rf55z7888?locale=en> accessed 26 April 2021

Wegner HC, 'Making Sense of KSR and Other Recent Patent Cases' (2007) 106 *Michigan Law Review First Impressions* 39

'What We Do: Finding New Ways to Treat Disease' (Benevolent AI) <www.benevolent.com/what-we-do> accessed 15 May 2021.

William HF and others, *Cases and Materials on Patent Law, Including Trade Secrets* (7th ed., West Academic Publishing 2017)

World Intellectual Property Organization (WIPO) Secretariat of the Standing Committee on the Law of Patents, 'Study on Inventive Step' (SCP/22/3, Geneva, July 6, 2015) 3 <www.wipo.int/edocs/mdocs/scp/en/scp_22/scp_22_3.pdf> accessed 15 January 2018

World Intellectual Property Organization, *Introduction to Intellectual Property: Theory and Practice* (2nd ed., Kluwer Law International 2017)

Zeitsch J, 'The Economic Value of the Australian Innovation Patent' (IP Australia, March 2013) <www.ipaustralia.gov.au/sites/default/files/economic_value_of_the_innovation_patent_-_final_report_-_verve_economics_-_24_mar_2013.pdf> accessed 22 May 2021

4 Conclusion and future outlook

4.1 Conclusion

This book was written in a time of uncertainty, where no accepted universal definition of AI is in place, and no clarity exists regarding the legal and policy directions in relation to the protection (or lack thereof) of AI-generated output. The topic of this book is thus dynamic and prone to constant change. However, an investigation into the notion of AI reveals that two elements should be considered part of any given AI definition: intelligence and autonomy.

In what concerns intelligence, it was argued that creativity is part of the concept of "intelligence." Creativity is defined differently according to the scientific domain which studies it, but it can generally be stated that both the product (i.e., the work or the invention) and the process of creation must be considered when assessing creativity. The process of creation must be heuristic, and not only intuition and spontaneity, but also conscious control and rationality, should be taken into account. That is, for a system to be "intelligent," thus falling under the definition of AI, it should be creative in the sense that its process of creation is heuristic and comprises the elements just mentioned.

With regard to autonomy, it was reasoned that it cannot be defined in a binary fashion (autonomous versus non-autonomous), but rather as a scale, with some AI systems and machines being more autonomous than others. A completely autonomous form of AI, however, doesn't exist yet – machine learning and programming still directly or indirectly dictate much of AI outcomes.

Given the state-of-the-art in AI, and as a few examples illustrate, there isn't at the moment an AI system that can generate works and inventions completely autonomously (even though it seems that AI creation in copyright has a higher level of autonomy than in patents, since in relation to the latter a human being is further needed to e.g., define the problem to be solved). A human being is thus always needed during the process of creating a work or an invention. The question is how that human intervention is computed under copyright and patent laws.

In fact, the impact of AI's intervention in the process of creation, and how that impact influences the application of copyright and patent law, is centred around the degree and type of human intervention vis-à-vis the degree of

DOI: 10.4324/9780367823290-4

intervention of the AI system. *De lege lata*, both copyright and patent laws require the intervention of a human author or inventor (even though copyright connects this requirement more clearly to protectability of the subject matter concerned, in the sense that the lack of a human author will cause the work to not be copyright-protected). The key question then becomes which type of human contribution can give rise to authorship and inventorship claims. In copyright law, a test that is jurisdiction-agnostic was proposed, whereby human intervention must be more than *de minimis* and the creative distance between that intervention and the final work must not be too great (as the creativity of the author, some expressive elements derived from his or her intellectual conception, must be reflected in the final work produced). In patent law, the inventorship bar differs from one jurisdiction to another (and in Europe, it has to be assessed on a country-by-country basis), and this question was left open. In any case, in both copyright and patent law it would be possible in many situations to forge a human proxy as an author or inventor – in copyright law, it would be enough that the name of a (human) author appears in the work "in the usual manner"[1]; in patent law, it is possible to designate the name of a human as an inventor in the patent application, knowing that patent offices do not usually object to the (reported) human inventor (if such fake authorship or inventorship would withstand court proceedings is of course another matter).

Beyond the apparent easiness in circumventing the need for a human creator, a few issues are deserving of attention. First, justifications for the grant of copyright and patent should be a yardstick against which to decide on future copyright and patent policies. Common to both copyright and patent are the utilitarian theory (focusing on the incentive to create), the labour theory (focusing on the reward to the creator) and, to a lesser extent, the personality rights theory (focusing on the personality of the creator).[2] Independently of the theory at stake, these justifications bear difficulties in terms of copyright and patent regulatory policy. Namely, the scope of copyright or patent rights should be broad enough to perform its function of reward, incentive, or protection of creators' personality, but it should not be as broad as to generate unnecessary burdens for society. Conditions for protection in copyright and patent laws should also be set to reflect this. For example, the patent system implies a trade-off between granting a time-limited monopoly in exchange for a disclosure of the invention in an enabling manner (so that others can produce and learn from the patent, subject of course to the limits of the mentioned monopoly). Translating this premise into concrete patent policies is the ultimate challenge; too lax patentability requirements and broad patent scope may lead to patent flooding, but too strict patentability requirements and narrow patent scope may halt innovation and inventive activities. A similar trade-off can be observed in copyright – the exclusionary space given by copyright to a right holder has to be balanced against certain exceptions and limitations that

---

1 Article 15(1) of the Berne Convention for the Protection of Literary Works (1886).
2 See supra Sections 2.3. and 3.3.

allow others to use the work to a limited extent, and the conditions for protection should be set at an optimal level.

It was against this background that a few recommendations were put forth. For copyright, it was suggested that a new neighbouring right (or similar regime) could be created to incentivise the dissemination of AI-generated works. However, this option has many drawbacks, which should be weighed against the advantages that such a right could bring. Namely, it should be assessed whether there is a need to incentivise the dissemination of AI-generated works in the first place, vis-à-vis the constraints that it would bring to users of said works.

For patents, the key recommendation was to revise and update Patent Offices' guidelines, namely in what concerns inventive step or non-obviousness. In that regard, a few measures were proposed: to broaden the scope of the concept of analogous/related arts; to take into account the use of AI when defining the person skilled in the art; and to consider the intervention of AI in the inventing process in the context of secondary indicia. These measures would in turn imply changing guidelines to make the disclosure of the inventing process mandatory in the framework of the sufficiency of disclosure or enablement requirement. Alternatively, a number of factors to assess sufficiency of disclosure or enablement – such as the quantity of experimentation necessary, the amount of guidance presented in the specification, or the relative skill of those in the art – could be introduced so that the disclosure of the use of an AI system in the inventing process would be indirectly required. Also in patents, it was suggested that the idea of introducing a regime similar to utility models for AI-generated inventions would have to be accompanied by economic studies to assess whether such introduction would be necessary or beneficial – namely, if having such a system would lead to more incremental innovation that would benefit society (which could only be assessed on a country-by-country basis).

An important pattern that cuts across patent and copyright emerges: the creation of new rights as an option for protection of new realities remains always a possibility, but it is not something that should be taken lightly. New rights can be created to the extent they are necessary to address a market failure, and/or to fulfil a natural rights justification, but the protection they afford should not be an end in itself. The costs inherent to intellectual property rights should be factored in. One of the main costs in having proprietary rights is of course the corresponding social cost of reducing the public's access to intellectual goods. But other costs should also be considered, such as the costs in transferring the rights (transaction costs) and in protecting the rights (e.g., costs in enforcement), as well as the costs produced by rent-seeking, where over-investment might not yield the corresponding benefits in return.[3]

At this point, it should be recalled that other options exist to incentivise the creation and/or dissemination of AI-generated output, such as technological protection measures or contract law. Moreover, several sectors thrive without

---

3 William M. Landes and Richard A. Posner, *The Economic Structure of Intellectual Property Law* (Harvard University Press 2003) 16–21.

the protection of intellectual property, either because that protection is simply not available, or it is thin/ineffective, or even due to other reasons such as a preference for informal governance norms.[4] What those sectors show is that sometimes intellectual property seeks exclusivity "without a careful examination of the conditions and motivations that define the creative environment."[5] More studies are therefore needed to assess what the creative landscape looks like in the field of AI-generated output. Chiefly, it is necessary to assess whether other reasons to create – such as social norms or first-mover advantages – are in place when it comes to AI creations.[6]

Nevertheless, if weighing the benefits and costs of having a new intellectual property right speaks in favour of creating it, then a second balancing exercise should come in, whereby the conditions for protection and scope of the right are carefully crafted to make sure the costs of the right do not outweigh its benefits. For example, in relation to copyright and neighbouring rights, it has been pointed out that neighbouring rights with no threshold and a corresponding rule of scope are "outdated and inherently unbalanced."[7] Likewise, empirical research suggests that higher creativity thresholds produce better creativity and better works.[8] With regard to patents, studies have found that weakened patent protection might incentivise innovation, while excessive patent protection might hinder it.[9] It is thus suggested that any new right for AI-generated output, be it in the field of copyright/neighbouring rights or patents/utility models, should combine clear rules on (likely high) protection thresholds with severe limitations on scope, namely on rights granted and duration of protection.

4 Examples of these industries, and an investigation of their workings, can be found in Kate Darling and Aaron Perzanowski (eds.), *Creativity Without Law* (New York University Press 2017). They include roller derbys, pornography, Nigerian cinema, or physicians anti-patenting norms, to name but a few.

5 Aaron Perzanowski and Kate Darling, 'Introduction', in Kate Darling and Aaron Perzanowski (eds.), *Creativity Without Law* (New York University Press 2017) 2.

6 See Christopher J. Sprigman, 'Copyright and Creative Incentives: What We Know (and Don't)' (2017) 55 *Houston Law Review* 451, 468: "Looking in those negative spaces, we can see other factors beyond formal IP that support creativity: market incentives, cognitive psychology, social norms, first-mover advantages, path-dependency, or even plain happenstance." See also Jessica Silbey, *The Eureka Myth: Creators, Innovators, and Everyday Intellectual Property* (Stanford University Press 2014) 274, drawing conclusions from her interviews with authors and scientists: "When interviewees focus on finances, they do so to enable more art or science or to form relationships, not to collect money for its own sake. (. . .) The objects they produce or the services they render are not everyday work goals, despite their likely monetization or distribution to develop fans and consumers. Work itself is the goal. They enjoy doing the work, meeting the challenges, thinking about and achieving the next step with cultivated skills and interests. (. . .) These people work to be free, and free to pursue what interests them."

7 Bernt Hugenholtz, 'Neighbouring Rights are Obsolete' (2019) 50 *IIC – International Review of Intellectual Property and Competition Law* 1006.

8 Christopher Buccafusco and others, 'Experimental Tests of Intellectual Property Laws' Creativity Thresholds' (2014) 92 *Texas Law Review* 1921, 1976.

9 Sridhar Srinivasan, 'Do Weaker Patents Induce Greater Research Investments?' (2018) <https://papers.ssrn.com/sol3/papers.cfm?abstract_id=3185148> accessed 3 June 2021.

4.2 Future outlook

Going forward, a few points of attention for policy-making, as well as avenues for future research, can be discussed.

A first question to be considered is that, as mentioned in Sections 2.2. and 3.2., AI systems need to be trained in order to produce works or inventions; the production of creative output is thus dependent on a previous stage of machine learning. Machine learning relies on large datasets that will often comprise copyright works, and these will technically be reproduced in the process of training the AI system. This raises copyright issues to the extent that reproduction is an exclusive right of the author, and that the reproduction that takes place during machine learning may be subsumed under the legal notion of reproduction. Should that be the case, absent an applicable exception, reproduction in the context of machine learning could amount to copyright infringement. These issues do not have a straightforward answer across jurisdictions. For instance in the EU the reproduction in machine learning is probably covered by a broad right of reproduction, even though some exceptions might be applicable to some situations (most notably, the exceptions for text and data mining in the recent Directive 2019/790 on copyright and related rights in the Digital Single Market).[10] The narrow exceptions applicable and the uncertainty that ensues for machine learning activities have been extensively criticised by the academic community.[11] By contrast, in the US, reproductions in the context of machine learning activities might amount to non-expressive uses covered by fair use and should therefore be permitted.[12] Yet another radically different regime can be found in Australia, which does not have any exception for text and data mining, while existing exceptions such as fair dealing do not seem to apply to the majority of cases of text and data mining.[13] Japan recognises an exception for

---

10 Article 3 of the Directive creates an exception for text and data mining for the purposes of scientific research, and Article 4 establishes an exception for text and data mining for any purposes (but the latter provision applies only in case the exception has not been expressly reserved by right holders "in an appropriate manner").

11 See e.g., Christophe Geiger, 'The Missing Goal-Scorers in the Artificial Intelligence Team: Of Big Data, the Fundamental Right to Research and the failed Text and Data Mining imitations in the CSDM Directive' (2021) PIJIP/TLS Research Paper Series 66 <https://digitalcommons.wcl. american.edu/research/66/> accessed 3 June 2021; Alain Strowel and Rossana Ducato, 'Artificial Intelligence and Data Mining. A Copyright Carol', in Eleonora Rosati (ed.), *Routledge Handbook of EU Copyright Law* (Routledge 2021) 281–298; Theodoros Chiou, 'Copyright Lessons on Machine Learning: What Impact on Algorithmic Art?' (2019) 10 *JIPITEC* 2019, 398; Eleonora Rosati, 'Copyright as an Obstacle or an Enabler? A European Perspective on Text and Data Mining and Its Role in the Development of AI Creativity' (2019) <https://papers.ssrn.com/sol3/papers. cfm?abstract_id=3452376> accessed 3 June 2021.

12 As defended by e.g., Matthew Sag, 'The New Legal Landscape for Text Mining and Machine Learning' (2020) <https://papers.ssrn.com/sol3/papers.cfm?abstract_id=3331606 > accessed 3 June 2021. See also James Grimmelmann, 'Copyright for Literate Robots' (2016) 101 *Iowa Law Review* <https:// scholarship.law.cornell.edu/cgi/viewcontent.cgi?article=2615&context=facpub> accessed 3 June 2021.

13 Rita Matulionyte, 'Australian Copyright Law Impedes the Development of Artificial Intelligence: What Are the Options?' (2021) 52 *IIC – International Review of Intellectual Property and Competition Law*

the purpose of "information analysis" which does not have a non-commercial requirement or an obligation to be carried out for scientific purposes,[14] but which does not cover the mining of works in databases meant for text and data mining purposes.[15] The widely different regimes provide a fertile ground for a comparative empirical research into how the existence or lack of exceptions such as fair use and data mining (and their respective scope where they exist) impact machine learning activities and subsequent AI-generated works and inventions. Such research could also highlight how those differences might impact cross-border uses of datasets, and how they may contribute to AI development silos across national borders. The resulting findings could be used by policymakers to design exceptions conducive to the flourishing of machine learning activities, building on already existing research that investigates the relevant elements that should be tackled when designing text and data mining exceptions.[16]

Another issue that should be the object of more in-depth research is ownership. As explained in the introduction of this book, ownership was not dealt with as it is beyond the scope of this work. However, the intervention of AI-systems in the process of creation exacerbates problems of ownership determination. In the context of AI-generated content, several human beings might have contributed to the production of that content, namely the programmer, the developer of the dataset used to train the AI, the owner, or the user. In the

---

2021, 417. See also Australian Government, Copyright and the Digital Economy (2013) <www. alrc.gov.au/publication/copyright-and-the-digital-economy-dp-79/> accessed 3 June 2021, Section 8.47: "One issue is whether text mining, if done for the purposes of research or study, would be covered by the fair dealing exceptions. The reach of the fair dealing exceptions may not extend to text mining if the whole dataset needs to be copied and converted into a suitable format. Such copying would be more than a 'reasonable portion' of the work concerned. (. . .) Nor is it clear whether copying for text mining would fall under the exception relating to temporary reproduction of works as part of a technical process, under s 43B of the Copyright Act, but it seems unlikely." (footnotes omitted)

14 Article 47–7 JCA.

15 FutureTDM, 'Reducing Barriers and Increasing Uptake of Text and Data Mining for Research Environments using a Collaborative Knowledge and Open Information Approach' (2016) 75–76 <www.futuretdm.eu/knowledge-library/?b5-file=4588&b5-folder=2227> accessed 3 June 2021; Jean-Paul Triaille and others, 'Study on the Legal Framework of Text and Data Mining (TDM)' (2014) 11–12 <https://op.europa.eu/en/publication-detail/-/publication/074ddf78-01e9-4a1d-9895-65290705e2a5/language-en> accessed 3 June 2021.

16 Daniel Gervais, 'Exploring the Interfaces Between Big Data and Intellectual Property Law' (2019) 10 *JIPITEC* 3, 11, suggests that policymakers should look into which rights the exception would apply to (reproduction, adaptation, etc); whether contractual overrides are possible; the lawfulness of the source; what dissemination of the data is possible; and whether the purpose of the text and data mining activity is non-commercial. Sean Flynn and others, 'Implementing User Rights for Research in the Field of Artificial Intelligence: A Call for International Action' (2020) 42 *European Intellectual Property Review* 393, 396 identify the main elements of exceptions that accommodate text and data mining activities throughout the world, namely "subject matter covered, rights covered, commercial use restrictions, transfer and sharing of data (including cross-border), lawful access requirements, and contractual and technical restrictions."

field of patent law, authors have suggested different solutions, namely: a default rule assigning ownership to the owner of the AI as a way to minimize transaction costs and encourage innovation (as that would incentivise the owner to allow others to use the AI);[17] and allocating ownership to users as the most likely market participants (and thus most likely to value patent rights).[18] In copyright, as a general rule, the author is the initial copyright owner. However, many jurisdictions allocate initial ownership to entities other than the author, often to protect investment of e.g., producers or intermediaries.[19] Given the need to trace the author of an AI-generated work for it to qualify for copyright protection and the difficulties that might be associated with that exercise, the corresponding rules of ownership also become an important topic to explore. Empirical research in this area is lacking, namely investigation into contractual practices of ownership allocation in case of AI-generated works, the breathing space left by legislation to such practices, and how they might contribute or not to the development of AI technology in the field of algorithmic creation. This type of research could then inform future policy directions on this subject (namely whether there is a need for further legislative intervention).

Finally, yet another topic worthy of attention is how the centrality of a human being in AI-generated creations – i.e., the need for a human author or inventor in the creative process – interacts with existing regimes of moral rights.[20] In copyright, as it was argued, protection of AI-generated output will ultimately depend on the "creative distance" between a putative author and the creative result, in the sense that the creative choices of the author need to be reflected in the final work. How the relationship between the author and her work changes in the context of AI-generated works, and the role that moral rights may play in that relationship, is something that hasn't been extensively covered.[21] In patent law, the inventor has the right to be named as such in the patent,[22] which

---

17 Ryan Abbott, *The Reasonable Robot: Artificial Intelligence and the Law* (Cambridge University Press 2020) 87–88. See also Erica Fraser, 'Computer as Inventors – Legal and Policy Implications of Artificial Intelligence on Patent Law' (2016) 13 *ScriptEd* 305, 331–332.

18 W. Michael Schuster, 'Artificial Intelligence and Patent Ownership' (2018) 75 *Washington and Lee Law Review* 1945, 1988.

19 Paul Goldstein and Bernt Hugenholtz, *International Copyright. Principles, Law and Practice* (2nd ed., Oxford University Press 2010) 245–246.

20 The Berne Convention requires countries to grant the moral rights of paternity (i.e., the right to claim authorship) and integrity (i.e., the right to object to any distortion of the work that prejudices his honour or reputation) – cf. Article 6*bis* Berne Convention. However, the ways that different countries chose to implement moral rights in their national legislations vary widely.

21 Conversely, the issue of moral rights in the specific regime of computer-generated works such as the one found in the UK (see supra section 2.5.2.1.) is explored in Mira Sundara Rajan, *Moral Rights: Principles, Practice and New Technology* (Oxford University Press 2011) 309–311. In her recommendations, the author tentatively foresees that "[t]he area of technology-based artistic creation is (. . .) likely to generate new kinds of moral rights. For example, the relationship between the author and the work may not be as important in relation to these kinds of works."

22 Article 4*ter* of the Paris Convention for the Protection of Industrial Property (1883).

is seen as his moral right.[23] It has been pointed out that the moral right of the inventor performs three essential roles: publicly acknowledging the inventor's value, affording moral legitimacy to the patent system, and tracing the invention to a certain space and time.[24] The extent to which these roles still hold up in the context of AI-generated inventions, and the question whether the moral rights on the inventor play, or should play, new roles therein, is an issue that hasn't been explored and that would add to a holistic understanding of the interplay between AI-generated inventions and patent law.

References

Primary sources

Berne Convention for the Protection of Literary and Artistic Works (1886)
Directive (EU) 2019/790 of the European Parliament and of the Council of 17 April 2019 on copyright and related rights in the Digital Single Market and amending Directives 96/9/EC and 2001/29/EC [2019] OJ L130/92
Paris Convention for the Protection of Industrial Property (1883)

Secondary sources

Abbott R, *The Reasonable Robot: Artificial Intelligence and the Law* (Cambridge University Press 2020)
Buccafusco C and others, 'Experimental Tests of Intellectual Property Laws' Creativity Thresholds' (2014) 92 *Texas Law Review* 1921
Chiou T, 'Copyright Lessons on Machine Learning: What Impact on Algorithmic Art?' (2019) 10 *JIPITEC* 398
Darling K and Perzanowski A (eds.), *Creativity Without Law* (New York University Press 2017)
Dutfield G, 'Collective Invention and Patent Law Individualism, 1877–2012 – or, the Curious Persistence of the Inventor's Moral Right', in Stathis Arapostathis and Graham Dutfield (eds.), *Knowledge Management and Intellectual Property. Concepts, Actors and Practices from the Past to the Present* (Edward Elgar 2013)
Flynn S and others, 'Implementing User Rights for Research in the Field of Artificial Intelligence: A Call for International Action' (2020) 42 *European Intellectual Property Review* 393
Fraser E, 'Computer as Inventors – Legal and Policy Implications of Artificial Intelligence on Patent Law' (2016) 13 *ScriptEd* 305
FutureTDM, 'Reducing Barriers and Increasing Uptake of Text and Data Mining for Research Environments using a Collaborative Knowledge and Open Information Approach' (2016) 75–76 <www.futuretdm.eu/knowledge-library/?b5-file=4588&b5-folder=2227> accessed 3 June 2021

---

23 Graham Dutfield, 'Collective Invention and Patent Law Individualism, 1877–2012 – or, the Curious Persistence of the Inventor's Moral Right', in Stathis Arapostathis and Graham Dutfield (eds.), *Knowledge Management and Intellectual Property. Concepts, Actors and Practices from the Past to the Present* (Edward Elgar 2013) 109–126.
24 Ibid., 122–123.

Geiger C, 'The Missing Goal-Scorers in the Artificial Intelligence Team: Of Big Data, the Fundamental Right to Research and the failed Text and Data Mining Imitations in the CSDM Directive' (2021) PIJIP/TLS Research Paper Series 66 <https://digitalcommons.wcl.american.edu/research/66/> accessed 3 June 2021

Gervais D, 'Exploring the Interfaces Between Big Data and Intellectual Property Law' (2019) 10 *JIPITEC* 3

Goldstein P and Hugenholtz B, *International Copyright. Principles, Law and Practice* (2nd ed., Oxford University Press 2010)

Grimmelmann J, 'Copyright for Literate Robots' (2016) 101 *Iowa Law Review* <https://scholarship.law.cornell.edu/cgi/viewcontent.cgi?article=2615&context=facpub> accessed 3 June 2021

Hugenholtz B, 'Neighbouring Rights are Obsolete' (2019) 50 *IIC – International Review of Intellectual Property and Competition Law* 1006

Landes WM and Posner RA, *The Economic Structure of Intellectual Property Law* (Harvard University Press 2003)

Matulionyte R, 'Australian Copyright Law Impedes the Development of Artificial Intelligence: What Are the Options?' (2021) 52 *IIC – International Review of Intellectual Property and Competition Law* 417

Perzanowski A and Darling K, 'Introduction', in Darling K and Perzanowski A (eds.), *Creativity Without Law* (New York University Press 2017)

Rosati E, 'Copyright as an Obstacle or an Enabler? A European Perspective on Text and Data Mining and Its Role in the Development of AI Creativity' (2019) <https://papers.ssrn.com/sol3/papers.cfm?abstract_id=3452376> accessed 3 June 2021

Sag M, 'The New Legal Landscape for Text Mining and Machine Learning' (2020) <https://papers.ssrn.com/sol3/papers.cfm?abstract_id=3331606

Schuster WM, 'Artificial Intelligence and Patent Ownership' (2018) 75 *Washington and Lee Law Review* 1945

Silbey J, *The Eureka Myth: Creators, Innovators, and Everyday Intellectual Property* (Stanford University Press 2014)

Sprigman CJ, 'Copyright and Creative Incentives: What We Know (and Don't)' (2017) 55 *Houston Law Review* 451

Srinivasan S, 'Do Weaker Patents Induce Greater Research Investments?' (2018) <https://papers.ssrn.com/sol3/papers.cfm?abstract_id=3185148> accessed 3 June 2021

Strowel A and Ducato R, 'Artificial Intelligence and Data Mining. A Copyright Carol', in Rosati E (ed.), *Routledge Handbook of EU Copyright Law* (Routledge 2021)

Sundara Rajan M, *Moral Rights: Principles, Practice and New Technology* (Oxford University Press 2011)

Triaille J-P and others, 'Study on the Legal Framework of Text and Data Mining (TDM)' (2014) <https://op.europa.eu/en/publication-detail/-/publication/074ddf78-01e9-4a1d-9895–65290705e2a5/language-en> accessed 3 June 2021

Index

Printed in Great Britain
by Amazon

62778598R00098